The Art of Fiction

Also by David Lodge

THE ART OF
FICTION

Illustrated from Classic and Modern Texts

DAVID LODGE

VIKING

VIKING
Published by the Penguin Group
Penguin Books USA Inc., 375 Hudson Street,
New York, New York 10014, U.S.A.
Penguin Books Ltd, 27 Wrights Lane,
London W8 5TZ, England
Penguin Books Australia Ltd, Ringwood,
Victoria, Australia
Penguin Books Canada Ltd, 10 Alcorn Avenue,
Toronto, Ontario, Canada M4V 3B2
Penguin Books (N.Z.) Ltd, 182–190 Wairau Road,
Auckland 10, New Zealand

Penguin Books Ltd, Registered Offices:
Harmondsworth, Middlesex, England

First American Edition
Published in 1993 by Viking Penguin, a division of Penguin Books USA Inc.

3   5   7   9   10   8   6   4

The essays in this book first appeared in different form in
The Independent on Sunday in Great Britain and in *The Washington Post
Book World* in the United States.

LIBRARY OF CONGRESS CATALOGING-IN-PUBLICATION DATA
Lodge, David, 1935–
The art of fiction : illustrated from classic and modern texts /
David Lodge.
p.   cm.
Includes bibliographical references and index.
ISBN 0–670–84848–4
1. English fiction — History and criticism — Theory, etc.
2. American fiction — History and criticism — Theory, etc.
3. Criticism — Terminology.   4. Fiction — Technique.   I. Title.
PR826.L63   1993
823.009 — dc20   92-50751

Printed in the United States of America
Set in Ehrhardt

To John Blackwell

"genius among editors" (*The Writing Game*, Act Two Scene Two)

Contents

Preface

For twelve months between 1990 and 1991, the poet James Fenton contributed a weekly column to the book pages of *The Independent on Sunday* entitled "*Ars Poetica*", the title of a famous treatise on poetry by the Roman poet Horace. Each week Fenton printed a short poem or extract from a poem, and wrote a commentary designed to throw light on both the text and some aspect of the art of poetry in general. Early in 1991 the literary editor of the newspaper, Blake Morrison, rang me up and asked if I would be interested in writing something similar about prose fiction when James Fenton had finished his stint.

Usually I take time to consider journalistic proposals, and more often than not I say no in the end; but on this occasion I had decided to say yes almost before Blake had finished his pitch. For nearly thirty years, between 1960 and 1987, I was an academic as well as a novelist, teaching English Literature at Birmingham University. Over that time I published several books of literary criticism, mainly concerned with novels and "The Novel", and for many of those years I offered a course called Form in Fiction. After taking early retirement from my university post in 1987 I found that I had little inclination or incentive to go on writing criticism for an essentially academic audience; but I felt that I still had things to say on the art of fiction and the history of the novel that might be of interest to a more general reading public, and sensed that a weekly newspaper column might provide an ideal platform.

I settled quite quickly on a format that was topic-centred rather than text-centred, since a novel, unlike many excellent poems, cannot be quoted in its entirety in a newspaper article. Each week I chose one or two short extracts from novels or stories, classic and modern, to illustrate some aspect of "The Art of Fiction".

(Following on Fenton's "*Ars Poetica*", this was a more or less inevitable name for the series, and I have retained it for the book in spite of some uneasiness at trespassing on the title of a venerated essay by Henry James.) With a few exceptions – Jane Austen, George Eliot, Henry James – I took my examples from a different author, or brace of authors, each week. I confined myself almost exclusively to English and American writers, because this is, as academics say, "my field" and I am less confident of doing accurate close analysis of novels outside it. I have commented on some of these passages before in print, but not in exactly the same terms.

I began with "Beginning" and always intended to end with "Ending". In between these two, one week's article sometimes suggested the topic for the following week, but I did not design the series as a systematic, progressive introduction to the theory of the novel. In revising the pieces for book publication I have inserted a number of cross-references, and provided an index, which should compensate for the somewhat random sequence of topics. Once a teacher, always a teacher. Although the book is intended for the "general reader" I have deliberately used, with explanations, a number of technical terms which may be unfamiliar to such a reader, because you cannot analyse a literary text without an appropriate descriptive vocabulary, any more than you can strip down an engine without an appropriate set of tools. Some of these terms are modern, like "intertextuality" and "metafiction", and some are ancient, like the names of figures of speech in classical rhetoric ("metonymy", "synecdoche" etc.), which modern linguistics has not yet improved upon. An alternative title for this book, if Wayne Booth hadn't used it already, would be *The Rhetoric of Fiction*. I have always regarded fiction as an essentially rhetorical art – that is to say, the novelist or short story-writer *persuades* us to share a certain view of the world for the duration of the reading experience, effecting, when successful, that rapt immersion in an imagined reality that Van Gogh caught so well in his painting "The Novel Reader". Even novelists who, for their own artistic purposes, deliberately break that spell have to cast it first.

The original articles were written to a prescribed length, but I usually submitted my copy slightly over-long, leaving the task of trimming it to fit the available space in the capable hands of Blake Morrison and his assistant Jan Dalley. (I should like to record here my appreciation of the skill and tact with which they carried out this task.) In revising the articles for book publication I have restored some of the passages which they were obliged to cut, and some which I deleted myself from earlier drafts, and have added new material, both illustrative and argumentative, to nearly all of them. One item has been replaced by a new piece on "Chapters". To throw light on the nuts and bolts of fiction, I have drawn more frequently on my own experience as a writer than seemed either appropriate or practicable in the original newspaper articles.

The book is approximately thirty per cent longer than the original series. But I have not attempted to "cover" any of the topics exhaustively. Most of them, after all, could be the subject of full-length essays or whole volumes, and in many cases already have been. This is a book for people who prefer to take their Lit. Crit. in small doses, a book to browse in, and dip into, a book that does not attempt to say the definitive word on any of the topics it touches on, but one that will, I hope, enhance readers' understanding and enjoyment of prose fiction, and suggest to them new possibilities of reading – and, who knows, even writing – in this most various and rewarding of literary forms.

The Art of Fiction

1 Beginning

Emma Woodhouse, handsome, clever, and rich, with a comfortable home and happy disposition, seemed to unite some of the best blessings of existence; and had lived nearly twenty-one years in the world with very little to distress or vex her.

She was the youngest of the two daughters of a most affectionate, indulgent father, and had, in consequence of her sister's marriage, been mistress of his house from a very early period. Her mother had died too long ago for her to have more than an indistinct remembrance of her caresses, and her place had been supplied by an excellent woman as governess, who had fallen little short of a mother in affection.

Sixteen years had Miss Taylor been in Mr Woodhouse's family, less as a governess than a friend, very fond of both daughters, but particularly of Emma. Between *them* it was more the intimacy of sisters. Even before Miss Taylor had ceased to hold the nominal office of governess, the mildness of her temper had hardly allowed her to impose any restraint; and the shadow of authority being now long passed away, they had been living together as friend and friend very mutually attached, and Emma doing just what she liked; highly esteeming Miss Taylor's judgment, but directed chiefly by her own.

The real evils indeed of Emma's situation were the power of having rather too much her own way, and a disposition to think a little too well of herself; these were the disadvantages which threatened alloy to her many enjoyments. The danger, however, was at present so unperceived, that they did not by any means rank as misfortunes with her.

Sorrow came – a gentle sorrow – but not at all in the shape of any disagreeable consciousness. – Miss Taylor married.

JANE AUSTEN *Emma* (1816)

This is the saddest story I have ever heard. We had known the Ashburnhams for nine seasons of the town of Nauheim with an extreme intimacy – or, rather, with an acquaintanceship as loose and easy and yet as close as a good glove's with your hand. My wife and I knew Captain and Mrs. Ashburnham as well as it was possible to know anybody, and yet, in another sense, we knew nothing at all about them. This is, I believe, a state of things only possible with English people of whom, till today, when I sit down to puzzle out what I know of this sad affair, I knew nothing whatever. Six months ago I had never been to England, and, certainly, I had never sounded the depths of an English heart. I had known the shallows.

FORD MADOX FORD The Good Soldier (1915)

WHEN DOES A NOVEL BEGIN? The question is almost as difficult to answer as the question, when does the human embryo become a person? Certainly the creation of a novel rarely begins with the penning or typing of its first words. Most writers do some preliminary work, if it is only in their heads. Many prepare the ground carefully over weeks or months, making diagrams of the plot, compiling C.V.s for their characters, filling a notebook with ideas, settings, situations, jokes, to be drawn on in the process of composition. Every writer has his or her own way of working. Henry James made notes for *The Spoils of Poynton* almost as long and almost as interesting as the finished novel. Muriel Spark, I understand, broods mentally on the concept of a new novel and does not set pen to paper until she has thought of a satisfactory title and opening sentence.

For the reader, however, the novel always begins with that opening sentence (which may not, of course, be the first sentence the novelist originally wrote). And then the next sentence, and then the sentence after that ... When does the beginning of a novel end, is another difficult question to answer. Is it the first paragraph, the first few pages, or the first chapter? However one defines it,

4

the beginning of a novel is a threshold, separating the real world we inhabit from the world the novelist has imagined. It should therefore, as the phrase goes, "draw us in".

This is not an easy task. We are not yet familiar with the author's tone of voice, range of vocabulary, syntactic habits. We read a book slowly and hesitantly, at first. We have a lot of new information to absorb and remember, such as the characters' names, their relationships of affinity and consanguinity, the contextual details of time and place, without which the story cannot be followed. Is all this effort going to be worthwhile? Most readers will give an author the benefit of the doubt for at least a few pages, before deciding to back out over the threshold. With the two specimens shown here, however, our hesitation is likely to be minimal or non-existent. We are "hooked" by the very first sentence in each case.

Jane Austen's opening is classical: lucid, measured, objective, with ironic implication concealed beneath the elegant velvet glove of the style. How subtly the first sentence sets up the heroine for a fall. This is to be the reverse of the Cinderella story, the triumph of an undervalued heroine, that previously attracted Jane Austen's imagination from *Pride and Prejudice* to *Mansfield Park*. Emma is a Princess who must be humbled before she finds true happiness. "Handsome" (rather than conventionally pretty or beautiful – a hint of masculine will-to-power, perhaps, in that androgynous epithet), "clever" (an ambiguous term for intelligence, sometimes applied derogatively, as in "too clever for her own good") and "rich", with all its biblical and proverbial associations of the moral dangers of wealth: these three adjectives, so elegantly combined (a matter of stress and phonology – try rearranging them) encapsulate the deceptiveness of Emma's "seeming" contentment. Having lived "nearly twenty-one years in the world with very little to distress or vex her", she is due for a rude awakening. Nearly twenty-one, the traditional age of majority, Emma must now take responsibility for her own life, and for a woman in early nineteenth-century bourgeois society this meant deciding whether and whom to marry. Emma is unusually free in this respect, since she is already "mistress" of her household, a circumstance likely to breed arrogance, especially as she has been brought up by a governess who supplied a mother's affection but not (by implication) a mother's discipline.

This suggestion is made more emphatically in the third paragraph; but at the same time, interestingly enough, we begin to hear the voice of Emma herself in the discourse, as well as the judicious, objective voice of the narrator. "Between *them* it was more the intimacy of sisters." "They had been living together as friend and friend . . ." In these phrases we seem to hear Emma's own, rather self-satisfied description of her relationship with her governess, one which allowed her to do "just what she liked." The ironic structure of the paragraph's conclusion, "highly esteeming Miss Taylor's judgment, but directed chiefly by her own," symmetrically balances two statements that are logically incompatible, and thus indicates the flaw in Emma's character that is explicitly stated by the narrator in the fourth paragraph. With the marriage of Miss Taylor, the story proper begins: deprived of Miss Taylor's company and mature counsel, Emma takes up a young protégée, Harriet, who encourages her vanity, and on whose behalf she begins to indulge in a matchmaking intrigue, with disastrous results.

Ford Madox Ford's famous opening sentence is a blatant ploy to secure the reader's attention, virtually dragging us over the threshold by the collar. But almost at once a characteristically modern obscurity and indirection, an anxiety about the possibility of discovering any truth, infect the narrative. Who is this person addressing us? He uses English yet is not English himself. He has known the English couple who seem to be the subject of the "saddest story" for at least nine years, yet claims to have "known nothing" about the English until this very moment of narration. "Heard" in the first sentence suggests that he is going to narrate someone else's story, but almost immediately it is implied that the narrator, and perhaps his wife, were themselves part of it. The narrator knows the Ashburnhams intimately – and not at all. These contradictions are rationalized as an effect of Englishness, of the disparity between appearance and reality in English middle-class behaviour; so this beginning strikes a similar thematic note to *Emma*'s, though tragic rather than comic in its premonitory under-

6

tones. The word "sad" is repeated towards the end of the paragraph, and another keyword, "heart" (two of the characters have supposed heart-conditions, all of them have disordered emotional lives), is dropped into the penultimate sentence.

I used the metaphor of a glove to describe Jane Austen's style, a style which itself claims authority partly by eschewing metaphor (metaphor being an essentially poetic figure of speech, at the opposite pole to reason and common sense). That same metaphor of a glove actually occurs in the opening paragraph of *The Good Soldier*, though with a different meaning. Here it signifies polite social behaviour, the easy but restrained manners that go with affluence and discriminating taste (a "good" glove is specified), but with a hint of deceptive concealment or "covering up". Some of the enigmas raised in the first paragraph are quickly explained – by, for instance, the information that the narrator is an American living in Europe. But the reliability of his testimony, and the chronic dissembling of the other characters, are to be crucial issues in this, the saddest story.

There are, of course, many other ways of beginning a novel, and readers browsing through this book will have opportunities to consider some of them, because I have often chosen the opening paragraph of a novel or story to illustrate other aspects of the art of fiction (it spares me from having to summarize the plot). But perhaps it is worth indicating the range of possibilities here. A novel may begin with a set-piece description of a landscape or townscape that is to be the primary setting of the story, the *mise-en-scène* as film criticism terms it: for example, the sombre description of Egdon Heath at the beginning of Thomas Hardy's *The Return of the Native*, or E. M. Forster's account of Chandrapore, in elegant, urbane guide-book prose, at the outset of *A Passage to India*. A novel may begin in the middle of a conversation, like Evelyn Waugh's *A Handful of Dust*, or Ivy Compton-Burnett's idiosyncratic works. It may begin with an arresting self-introduction by the narrator, "Call me Ishmael" (Herman Melville's *Moby Dick*), or with a rude gesture at the literary tradition of autobiography: ". . . the first thing you'll probably want to know is where I was born, and what my lousy childhood was like, and how my parents were occupied and all before they had me, and all that David Copperfield kind of crap, but I don't feel like going into it" (J. D. Salinger's *The Catcher in the Rye*). A novelist may begin with a philosophical reflection – "The past is a foreign country: they do things differently there" (L. P. Hartley, *The Go-Between*), or pitch a character into extreme jeopardy with the very first sentence: "Hale knew they meant to murder him before he had been in Brighton three hours" (Graham Greene, *Brighton Rock*). Many novels begin with a "frame-story" which explains how the main story was discovered, or describes it being told to a fictional audience. In Conrad's *Heart of Darkness* an anonymous narrator describes Marlow relating his Congo experiences to a circle of friends sitting on the deck of a cruising yawl in the Thames estuary ("And this also," Marlow begins, "has been one of the dark places of the earth"). Henry James's *The Turn of the Screw* consists of a deceased woman's memoir, which is read aloud to guests at a country-house party who have been entertaining themselves with ghost stories, and get, perhaps, more than they bargained for. Kingsley Amis begins his ghost story, *The Green Man*, with a witty pastiche of the *The Good Food Guide*: "No sooner has one got over one's surprise at finding a genuine coaching inn less than 40 miles from London – and 8 from the M1 – than one is marvelling at the quality of the equally English fare ..." Italo Calvino's *If on a winter's night a traveller* begins, "You are about to begin reading Italo Calvino's new novel, *If on a winter's night a traveller*." James Joyce's *Finnegans Wake* begins in the middle of a sentence: "riverrun, past Eve and Adam's, from swerve of shore to bend of bay, brings us by a commodius vicus of recirculation back to Howth Castle and Environs." The missing fragment concludes the book: "A way a lone a last a loved a long the" – thus returning us to the beginning again, like the recirculation of water in the environment, from river to sea to cloud to rain to river, and like the unending production of meaning in the reading of fiction.

2 The Intrusive Author

With a single drop of ink for a mirror, the Egyptian sorcerer undertook to reveal to any chance comer far-reaching visions of the past. This is what I undertake to do for you, reader. With this drop of ink at the end of my pen, I will show you the roomy workshop of Jonathan Burge, carpenter and builder in the village of Hayslope, as it appeared on the 18th of June, in the year of Our Lord, 1799.

GEORGE ELIOT *Adam Bede* (1859)

To Margaret – I hope that it will not set the reader against her – the station of King's Cross had always suggested Infinity. Its very situation – withdrawn a little behind the facile splendours of St Pancras – implied a comment on the materialism of life. Those two great arches, colourless, indifferent, shouldering between them an unlovely clock, were fit portals for some eternal adventure, whose issue might be prosperous, but would certainly not be expressed in the ordinary language of prosperity. If you think this ridiculous, remember that it is not Margaret who is telling you about it; and let me hasten to add that they were in plenty of time for the train; that Mrs Munt secured a comfortable seat, facing the engine, but not too near it; and that Margaret, on her return to Wickham Place, was confronted with the following telegram:

All over. Wish I had never written. Tell no one. – Helen.

But Aunt Juley was gone – gone irrevocably, and no power on earth could stop her.

E. M. FORSTER *Howards End* (1910)

THE SIMPLEST WAY of telling a story is in the voice of a storyteller, which may be the anonymous voice of folk-tale ("Once upon a time there was a beautiful princess") or the voice of the epic bard (e.g., Virgil's "Arms and the man I sing") or the confiding, companionable, sententious authorial voice of classic fiction from Henry Fielding to George Eliot.

At the beginning of *Adam Bede*, by a neat rhetorical trick with the drop of ink, which is both mirror and medium, George Eliot transforms the act of writing into a kind of speaking, a direct yet intimate address to the reader, inviting us "over the threshold" of the novel, and literally over the threshold of Jonathan Burge's workshop. By implication she contrasts her own, minutely particular, scrupulously historical kind of story-telling, with the dubious revelations of magic and superstition. The nugget of information about the techniques of Egyptian sorcerers has no other narrative function, but is not without interest in itself. We read fiction, after all, not just for the story, but to enlarge our knowledge and understanding of the world, and the authorial narrative method is particularly suited to incorporating this kind of encyclopedic knowledge and proverbial wisdom.

Around the turn of the century, however, the intrusive authorial voice fell into disfavour, partly because it detracts from realistic illusion and reduces the emotional intensity of the experience being represented, by calling attention to the act of narrating. It also claims a kind of authority, a God-like omniscience, which our sceptical and relativistic age is reluctant to grant to anyone. Modern fiction has tended to suppress or eliminate the authorial voice, by presenting the action through the consciousness of the characters, or by handing over to them the narrative task itself. When the intrusive authorial voice *is* employed in modern fiction, it's usually with a certain ironic self-consciousness, as in the passage from *Howards End*. This concludes the second chapter, in which the Bloomsburyite Margaret Schlegel, having heard that her sister Helen has fallen in love with the younger son of a *nouveau-riche* captain of industry, Henry Wilcox, despatches her aunt (Mrs Munt) to investigate.

Howards End is a Condition-of-England novel, and the sense of the country as an organic whole, with a spiritually inspiring, essentially agrarian past, and a problematic future overshadowed by commerce and industry, is what gives a representative significance to the characters and their relationships. This theme reaches its visionary climax in Chapter 19, where, from the high vantage-point of the Purbeck hills, the question is posed by the author, whether England belongs to those who have created her wealth and power or "to those who ... have somehow seen her, seen the whole island at once, lying as a jewel in a silver sea, sailing as a ship of souls, with all the brave world's fleet accompanying her towards eternity."

Both the author and Margaret clearly belong to the visionary company. The Infinity that Margaret associates with King's Cross station is equivalent to the eternity towards which the ship of England is sailing, while the materialism and prosperity on which King's Cross adversely comments belong to the world of the Wilcoxes. The solidarity of sentiment between author and heroine is obvious in the style: only the shift to a past tense (*"implied* a comment", *"were* fit portals") distinguishes Margaret's thoughts, grammatically, from the authorial voice. Forster is overtly – some might say, overly – protective towards his heroine.

"To Margaret – I hope that it will not set the reader against her ..." "If you think this ridiculous, remember that it is not Margaret who is telling you about it," are risky moves, which come near to creating the effect Erving Goffman calls "breaking frame" – when some rule or convention that governs a particular type of experience is transgressed. These phrases bring into the open what realistic illusion normally requires us to suppress or bracket off – our knowledge that we are reading a novel about invented characters and actions.

This is a device much favoured by postmodern writers, who disown a naive faith in traditional realism by exposing the nuts and bolts of their fictional constructs. Compare, for example, this startling authorial intrusion in the middle of Joseph Heller's *Good as Gold* (1980):

Once again Gold found himself preparing to lunch with someone – Spotty Weinrock – and the thought arose that he was spending an awful lot of time in this book eating and talking. There was not much else to be done with him. I was putting him into bed a lot with Andrea and keeping his wife and children conveniently in the background ... Certainly he would soon meet a school-teacher with four children with whom he would fall madly in love, and I would shortly hold out to him the tantalizing promise of becoming the country's first Jewish Secretary of State, a promise I did not intend to keep.

Forster does not undermine, as radically as that, the illusion of life generated by his story, and invites our sympathetic interest in the characters and their fortunes by referring to them as if they are real people. So what is he trying to achieve by drawing attention to the gap between Margaret's experience and his narration of it? I suggest that, by making a playful, self-deprecating reference to his own rhetorical function, he obtains permission, as it were, to indulge in those high-flown authorial disquisitions about history and metaphysics (like the vision of England from the Purbeck hills) which are scattered throughout the novel, and which he saw as essential to its thematic purpose. Urbane humour is an effective way of deflecting and disarming the possible reader-response of "*Come off it!*" which this kind of authorial generalizing invites. Forster also makes a joke out of the interruption of narrative momentum which such passages inevitably entail, by apologetically "hastening" to return us to the story, and ending his chapter with a fine effect of suspense.

But suspense is a separate subject.

3 Suspense

At first, when death appeared improbable because it had never visited him before, Knight could think of no future, nor of anything connected with his past. He could only look sternly at Nature's treacherous attempt to put an end to him, and strive to thwart her.

From the fact that the cliff formed the inner face of the segment of a hollow cylinder, having the sky for a top and the sea for a bottom, which enclosed the bay to the extent of nearly a semicircle, he could see the vertical face curving round on each side of him. He looked far down the façade, and realized more thoroughly how it threatened him. Grimness was in every feature, and to its very bowels the inimical shape was desolation.

By one of those familiar conjunctions of things wherewith the inanimate world baits the mind of man when he pauses in moments of suspense, opposite Knight's eyes was an imbedded fossil, standing forth in low relief from the rock. It was a creature with eyes. The eyes, dead and turned to stone, were even now regarding him. It was one of the early crustaceans called *Trilobites*. Separated by millions of years in their lives, Knight and this underling seemed to have met in their place of death. It was the single instance within reach of his vision of anything that had ever been alive and had had a body to save, as he himself had now.

THOMAS HARDY *A Pair of Blue Eyes* (1873)

NOVELS ARE NARRATIVES, and narrative, whatever its medium – words, film, strip-cartoon – holds the interest of an audience by raising questions in their minds, and delaying the answers. The questions are broadly of two kinds, having to do with causality (e.g. whodunnit?) and temporality (e.g. what will happen next?) each exhibited in a very pure form by the classic detective story and the adventure story, respectively. Suspense is an effect especially associated with the adventure story, and with the hybrid of detective story and adventure story known as the thriller. Such narratives are designed to put the hero or heroine repeatedly into situations of extreme jeopardy, thus exciting in the reader emotions of sympathetic fear and anxiety as to the outcome.

Because suspense is particularly associated with popular forms of fiction it has often been despised, or at least demoted, by literary novelists of the modern period. In *Ulysses*, for instance, James Joyce superimposed the banal and inconclusive events of a day in modern Dublin upon the heroic and satisfyingly closed story of Odysseus's return from the Trojan War, implying that reality is less exciting and more indeterminate than traditional fiction would have us believe. But there have been writers of stature, especially in the nineteenth century, who consciously borrowed the suspense-creating devices of popular fiction and turned them to their own purposes.

One such was Thomas Hardy, whose first published novel, *Desperate Remedies* (1871), was a "sensation-novel" in the style of Wilkie Collins. His third, *A Pair of Blue Eyes* (1873), was more lyrical and psychological, drawing on Hardy's courtship of his first wife in the romantic setting of north Cornwall, and was the favourite novel of that master of modern autobiographical fiction, Marcel Proust. But it contains a classic scene of suspense that was, as far as I know, entirely invented. The word itself derives from the Latin word meaning "to hang", and there could hardly be a situation more productive of suspense than that of a man clinging by his finger-tips to the face of a cliff, unable to climb to safety – hence the generic term, "cliffhanger".

About halfway through *A Pair of Blue Eyes*, the young and somewhat fickle heroine, Elfride, daughter of a Cornish vicar,

14

takes a telescope to the top of a high cliff overlooking the Bristol Channel, to view the ship that is bringing home from India the young architect to whom she is secretly engaged. She is accompanied by Henry Knight, a friend of her stepmother's, a man of maturer years and intellectual interests, who has made overtures to her, and to whom she is becoming guiltily attracted. As they sit on the cliff top, Knight's hat is blown towards the edge, and when he tries to retrieve it he finds himself unable to climb back up the slippery one-in-three slope that terminates in a sheer drop of several hundred feet. Elfride's impetuous efforts to assist him only make things worse, and as she clambers back to safety she inadvertently sends him sliding further towards disaster. "As he slowly slid inch by inch ... Knight made a last desperate dash at the lowest tuft of vegetation – the last outlying knot of starved herbage where the rock appeared in all its bareness. It arrested his further descent. Knight was now literally *suspended* by his arms ..." (*my italics*). Elfride disappears from Knight's view, presumably seeking assistance, though he knows they are miles from any human habitation.

What happens next? Will Knight survive, and if so, how? Suspense can only be sustained by delaying the answers to these questions. One way of doing this, beloved of the cinema (whose effects Hardy often anticipated in his intensely visual fiction) would be to crosscut between the anguish of Knight and the frantic efforts of the heroine to effect a rescue. But Hardy wants to surprise Knight (and the reader) with Elfride's response to the emergency, and therefore restricts the narration of the scene to Knight's point of view. The suspense is extended by a detailed account of his thoughts as he clings to the cliff-face, and these thoughts are those of a Victorian intellectual, on whom recent discoveries in geology and natural history, especially the work of Darwin, have made a deep impression. The passage in which Knight realizes that he is staring into the eyes, "dead and turned to stone", of a fossilized arthropod millions of years old, is one that perhaps only Hardy could have written. His work is notable for such breathtaking shifts of perspective, which display the fragile human figure dwarfed by a Universe whose vast dimensions of space and time were just beginning to be truly apprehended. And invariably his characters, fallaciously but understandably, read into this disparity of scale a kind of cosmic malice. Confronting the dead eyes of the fossil, which have replaced the living, seductive blue eyes of Elfride in his field of vision, Knight acquires a new understanding, both poignant and bleak, of his own mortality.

The scene is extended for some pages by the same means: philosophical reflections on geology, prehistory and the apparent spitefulness of Nature (the wind whips Knight's clothing, the rain stings his face, a red sun looks on "with a drunken leer") punctuated by questions that keep the wire of narrative suspense taut: "Was he to die? . . . He had hoped for deliverance, but what could a girl do? He dared not move an inch. Was Death really stretching out his hand?"

Elfride, of course, rescues him. How she does it I will not divulge, except to say, by way of encouragement to those of you who haven't yet got round to reading this delightful book, that it entails taking off all her clothes.

4 Teenage *Skaz*

Old Sally didn't talk much, except to rave about the Lunts, because she was busy rubbering and being charming. Then, all of a sudden, she saw some jerk she knew on the other side of the lobby. Some guy in one of those very dark grey flannel suits and one of those checkered vests. Strictly Ivy League. Big deal. He was standing next to the wall, smoking himself to death and looking bored as hell. Old Sally kept saying, "I *know* that boy from somewhere." She always *knew* somebody, any place you took her, or thought she did. She kept saying that till I got bored as hell, and I said to her, "Why don't you go on over and give him a big soul kiss, if you know him. He'll enjoy it." She got sore when I said that. Finally, though, the jerk noticed her and came over and said hello. You should've seen the way they said hello. You'd have thought they hadn't seen each other in twenty years. You'd have thought they'd taken baths in the same bathtub or something when they were little kids. Old buddyroos. It was nauseating. The funny part was, they probably met each other just *once*, at some phoney party. Finally, when they were all done slobbering around, old Sally introduced us. His name was George something – I don't even remember – and he went to Andover. Big, big deal. You should've seen him when old Sally asked him how he liked the play. He was the kind of a phoney that have to give themselves *room* when they answer somebody's question. He stepped back, and stepped right on the lady's foot behind him. He probably broke every toe in her body. He said the play itself was no masterpiece, but that the Lunts, of course, were absolute angels. Angels. For Chrissake. *Angels*. That killed me. Then he and old Sally started talking about a lot of people they both knew. It was the phoniest conversation you ever heard in your life.

J. D. SALINGER *The Catcher in the Rye* (1951)

Skaz IS A RATHER APPEALING Russian word (suggesting "jazz" and "scat", as in "scat-singing", to the English ear) used to designate a type of first-person narration that has the characteristics of the spoken rather than the written word. In this kind of novel or story, the narrator is a character who refers to himself (or herself) as "I", and addresses the reader as "you". He or she uses vocabulary and syntax characteristic of colloquial speech, and appears to be relating the story spontaneously rather than delivering a carefully constructed and polished written account. We don't so much read it as listen to it, as to a talkative stranger encountered in a pub or railway carriage. Needless to say, this is an illusion, the product of much calculated effort and painstaking rewriting by the "real" author. A narrative style that faithfully imitated actual speech would be virtually unintelligible, as are transcripts of recorded conversations. But it is an illusion that can create a powerful effect of authenticity and sincerity, of truth-telling.

For American novelists *skaz* was an obvious way to free themselves from the inherited literary traditions of England and Europe. The crucial impetus was given by Mark Twain. "All modern American literature comes from one book by Mark Twain called *Huckleberry Finn*," said Ernest Hemingway – an overstatement, but an illuminating one. Twain's masterstroke was to unite a vernacular colloquial style with a naive, immature narrator, an adolescent boy who is wiser than he knows, whose vision of the adult world has a devastating freshness and honesty. This, for example, is Huck's reaction to different types of Christian faith:

> Sometimes the widow would take me one side and talk about Providence in a way to make a body's mouth water; but maybe next day Miss Watson would take hold and knock it all down again. I judged I could see there were two Providences and a poor chap would stand considerable show with the widow's Providence, but if Miss Watson's got him there warn't no hope for him any more.

J. D. Salinger's Holden Caulfield is a literary descendant of Huck Finn: more educated and sophisticated, the son of affluent

New Yorkers, but like Huck a youthful runaway from a world of adult hypocrisy, venality and, to use one of his own favourite words, phoniness. What particularly appals Holden is the eagerness of his peers to adopt that corrupt grownup behaviour. In the course of the story, Holden takes a girlfriend to a matinée of a Broadway play starring a famous acting couple, Alfred and Lynn Lunt. "Old Sally", and the acquaintance she meets in the lobby during the interval, are described in this extract as acting out a wholly inauthentic type of adult social behaviour.

The features of Holden's narrative style that make it sound like speech rather than writing, and a teenager's speech at that, are easy enough to identify. There's a lot of repetition (because elegant variation in vocabulary requires careful thought) especially of slang expressions like "jerk", "bored as hell", "phoney", "big deal", "killed me" and "old" (an epithet applied promiscuously to anything familiar, whatever its age). Like many young people, Holden expresses the strength of his feelings by exaggeration, the device rhetoricians call hyperbole: "smoking himself to death", "You'd have thought they hadn't seen each other in twenty years", "slobbering around". The syntax is simple. Sentences are typically short and uncomplicated. Many of them aren't properly formed, lacking a finite verb ("Strictly Ivy League. Big deal.") There are grammatical mistakes such as speakers often make ("He was the kind of a phoney that have to give themselves *room* . . ."). In longer sentences, clauses are strung together as they seem to occur to the speaker, rather than being subordinated to each other in complex structures.

The informality of Holden's discourse is the guarantee of his spontaneity and authenticity. It is thrown into relief by the well-formed but pretentious small talk of George: "He said the play itself was no masterpiece, but that the Lunts, of course, were absolute angels." This utterance is further downgraded, and made to seem especially stilted, by being rendered as indirect or reported speech, in contrast to Holden's exasperated outburst to Sally, which is quoted directly: "Why don't you go on over and give him a big soul kiss . . ."

It is, as I say, easy enough to describe Holden's style of narration;

but more difficult to explain how it holds our attention and gives us pleasure for the length of a whole novel. For, make no mistake, it's the style that makes the book interesting. The story it tells is episodic, inconclusive and largely made up of trivial events. Yet the language is, by normal literary criteria, very impoverished. Salinger, the invisible ventriloquist who speaks to us through Holden, must say everything he has to say about life and death and ultimate values within the limitations of a seventeen-year-old New Yorker's argot, eschewing poetic metaphors, periodic cadences, fine writing of any kind.

Part of the answer is certainly the derisive humour created by the application of Holden's "low" language to the polite pretences of social and cultural life as exhibited by Sally and George. The formal incorrectness of his English is also a source of humour – the funniest line in the extract is, "He probably broke every toe in her body", a distortion of "every bone in her body", and another hyperbolic expression. A further reason is that Holden's language implies more than it states. In this extract, for instance, there is clearly an unacknowledged theme of jealousy on Holden's part, towards the rival male figure of George, much as Holden claims to despise his status-conferring Ivy-League clothes and suave manners. The pathos of Holden Caulfield's situation, here and throughout the book, is more effective for not being explicitly spoken.

In the last analysis, though, there's something surprisingly poetic about this prose, a subtle manipulation of the rhythms of colloquial speech which makes it an effortless pleasure to read, and re-read. As jazz musicians say, it swings.

5 The Epistolary Novel

What I can't bear is that for one moment she recognized my claims, acknowledged my rights. What makes me want to hammer my fist on the table . . .

Phone. Ringing. Hold on.

No. Just some student having a breakdown. Yes, what makes me want to howl at the moon is the thought of her scratching away down there in London as if nothing had happened. I'd just like to know that she had lifted her head from her imaginary world for one moment, and said . . .

Another thought has just occurred to me, though. She may not be scratching away as if nothing had happened. She may be putting down some version of the events in the guest room. One of her maddeningly percipient, odd, crabwise heroines may be scuttering bizarrely sideways at the sight of some bumptious young academic's aubergine underpants. No need for one of your looks, thank you – I have managed to grasp the irony of this unprompted. It's different, though – she's not writing privately to a friend of hers in some comfortingly remote country. She's writing to friends of mine. And enemies of mine. And colleagues of mine. And students of mine . . .

What? *Are* my underpants aubergine? Of course they're not aubergine! Don't you know anything about my taste at all? But she may be saying they're aubergine! That's what they do, these people. They embroider, they improve on the truth – they tell lies.

MICHAEL FRAYN *The Trick of It* (1989)

NOVELS WRITTEN in the form of letters were hugely popular in the eighteenth century. Samuel Richardson's long, moralistic and psychologically acute epistolary novels of seduction, *Pamela* (1741) and *Clarissa* (1747), were landmarks in the history of European fiction, inspiring many imitators such as Rousseau (*La Nouvelle Héloïse*) and Laclos (*Les Liaisons dangereuses*). Jane Austen's first draft of *Sense and Sensibility* was in letter form, but her second thoughts were prophetic of the decline of the epistolary novel in the nineteenth century. In the age of the telephone it became a very rare species indeed, though, as Michael Frayn's *The Trick of It* recently demonstrated, not altogether extinct, and well worth preserving.

The invention of the fax machine may provoke a revival of the form (the title story of Andrew Davies's *Dirty Faxes*, 1990, being perhaps a straw in the wind) but, generally speaking, the modern epistolary novelist is obliged to separate his correspondents by some considerable distance to make the convention seem plausible. Frayn's hero, or antihero, is a nameless thirtysomething British academic specializing in the work of a contemporary woman novelist of slightly more mature years, referred to in the text by her initials, JL. He invites her to speak at his University and, much to his surprise, is invited afterwards into her guestroom bed. This event, and the sequel, he describes in a series of letters to an academic friend based in Australia.

He is divided between infatuation and suspicion. On the one hand he glories in his intimate relationship with the woman to the study of whose work he has dedicated his professional career; on the other hand he fears that she will exploit this relationship by turning it into new fictions, both publicizing it and misrepresenting it in the process. He reveres her literary ability, but he also envies it, and in a paradoxical way resents it. He is vexed that in spite of possessing her body (and eventually marrying her) he does not at the same time control her fictive imagination. He ends by vainly attempting to acquire "the trick of it" (i.e. writing fiction) himself. It's a familiar satirical theme – the contrast between the critical and the creative faculties – rendered fresh and amusing by the artfulness of the telling.

The epistolary novel is a type of first-person narrative, but it has certain special features not found in the more familiar autobiographical mode. Whereas the story of an autobiography is known to the narrator before he starts, letters chronicle an ongoing process; or as Richardson put it: *"Much more* lively and affecting ... must be the style of those who write in the height of a *present* distress, the mind tortured by the pangs of uncertainty ... than the dry, narrative unanimated style of a person relating difficulties and danger surmounted can be ...."

The same effect can of course be obtained by using the form of a journal, but the epistolary novel has two additional advantages. Firstly, you can have more than one correspondent, and thus show the same event from different points of view, with quite different interpretations, as Richardson brilliantly demonstrated in *Clarissa*. (For example, Clarissa writes to her friend Miss Howe about an interview with Lovelace in which he seemed to be showing a genuine disposition to renounce his licentious past; Lovelace reports the same conversation to his friend Belford as a stage in his cunning plot to seduce her.) Secondly, even if you limit yourself, as Frayn does, to one writer, a letter, unlike a journal, is always addressed to a specific addressee, whose anticipated response conditions the discourse, and makes it rhetorically more complex, interesting and obliquely revealing.

Frayn exploits this latter opportunity to particularly good effect. His academic is a comically flawed character, full of vanity, anxiety and paranoia, which he constantly betrays by anticipating or imagining his Australian friend's reactions ("No need for one of your looks, thank you ..."). Sometimes the letters read like dramatic monologues, in which we overhear one side only of a dialogue, and infer the rest: "What? *Are* my underpants aubergine? Of course they're not aubergine! Don't you know anything about my taste at all?" There, the style approaches *skaz*, the imitation of oral narrative I discussed in the previous section; but it can also comfortably accommodate selfconsciously literary writing, like, "One of her maddeningly percipient, odd, crabwise heroines may be scuttering bizarrely sideways at the sight of some bumptious young academic's aubergine underpants." If that sentence seems a shade over-written, weighed down with too many adjectives and adverbs, that is all part of Frayn's purpose. The narrator must vividly convey the comedy of his plight, but he cannot be allowed true eloquence, for that would contradict his inability to master the "trick of it".

Writing, strictly speaking, can only faithfully imitate other writing. Its representation of speech, and still more of non-verbal events, is highly artificial. But a fictional letter is indistinguishable from a real letter. A reference to the circumstances in which a novel is being written, in the text itself, would normally draw attention to the existence of the "real" author behind the text, and thus break the fictional illusion of reality, but in the epistolary novel it contributes to the illusion. I do not, for example, incorporate telephone calls from my agent into the text of my novel-in-progress, but the call from the student which interrupts Frayn's academic in mid-sentence is both realistic and character-revealing (he is so self-obsessed that he ignores his pastoral responsibilities).

The pseudo-documentary realism of the epistolary method gave the early novelists an unprecedented power over their audiences, comparable to the spell exerted on modern television audiences by certain soap-operas. While the enormously long *Clarissa* was being published, volume by volume, Richardson was frequently begged by readers not to allow the heroine to die, and many of the first readers of *Pamela* supposed it was an actual correspondence, of which Richardson was merely the editor. Modern readers of literary fiction will not be thus taken in, of course; but it is a neat trick on Frayn's part to make his academic complain of the way novelists turn fact into fiction ("That's what they do, these people. They embroider, they improve on the truth – they tell lies") in a kind of novel originally designed to make fiction look like fact.

6 Point of View

It must not be supposed that her ladyship's intermissions were not qualified by demonstrations of another order – triumphal entries and breathless pauses during which she seemed to take of everything in the room, from the state of the ceiling to that of her daughter's boot-toes, a survey that was rich in intentions. Sometimes she sat down and sometimes she surged about, but her atttitude wore equally in either case the grand air of the practical. She found so much to deplore that she left a great deal to expect, and bristled so with calculation that she seemed to scatter remedies and pledges. Her visits were as good as an outfit; her manner, as Mrs Wix once said, as good as a pair of curtains; but she was a person addicted to extremes – sometimes barely speaking to her child and sometimes pressing this tender shoot to a bosom cut, as Mrs Wix had also observed, remarkably low. She was always in a fearful hurry, and the lower the bosom was cut the more it was to be gathered she was wanted elsewhere. She usually broke in alone, but sometimes Sir Claude was with her, and during all the earlier period there was nothing on which these appearances had had so delightful a bearing as on the way her ladyship was, as Mrs Wix expressed it, under the spell. "But *isn't* she under it!" Maisie used in thoughtful but familiar reference to exclaim after Sir Claude had swept mamma away in peals of natural laughter. Not even in the old days of the convulsed ladies had she heard mamma laugh so freely as in these moments of conjugal surrender, to the gaiety of which even a little girl could see she had at last a right – a little girl whose thoughtfulness was now all happy selfish meditation on good omens and future fun.

HENRY JAMES *What Maisie Knew* (1897)

A REAL EVENT may be – and usually is – experienced by more than one person, simultaneously. A novel can provide different perspectives on the same event – but only one at a time. And even if it adopts an "omniscient" narrative method, reporting the action from a God-like altitude, it will usually privilege just one or two of the possible "points of view" from which the story could be told, and concentrate on how events affect *them*. Totally objective, totally impartial narration may be a worthy aim in journalism or historiography, but a fictional story is unlikely to engage our interest unless we know whose story it is.

The choice of the point(s) of view from which the story is told is arguably the most important single decision that the novelist has to make, for it fundamentally affects the way readers will respond, emotionally and morally, to the fictional characters and their actions. The story of an adultery, for instance – any adultery – will affect us differently according to whether it is presented primarily from the point of view of the unfaithful person, or the injured spouse, or the lover – or as observed by some fourth party. *Madame Bovary* narrated mainly from the point of view of Charles Bovary would be a very different book from the one we know.

Henry James was something of a virtuoso in the manipulation of point of view. In *What Maisie Knew* he presents a story of multiple adulteries – or adulteries thinly legitimized by divorce and re-marriage – exclusively through the eyes of a child who is affected by, but largely uncomprehending of them. Maisie's parents divorce when her father has an affair with her governess, whom he marries. Maisie's mother, Ida, marries a young admirer, Sir Claude, and puts Maisie in the charge of another governess, Mrs Wix. Before long, the step-parents become lovers. Maisie is used by these selfish and unscrupulous adults as a pawn in their quarrels and an intermediary in their amorous intrigues. While they pursue their selfish pleasures, she is confined to a dreary schoolroom with the frumpish Mrs Wix, who is herself infatuated with Sir Charles, and mature only in years.

The passage quoted comes early in the book, and concerns Ida's empty promises, in the honeymoon period of her second marriage, to improve the quality of Maisie's life. It is narrated from Maisie's point of view – but not in her own voice, nor in a style that in any way attempts to imitate a child's discourse. James explained his reason in the Preface he wrote to the New York Edition: "Small children have many more perceptions than they have terms to translate them: their vision is at any moment richer, their apprehension even constantly stronger, than their prompt, their at all producible, vocabulary." Stylistically, then, *What Maisie Knew* is antithetical to *The Catcher in the Rye*. A naive viewpoint is articulated in a mature style: elegant, complex, subtle.

Nothing is described which Maisie could not plausibly perceive and, in her own childish terms, understand. Her mamma makes exciting, energetic proposals for redecorating the schoolroom and renewing Maisie's wardrobe. Ida's visitations are sudden and brief, her behaviour volatile and unpredictable. She is usually glamorously dressed, and on her way to some social engagement. She seems to be much in love with her new husband, and in good spirits. Maisie observes all these things accurately, but innocently. She still trusts her mamma, and looks forward hopefully to "future fun". The reader, however, is under no such illusions, because the highly sophisticated language in which these observations are communicated is devastatingly ironic at Ida's expense.

The very first sentence of this paragraph contains most of the features that place its style at the opposite pole from the language of a child. It begins with a passive verbal construction ("It must not be supposed"), proceeds to a double negative ("were not qualified"), prefers polysyllabic abstract nouns ("intermissions", "demonstrations", "intentions") to concrete or homely words, and favours elegantly symmetrical pairings ("triumphal entries and breathless pauses", "from . . . ceiling . . . to . . . boot-toes"). The structure of the whole sentence is what grammarians call periodic – in other words, you have to wait till the end, holding the accumulating information in your head, for the clinching clause that delivers the main point (which is, that Ida's apparent concern is all show). This makes reading James a strenuous, but rewarding experience: nod in mid-sentence, and you are lost.

His fondness for parallelism and antithesis is particularly marked, and particularly effective, in this excerpt. "Sometimes she

27

sat down and sometimes she surged about." "She found so much to deplore that she left a good deal to expect." "Her visits were as good as an outfit; her manner, as Mrs Wix once said, as good as a pair of curtains." These deftly balanced structures underline the contradictions between Ida's promises and her performance, her pretensions to generosity and her actual selfishness.

One of the commonest signs of a lazy or inexperienced writer of fiction is inconsistency in handling point of view. A story – let us say it is the story of John, leaving home for the first time to go to University, as perceived by John – John packing his bag, taking a last look round his bedroom, saying goodbye to his parents – and suddenly, for just a couple of sentences, we are told what his mother is thinking about the event, merely because it seemed to the writer an interesting bit of information to put in at that point; after which the narrative carries on from John's point of view. Of course, there is no rule or regulation that says a novel may not shift its point of view whenever the writer chooses; but if it is not done according to some aesthetic plan or principle, the reader's involvement, the reader's "production" of the meaning of the text, will be disturbed. We may wonder, consciously or subliminally, why, if we have been told what John's mother was thinking at one point in the scene, we haven't been given the same access to her mind at other moments. The mother, who was up to that point an object of John's perception, has suddenly become a subject in her own right, but an incompletely realized one. And, if we are given access to the mother's point of view, why not the father's too?

There is in fact a certain enhancement of intensity and immediacy to be gained by restricting the narrative to a single point of view – or so James certainly believed. But how artfully he uses Mrs Wix to convey adult judgments on Ida, judgments of which Maisie would be incapable, without deviating from Maisie's perspective. Maisie assimilates the comment about Ida's manner being as good as a pair of curtains as a kind of compliment, whereas the reader interprets it as a tart criticism. Likewise Mrs Wix's observation of Ida's décolletage is motivated by jealousy and moral disapproval, whereas Maisie, seeing no erotic significance in the exposure of the female bosom, is struck only by the ratio between the lowness of the necklines and the duration of her mother's visits.

Later in the story, as Maisie moves from childhood to adolescence, such innocence yields to a dawning awareness of what her adult relations are up to, but the gap between language and point of view is never closed, and the question of what Maisie knew never entirely resolved. "Beauty is truth," said Keats. "Beauty is information," says the great Russian semiotician, Juri Lotman, a formula more in tune with the modern mind. Henry James, the first truly modern novelist in the English language, did not believe that the ultimate truth about human experience could ever be established, but developed a fictional technique that loaded every rift with the ore of information.

7 Mystery

"Mr Vickery would go up-country that same evening to take over certain naval ammunition left after the war in Bloemfontein Fort. No details was ordered to accompany Master Vickery. He was told off first person singular – as a unit – by himself."

The marine whistled penetratingly. "That's what I thought," said Pyecroft. "I went ashore with him an' 'e asked me to walk through the station. He was clickin' audibly, but otherwise seemed happy-ish.

"'You might like to know,' he says, 'that Phyllis's Circus will be performin' at Worcester tomorrow night. So I shall see 'er yet once again. You've been very patient with me,' he says.

"'Look here, Vickery,' I said, 'this thing's come to be just as much as I can stand. Consume your own smoke. I don't want to know any more.'

"'You!' he said. 'What have you got to complain of? – you've only had to watch. I'm *it*,' he says, 'but that's neither here nor there,' he says. 'I've one thing to say before shakin' 'ands. Remember,' 'e says – we were just by the admiral's garden-gate then – 'remember that I am not a murderer, because my lawful wife died in childbed six weeks after I came out. That much at least I am clear of,' 'e says.

"'Then what have you done that signifies?' I said. 'What's the rest of it?'

"'The rest,' 'e says, 'is silence,' an' he shook 'ands and went clickin' into Simonstown station."

"Did he stop to see Mrs Bathurst at Worcester?" I asked.

"It's not known. He reported at Bloemfontein, saw the ammunition into the trucks, and then 'e disappeared. Went out – deserted, if you care to put it so – within eighteen months of his pension, an' if what 'e said about 'is wife was true he was a free man as 'e then stood. How do you read it off?"

RUDYARD KIPLING "Mrs Bathurst" (1904)

A FEW PAGES EARLIER, discussing a "cliffhanging" episode in Thomas Hardy's *A Pair of Blue Eyes*, I revealed that the heroine eventually rescued the hero, but gave only a clue as to how she contrived to do so. For readers unfamiliar with the novel I thus converted an effect of suspense ("what will happen?") to one of enigma or mystery ("how did she do it?"). These two questions are the mainsprings of narrative interest and as old as storytelling itself.

One of the staple ingredients of traditional romance, for example, was mystery concerning the origins and parentage of characters, invariably resolved to the advantage of the hero and/or heroine, a plot motif that persists deep into nineteenth-century fiction and is still common in popular fiction today (in literary fiction it tends to be used parodically, as in Anthony Burgess's *M/F*, or my own *Small World*). Victorian novelists like Dickens and Wilkie Collins exploited mystery in connection with crimes and misdemeanours, leading eventually to the evolution of a separate subgenre, the classic detective story of Conan Doyle and his successors.

A solved mystery is ultimately reassuring to readers, asserting the triumph of reason over instinct, of order over anarchy, whether in the tales of Sherlock Holmes or in the case histories of Sigmund Freud which bear such a striking and suspicious resemblance to them. That is why mystery is an invariable ingredient of popular narrative, whatever its form – prose fiction or movies or television soaps. Modern literary novelists, in contrast, wary of neat solutions and happy endings, have tended to invest their mysteries with an aura of ambiguity and to leave them unresolved. We never discover for certain what Maisie knew about her adult relations' sexual behaviour, whether Conrad's Kurtz in *Heart of Darkness* was a tragic hero or a human devil, or which of the alternative endings of John Fowles' *The French Lieutenant's Woman* is the "true" one.

Kipling's story "Mrs Bathurst" is a famous example of such a text, and particularly interesting in coming from a writer who commanded a huge popular audience, most of whom must have been baffled and exasperated by its elaborate and undecidable mystifications. By the same token it shows that he was a much more selfconscious, artful and experimental writer than he is often given credit for.

The story is set in South Africa shortly after the end of the Boer War, and concerns the mysterious disappearance of a British sailor called Vickery, known as Click on account of his ill-fitting false teeth. The few known facts of the case emerge gradually in the course of a conversation between four men who meet by chance on a railway siding beside a Cape beach. They are: Vickery's shipmate Pyecroft, a Sergeant of Marines called Pritchard, a Railway Inspector called Hooper and an anonymous "I" narrator (by implication, Kipling himself) who frames the story by describing the circumstances of their meeting, and reports their conversation. Pyecroft describes how, in the days immediately preceding his disappearance, Vickery insisted on taking him with obsessive frequency to see a cinematic newsreel, part of a travelling entertainment for the troops called Phyllis's Circus, because it contained a fleeting glimpse of a woman alighting from a train at Paddington station. She was a widow called Mrs Bathurst, also known to Pyecroft and Pritchard as the friendly landlady of a pub in New Zealand, with whom Vickery evidently had a guilty relationship (though her own character, as Pritchard testifies, was spotless). Pyecroft's (which is to say Kipling's) remarkable account of this bit of film – the first he has ever seen – is one of the earliest literary descriptions of cinema, and encapsulates the elusiveness of the story's core:

> "Then the doors opened and the passengers came out and the porters got the luggage – just like life. Only – only when anyone came down too far towards us that was watchin', they walked right out o' the picture, so to speak . . . Quite slowly, from be'ind two porters – carryin' a little reticule an' lookin' from side to side – comes our Mrs Bathurst. There was no mistakin' the walk in a hundred thousand. She come forward – right forward – she looked out straight at us with the blindish look which Pritch alluded to. She walked on and on till she melted out of the picture – like – like a shadow jumping over a candle . . ."

Vickery, convinced that Mrs Bathurst is "looking for him",

becomes so disturbed by this repeated spectacle that his commanding officer is alarmed, and sends him off on a solitary mission on land, from which he never returns. In the passage quoted, Pyecroft describes his last sight of Vickery, as he escorted him ashore, and formulates the enigma of his disappearance.

The effect of mystery is impossible to illustrate with a single short quotation, because it is maintained by a steady stream of hints, clues and puzzling data. And in the case of "Mrs Bathurst" there is additional mystification about what the central mystery *is*. The frame story of the meeting of the four men, and their badinage, arguments and lengthy anecdotal reminiscences, seem to occupy more textual space than the story of Vickery. The passage quoted, where the enigma of his disappearance is most explicitly formulated, and which would have come near the beginning of a Sherlock Holmes story, in fact comes very near the end of this one.

As Vickery mentions murder only to declare his innocence of it, so Kipling invokes the detective story only to distance himself from it. "Inspector" Hooper (the title could be mistaken for a policeman's) has in his waistcoat pocket a set of false teeth, found on one of two corpses that have been discovered burned to death in a teak-forest fire up-country. This seems to be forensic evidence of how Vickery met his end. "Permanent things false teeth are. You read about 'em in all the murder trials," says Hooper; but at the end of the story the narrator reports that he "brought his hand away from his waistcoat pocket – empty." Though attributed to Hooper's sense of decorum, the empty hand also symbolizes the frustration of the reader's desire for a solution to the mystery. Even if we accept the identification of Vickery, and the account of his end, we do not know what deed drove him to this extremity, or the identity of the second corpse found beside him (numerous scholars have debated these questions, and offered ingenious, sometimes bizarre, and always inconclusive answers). Vickery, like Mrs Bathurst in the newsreel, has melted out of the picture, jumped out of the story's frame, and the ultimate truth about him is irrecoverable.

Why does Kipling tease his readers in this way? The reason is, I believe, that "Mrs Bathurst" is not essentially a mystery story at all, in the usual sense of that term, but a tragedy. The quotation from *Hamlet* that is Vickery's last recorded speech ("The rest is silence"), the echo of Marlowe's Faustus ("Why this is hell, nor am I out of it") in his earlier statement, "You've only had to watch. I'm *it*," are among several allusions to high tragedy in the story. Here, as elsewhere, Kipling shows that ordinary humble people, who drop their aitches and have ill-fitting dentures, are nevertheless capable of intense emotions, violent passions and crippling guilt; and that the greatest mystery of all is the human heart.

8 Names

... and a girl you have not yet been introduced to, who now comes forward from the shadows of the side aisle, where she has been lurking, to join the others at the altar rail. Let her be called Violet, no, Veronica, no Violet, improbable a name as that is for Catholic girls of Irish extraction, customarily named after saints and figures of Celtic legend, for I like the connotations of Violet – shrinking, penitential, melancholy – a diminutive, dark-haired girl, a pale, pretty face ravaged by eczema, fingernails bitten down to the quick and stained by nicotine, a smartly cut needlecord coat sadly creased and soiled; a girl, you might guess from all this evidence, with problems, guilts, hangups.

DAVID LODGE *How Far Can You Go?* (1980)

And there, for the time being, let us leave Vic Wilcox, while we travel back an hour or two in time, a few miles in space, to meet a very different character. A character who, rather awkwardly for me, doesn't herself believe in the concept of character. That is to say (a favourite phrase of her own), Robyn Penrose, Temporary Lecturer in English Literature at the University of Rummidge, holds that "character" is a bourgeois myth, an illusion created to reinforce the ideology of capitalism.

DAVID LODGE *Nice Work* (1988)

"In that case," he said, "I'm happy to oblige you. My name is Quinn."

"Ah," said Stillman reflectively, nodding his head. "Quinn."

"Yes, Quinn, Q-U-I-N-N."

"I see. Yes, yes, I see. Quinn. Hmmm. Yes. Very interesting. Quinn. A most resonant word. Rhymes with twin, does it not?"

"That's right. Twin."

"And sin, too, if I'm not mistaken."

"You're not."

"And also in – one n – or inn – two. Isn't that so?"

"Exactly."

"Hmmm. Very interesting. I see many possibilities for this word, this Quinn, this . . . quintessence . . . of quiddity. Quick, for example. And quill. And quack. And quirk. Hmmm. Rhymes with grin. Not to speak of kin. Hmmm. Very interesting. And win. And fin. And din. And gin. And pin. And tin. And bin. Even rhymes with djinn. Hmmm. And if you say it right, with been. Hmmm. Yes, very interesting. I like your name enormously, Mr Quinn. It flies off in so many little directions at once."

"Yes, I've often noticed that myself."

PAUL AUSTER *City of Glass* (1985)

ONE OF THE FUNDAMENTAL principles of structuralism is "the arbitrariness of the sign", the idea that there is no necessary, existential connection between a word and its referent. Not "rightly is they called pigs," as the man said, but by linguistic chance. Other words serve the same purpose in other languages. As Shakespeare observed, anticipating Ferdinand de Saussure by three centuries, "a rose by any other name would smell as sweet."

Proper names have an odd and interesting status in this respect. Our first names are usually given to us with semantic intent, having for our parents some pleasant or hopeful association which we may or may not live up to. Surnames however are generally perceived as arbitrary, whatever descriptive force they may once have had. We don't expect our neighbour Mr Shepherd to look after sheep, or mentally associate him with that occupation. If he is a character in a novel, however, pastoral and perhaps biblical associations will inevitably come into play. One of the great mysteries of literary history is what exactly the supremely respectable Henry James meant by calling one of his characters Fanny Assingham.

In a novel names are never neutral. They always signify, if it is only ordinariness. Comic, satiric or didactic writers can afford to be exuberantly inventive, or obviously allegorical, in their naming (Thwackum, Pumblechook, Pilgrim). Realistic novelists favour mundane names with appropriate connotations (Emma Wood-house, Adam Bede). The naming of characters is always an important part of creating them, involving many considerations, and hesitations, which I can most conveniently illustrate from my own experience.

The question in the title *How Far Can You Go?* applies to both the undermining of traditional religious belief by radical theology and the undermining of literary convention by the device of "breaking frame", which I referred to earlier in connection with the intrusive authorial voice (see Section 2). For an author to openly change his mind about the name of a character, in mid-text, is a particularly blatant admission that the whole story is "made up", something readers know but usually suppress, as religious believers suppress their doubts. Nor is it customary for novelists to explain the connotations of the names they give to their characters: such suggestions are supposed to work subliminally on the reader's consciousness.

The invention of the word processor has made it easy to change the name of a character at a late stage of composition, just by touching a few keys, but I would have a strong resistance to doing that to any but the most minor character in my fiction. One may hesitate and agonize about the choice of a name, but once made, it becomes inseparable from the character, and to question it seems to throw the whole project *en abîme*, as the deconstructionists say. I was made acutely aware of this in the process of writing *Nice Work*.

This novel concerns the relationship between the managing director of an engineering company and a young academic who is obliged to "shadow" him. Although it contains some frame-breaking asides, as the quotation above illustrates, it is generally a more straightforwardly realistic novel than *How Far Can You Go?* and in naming the characters I was looking for names that would seem "natural" enough to mask their symbolic appropriateness. I named the man Vic Wilcox to suggest, beneath the ordinariness and Englishness of the name, a rather aggressive, even coarse masculinity (by association with *victor, will* and *cock*), and I soon settled on Penrose for the surname of my heroine for its contrasting connotations of literature and beauty (*pen* and *rose*). I hesitated for some time, however, about the choice of her first name, vacillating between Rachel, Rebecca and Roberta, and I remember that this held up progress on Chapter Two considerably, because I couldn't imaginatively inhabit this character until her name was fixed. Eventually I discovered in a dictionary of names that Robin or Robyn is sometimes used as a familiar form of Roberta. An androgynous name seemed highly appropriate to my feminist and assertive heroine, and immediately suggested a new twist to the plot: Wilcox would be expecting a male Robin to turn up at his factory.

About halfway through writing the novel I realized that I had selected for Vic, perhaps by the same mental route as E. M. Forster, the surname of the chief male character in *Howards End*, Henry Wilcox – another man of business who becomes enamoured of an intellectual woman. Rather than change my hero's name, I incorporated *Howards End* into the intertextual level of the novel, emphasizing the parallels between the two books – by, for instance, the legend on the tee-shirt of Robyn's student, Marion, "ONLY CONNECT" (the epigraph to Forster's novel). And why Marion? Perhaps because she is a "maid" whose innocence and virtue Robyn (cf. Robin Hood) is anxious to protect, perhaps because the young, as it were potential, George Eliot (who figures prominently in Robyn's teaching) was called Marian Evans. I say "perhaps" because authors are not always conscious of their motivation in these matters.

The passage quoted from Paul Auster's *City of Glass*, one of the three remarkable novellas that make up his *New York Trilogy*, pushes the connotative significance of names in literary texts to an absurdist extreme. These three stories subject the clichés and stereotypes of the gumshoe detective story to a postmodernist scepticism about identity, causality and meaning. Quinn himself writes detective stories under the name of William Wilson, which happens to be the name of the eponymous hero of Poe's famous tale about a man in pursuit of his *Doppelgänger* (see Section 47). Misidentified as "Paul Auster of the Auster Detective Agency", Quinn is seduced into acting the part, tailing a former professor called Stillman who has recently been released from prison and is feared by the client of Quinn, alias Wilson, alias Auster. Stillman has written a book in which he concludes that the arbitrariness of the sign was a consequence of Original Sin.

> Adam's one task in the Garden had been to invent language, to give each creature and thing its name. In that state of innocence, his tongue had gone straight to the quick of the world. His words had not been merely appended to the things he saw, they had revealed their essences, had literally brought them to life. A thing and its name were interchangeable. After the fall, this was no longer true. Names became detached from things; words devolved into a collection of arbitrary signs; language had been severed from God. The story of the Garden, therefore, not only records the fall of man, but the fall of language.

As if to demonstrate the point, Stillman deconstructs Quinn's name, when they eventually meet, with a flow of whimsical free association. The connotations of Quinn stop nowhere, and therefore become useless to the reader as an interpretative key.

In the second story, *Ghosts*, all the characters have the names of colours.

> First of all there is Blue. Later there is White, and then there is Black, and before the beginning there is Brown. Brown broke him in, Brown taught him the ropes, and when Brown grew old, Blue took over. That is how it begins . . . The case seems simple enough. White wants Blue to follow a man named Black and to keep an eye on him for as long as possible.

By this manifestly artificial naming system, Auster again affirms the arbitrariness of language, introducing it (arbitrariness) where it doesn't usually belong (fictional names). In the third story, *The*

Locked Room, the narrator confesses how he faked government census returns, parodying the activity of a novelist:

> Most of all there was the pleasure of making up names. At times I had to curb my impulse towards the outlandish – the fiercely comical, the pun, the dirty word – but for the most part I was content to play within the bounds of realism.

In all three stories the impossibility of pinning the signifier to the signified, of recovering that mythical, prelapsarian state of innocence in which a thing and its name were interchangeable, is replicated on the level of plot by the futility of the routines of detection. Each narrative ends with the death or despair of the detective-figure, faced with an insoluble mystery, lost in a labyrinth of names.

9 The Stream of Consciousness

Mrs Dalloway said she would buy the flowers herself. For Lucy had her work cut out for her. The doors would be taken off their hinges; Rumpelmayer's men were coming. And then, thought Clarissa Dalloway, what a morning – fresh as if issued to children on a beach.

What a lark! What a plunge! For so it had always seemed to her when, with a little squeak of the hinges, which she could hear now, she had burst open the French windows and plunged at Bourton into the open air. How fresh, how calm, stiller than this of course, the air was in the early morning; like the flap of a wave; the kiss of a wave; chill and sharp and yet (for a girl of eighteen as she then was) solemn, feeling as she did, standing there at the open window, that something awful was about to happen; looking at the flowers, at the trees with the smoke winding off them and the rooks rising, falling; standing and looking until Peter Walsh said, "Musing among the vegetables?" – was that it? – "I prefer men to cauliflowers" – was that it? He must have said it at breakfast one morning when she had gone out on to the terrace – Peter Walsh. He would be back from India one of these days, June or July, she forgot which, for his letters were awfully dull; it was his sayings one remembered; his eyes, his pocket-knife, his smile, his grumpiness and, when millions of things had utterly vanished – how strange it was! – a few sayings like this about cabbages.

VIRGINIA WOOLF *Mrs Dalloway* (1925)

"THE STREAM OF CONSCIOUSNESS" was a phrase coined by William James, psychologist brother of the novelist, Henry, to characterize the continuous flow of thought and sensation in the human mind. Later it was borrowed by literary critics to describe a particular kind of modern fiction which tried to imitate this process, exemplified by, among others, James Joyce, Dorothy Richardson and Virginia Woolf.

The novel always was, of course, notable for its interiorized rendering of experience. *Cogito, ergo sum* ("I think, therefore I am") could be its motto, though the novelist's *cogito* includes not only reasoning but also emotions, sensations, memories and fantasies. Defoe's autobiographers, and Richardson's letter-writers, at the beginning of the novel's development as a literary form, were obsessively introspective. The classic nineteenth-century novel, from Jane Austen to George Eliot, combined the presentation of its characters as social beings with a subtle and sensitive analysis of their moral and emotional inner lives. Towards the turn of the century, however (you can see it happening in Henry James), reality was increasingly located in the private, subjective consciousness of individual selves, unable to communicate the fullness of their experience to others. It has been said that the stream-of-consciousness novel is the literary expression of solipsism, the philosophical doctrine that nothing is certainly real except one's own existence; but we could equally well argue that it offers us some relief from that daunting hypothesis by offering us imaginative access to the inner lives of other human beings, even if they are fictions.

Undoubtedly this kind of novel tends to generate sympathy for the characters whose inner selves are exposed to view, however vain, selfish or ignoble their thoughts may occasionally be; or, to put it another way, continuous immersion in the mind of a wholly unsympathetic character would be intolerable for both writer and reader. *Mrs Dalloway* is a particularly interesting case in point, because its heroine also appeared as a minor character in Virginia Woolf's first novel, *The Voyage Out* (1915). There a more traditional authorial narrative method is used to give a very satirical and prejudicial portrait of Clarissa Dalloway and her husband, as snobbish and reactionary members of the British upper class.

Here, for instance, is Mrs Dalloway in her earlier incarnation preparing to be introduced to a scholar called Ambrose and his wife:

> Mrs Dalloway, with her head a little on one side, did her best to recollect Ambrose – was it a surname? – but failed. She was made slightly uneasy by what she had heard. She knew that scholars married anyone – girls they met in farms on reading parties; or little suburban women who said disagreeably, "Of course I know it's my husband you want, not *me*." But Helen came in at that point, and Mrs Dalloway saw with relief that though slightly eccentric in appearance, she was not untidy, held herself well, and her voice had restraint in it, which she held to be the sign of a lady.

We are shown what Mrs Dalloway is thinking, but the style in which her thoughts are reported puts them and her at an ironic distance, and passes silent judgment on them. There is evidence that when Virginia Woolf began writing about this character again, it was originally with the same quasi-satirical intention; but by that time she had become committed to the stream-of-consciousness novel, and the method inevitably led her into a much more sympathetic portrait of Clarissa Dalloway.

There are two staple techniques for representing consciousness in prose fiction. One is interior monologue, in which the grammatical subject of the discourse is an "I", and we, as it were, overhear the character verbalizing his or her thoughts as they occur. I shall discuss this method in the next section. The other method, called free indirect style, goes back at least as far as Jane Austen, but was employed with ever-increasing scope and virtuosity by modern novelists like Woolf. It renders thought as reported speech (in the third person, past tense) but keeps to the kind of vocabulary that is appropriate to the character, and deletes some of the tags, like "she thought," "she wondered," "she asked herself" etc. that a more formal narrative style would require. This gives the illusion of intimate access to a character's mind, but without totally surrendering authorial participation in the discourse.

"Mrs Dalloway said she would buy the flowers herself," is the first sentence of the novel: the statement of an authorial narrator, but an impersonal and inscrutable one, who does not explain who Mrs Dalloway is or why she needed to buy flowers. This abrupt plunging of the reader into the middle of an ongoing life (we gradually piece together the heroine's biography by a process of inference) typifies the presentation of consciousness as a "stream". The next sentence, "For Lucy had her work cut out for her," moves the focus of the narrative into the character's mind by adopting free indirect style, omitting an intrusive authorial tag, such as "Mrs Dalloway reflected"; referring to the maid familiarly by her first name, as Mrs Dalloway herself would, not by her function; and using a casual, colloquial expression, "cut out for her", that belongs to Mrs Dalloway's own style of speech. The third sentence has the same form. The fourth moves back slightly towards an authorial manner to inform us of the heroine's full name, as well as her pleasure in the fine summer morning: "And then, *thought Clarissa Dalloway*, what a morning – fresh as if issued to children on a beach." (*Italics mine.*)

The ejaculations, "What a lark! What a plunge!" that follow look superficially like interior monologue, but they are not the mature heroine's responses to the morning in Westminster as she goes out to buy flowers. She is remembering herself at the age of eighteen remembering herself as a child. Or, to put it another way, the image "fresh as if issued to children on a beach", evoked by the Westminster morning, reminds her of how similar metaphors, of children larking in the sea, would come to mind as she "plunged" into the fresh, calm air of a summer morning, "like the flap of a wave; the kiss of a wave," at Bourton (some country house, we presume), where she would meet someone called Peter Walsh (the first hint of anything like a story). The actual and the metaphorical, time present and times past, interweave and interact in the long, meandering sentences, each thought or memory triggering the next. Realistically, Clarissa Dalloway cannot always trust her memory: " 'Musing among the vegetables?' – was that it? – 'I prefer men to cauliflowers' – was that it?"

Meandering the sentences may be, but they are, apart from the licence of free indirect style, well-formed and elegantly cadenced.

Virginia Woolf has smuggled some of her own lyrical eloquence into Mrs Dalloway's stream of consciousness without its being obvious. Transpose these sentences into the first person, and they would sound far too literary and considered to pass for a transcription of someone's random thoughts. They would sound indeed like *writing*, in a rather precious style of autobiographical reminiscence:

> What a lark! What a plunge! For so it always seemed to me when, with a little squeak of the hinges, which I can hear now, I burst open the French windows and plunged at Bourton into the open air. How fresh, how calm, stiller than this of course, the air was in the early morning; like the flap of a wave; the kiss of a wave; chill and sharp and yet (for a girl of eighteen as I then was) solemn, feeling as I did, standing there at the open window, that something awful was about to happen . . .

The interior monologues of Virginia Woolf's later novel, *The Waves*, suffer from such artificiality, to my mind. James Joyce was a more resourceful exponent of that way of rendering the stream of consciousness.

10 Interior Monologue

On the doorstep he felt in his hip pocket for the latchkey. Not there. In the trousers I left off. Must get it. Potato I have. Creaky wardrobe. No use disturbing her. She turned over sleepily that time. He pulled the halldoor to after him very quietly, more, till the footleaf dropped gently over the threshold, a limp lid. Looked shut. All right till I come back anyhow.

He crossed to the bright side, avoiding the loose cellarflap of number seventyfive. The sun was nearing the steeple of George's church. Be a warm day I fancy. Specially in these black clothes feel it more. Black conducts, reflects (refracts is it?), the heat. But I couldn't go in that light suit. Make a picnic of it. His eyelids sank quietly often as he walked in happy warmth.

*

They came down the steps from Leahy's terrace prudently, *Frauenzimmer:* and down the shelving shore flabbily their splayed feet sinking in the silted sand. Like me, like Algy, coming down to our mighty mother. Number one swung lourdily her midwife's bag, the other's gamp poked in the beach. From the liberties, out for the day. Mrs Florence MacCabe, relict of the late Patk MacCabe, deeply lamented, of Bride Street. One of her sisterhood lugged me squealing into life. Creation from nothing. What has she in the bag? A misbirth with a trailing navelcord, hushed in ruddy wool. The cords of all link back, strandentwining cable of all flesh. That is why mystic monks. Will you be as gods? Gaze in your omphalos. Hello. Kinch here. Put me on to Edenville. Aleph, alpha: nought, nought, one.

*

Yes because he never did a thing like that before as ask to get his breakfast in bed with a couple of eggs since the *City Arms* hotel when he used to be pretending to be laid up with a sick voice doing his highness to make himself interesting to that old

46

faggot Mrs Riordan that he thought he had a great leg of and
she never left us a farthing all for masses for herself and her
soul greatest miser ever was actually afraid to lay out 4d for her
methylated spirit telling me all her ailments she had too much
old chat in her about politics and earthquakes and the end of
the world let us have a bit of fun first God help the world if all
the women were her sort down on bathingsuits and lownecks of
course nobody wanted her to wear I suppose she was pious
because no man would look at her twice

JAMES JOYCE Ulysses (1922)

THE TITLE of James Joyce's *Ulysses* is a clue – the only absolutely
unmissable one in the entire text – that its account of a fairly
ordinary day in Dublin, 16 June 1904, re-enacts, mimics or
travesties the story of Homer's *Odyssey* (whose hero, Odysseus, was
called Ulysses in Latin). Leopold Bloom, middle-aged Jewish
advertising canvasser, is the unheroic hero, whose wife Molly falls
far short of her prototype, Penelope, in faithfulness to her spouse.
After crossing and recrossing the city of Dublin on various
inconclusive errands, as Odysseus was blown around the Mediter-
ranean by adverse winds on his way home from the Trojan war,
Bloom meets and paternally befriends Stephen Dedalus, the
Telemachus of the tale, and a portrait of Joyce's own, younger self
– a proud, penniless aspirant writer, alienated from his father.

Ulysses is a psychological rather than a heroic epic. We become
acquainted with the principal characters not by being told about
them, but by sharing their most intimate thoughts, represented as
silent, spontaneous, unceasing streams of consciousness. For the
reader, it's rather like wearing earphones plugged into someone's
brain, and monitoring an endless tape-recording of the subject's
impressions, reflections, questions, memories and fantasies, as they
are triggered either by physical sensations or the association of
ideas. Joyce was not the first writer to use interior monologue (he
credited the invention to an obscure French novelist of the late

nineteenth century, Edouard Dujardin), nor the last, but he brought it to a pitch of perfection that makes other exponents, apart from Faulkner and Beckett, look rather feeble in comparison.

Interior monologue is indeed a very difficult technique to use successfully, all too apt to impose a painfully slow pace on the narrative and to bore the reader with a plethora of trivial detail. Joyce avoids these pitfalls partly by his sheer genius with words, which renders the most commonplace incident or object as riveting as if we had never encountered them before, but also by cleverly varying the grammatical structure of his discourse, combining interior monologue with free indirect style and orthodox narrative description.

The first extract concerns Leopold Bloom leaving his house early in the morning to buy a pork kidney for his breakfast. "On the doorstep he felt in his hip pocket for the latchkey" describes Bloom's action from his point of view, but grammatically implies a narrator, however impersonal. "Not there" is interior monologue, a contraction of Bloom's unuttered thought, "It's not there." The omission of the verb conveys the instantaneousness of the discovery, and the slight sense of panic it entails. He remembers that the key is in another pair of trousers which he "left off" because he is wearing a black suit to attend a funeral later in the day. "Potato I have" is totally baffling to the first-time reader: in due course we discover that Bloom superstitiously carries a potato around with him as a kind of talisman. Such puzzles add to the authenticity of the method, for we should not expect to find another person's stream of consciousness totally transparent. Bloom decides against returning to his bedroom to fetch the key because the creaky wardrobe door might disturb his wife, still dozing in bed – an indication of his essentially kind and considerate nature. He refers to Molly simply as "her" (and in the last sentence as "she") because his wife looms so large in his consciousness that he does not need to identify her to himself by name – as a narrator, with a reader's interests in mind, would naturally do.

The next, brilliantly mimetic sentence, describing how Bloom pulled the house door almost shut, returns to the narrative mode, but it maintains Bloom's point of view and remains within his vocabulary range, so that a fragment of interior monologue, "more", can be incorporated in it without jarring. The past tense of the next sentence "Looked shut" marks it as free indirect style, and provides an easy transition back to interior monologue: "All right till I come back anyhow," in which "All right" is a contraction of "That will be all right." None of the sentences in this extract, apart from the narrative ones, are grammatically correct or complete by strict standards, because we do not think, or even speak spontaneously, in well-formed sentences.

The second quotation, describing Stephen Dedalus catching sight of two women as he walks on the beach, displays the same variety of discourse types. But whereas Bloom's thoughtstream is practical, sentimental and, in an uneducated fashion, scientific (he gropes uncertainly for the correct technical term for the reaction of black clothing to heat) Stephen's is speculative, witty, literary – and much more difficult to follow. "Algy" is a familiar reference to the poet Algernon Swinburne, who called the sea "a great sweet mother", and "lourdily" is either a literary archaism or a coinage influenced by Stephen's bohemian domicile in Paris (*lourd* being French for "heavy"). Mrs MacCabe's calling prompts Stephen's writerly imagination to evoke his own birth with startling concreteness: "One of her sisterhood lugged me squealing into life," another miraculously mimetic sentence that makes you feel the newborn infant's slippery body in the midwife's hands. The slightly morbid fancy that Mrs MacCabe has a miscarried foetus in her bag diverts Stephen's stream of consciousness into a complex and fantastical reverie in which the navel cord is likened to a cable linking all human beings to their first mother, Eve, which suggests why oriental monks contemplate their navels (Greek, *omphalos*) though Stephen does not complete the thought, his mind leaping on to another metaphorical conceit, the collective human navelcord as a telephone cable, by means of which Stephen (nicknamed Kinch by his associate, Buck Mulligan) whimsically imagines himself dialling the Garden of Eden.

Joyce did not write the whole of *Ulysses* in the stream-of-consciousness form. Having taken psychological realism as far as it would go, he turned, in later chapters of his novel, to various kinds of stylization, pastiche and parody: it is a linguistic epic, as well as a psychological one. But he ended it with the most famous of all interior monologues, Molly Bloom's.

In the last "episode" (as the chapters of *Ulysses* are called), Leopold Bloom's wife, Molly, who has hitherto been an object of his and other characters' thoughts, observations and memories, becomes a subject, a centre of consciousness. During the afternoon she has been unfaithful to Leopold with an impresario called Blazes Boylan (she is a semi-professional singer). Now it is late at night. Bloom has come to bed, disturbing Molly, and she lies beside him, half-awake, drowsily remembering the events of the day, and of her past life, especially her experiences with her husband and various lovers. The Blooms have not in fact enjoyed normal sexual relations for many years, following the trauma of losing their son in infancy, but they remain tied to each other by familiarity, a kind of exasperated affection and even jealousy. Bloom's day has been overcast by his awareness of Molly's assignation, and her long, almost entirely unpunctuated monologue begins with the speculation that Bloom must have had some erotic adventure, since he has uncharacteristically asserted himself by demanding that she bring him his breakfast in bed the next morning, something he hasn't done since a distant time when he pretended to be an invalid in order to impress a widow called Mrs Riordan (an aunt of Stephen Dedalus, in fact, one of many little coincidences that knit together the apparently random events of *Ulysses*) from whom he was hoping to receive a legacy, although in fact she left them nothing, all her money going to pay for masses to be said for the repose of her soul ... (In paraphrasing Molly Bloom's soliloquy one tends to fall into her own freeflowing style.)

Whereas Stephen's and Bloom's streams of consciousness are stimulated and made to change course by their sense-impressions, Molly, lying in the darkness, with only the occasional noise from the street to distract her, is borne along by her own memories, one memory triggering another by some kind of association. And whereas association in Stephen's consciousness tends to be metaphorical (one thing suggests another by resemblance, often of an arcane or fanciful kind) and in Bloom's metonymic (one thing suggests another because they are connected by cause and effect, or by contiguity in space/time), association in Molly's consciousness is simply literal: one breakfast in bed reminds her of another, as one man in her life reminds her of another. As thoughts of Bloom lead to thoughts of other lovers, it is not always easy to determine to whom the pronoun "he" refers.

11 Defamiliarization

This picture, I say, seemed to consider itself the queen of the collection.

It represented a woman, considerably larger, I thought, than the life. I calculated that this lady, put into a scale of magnitude suitable for the reception of a commodity of bulk, would infallibly turn from fourteen to sixteen stone. She was, indeed, extremely well fed; very much butcher's meat – to say nothing of bread, vegetables, and liquids – must she have consumed to attain that breadth and height, that wealth of muscle, that affluence of flesh. She lay half-reclined on a couch – why, it would be difficult to say; broad daylight blazed round her. She appeared in hearty health, strong enough to do the work of two plain cooks; she could not plead a weak spine; she ought to have been standing, or at least sitting bolt upright. She had no business to lounge away the noon on a sofa. She ought likewise to have worn decent garments – a gown covering her properly, which was not the case. Out of abundance of material – seven-and-twenty yards, I should say, of drapery – she managed to make inefficient raiment. Then for the wretched untidiness surrounding her there could be no excuse. Pots and pans – perhaps I ought to say vases and goblets – were rolled here and there on the foreground; a perfect rubbish of flowers was mixed amongst them, and an absurd and disorderly mass of curtain upholstery smothered the couch and cumbered the floor. On referring to the catalogue, I found that this notable production bore the name "Cleopatra".

CHARLOTTE BRONTË *Villette* (1853)

DEFAMILIARIZATION is the usual English translation of *ostranenie* (literally, "making strange"), another of those invaluable critical terms coined by the Russian Formalists. In a famous essay first published in 1917, Victor Shklovsky argued that the essential purpose of art is to overcome the deadening effects of habit by representing familiar things in unfamiliar ways:

> Habitualization devours works, clothes, furniture, one's wife, and the fear of war ... And art exists that one may recover the sensation of life; it exists to make one feel things, to make the stony *stony*. The purpose of art is to impart the sensation of things as they are perceived and not as they are known.

This theory vindicates the distortions and dislocations of modernist writing, but it applies equally well to the great exponents of the realistic novel. One of Shklovsky's examples was a passage where Tolstoy effectively ridicules opera by describing a performance as if through the eyes of someone who has never seen or heard an opera before (e.g., "Then still more people came running out and began to drag away the maiden who had been wearing a white dress but who now wore one of sky blue. They did not drag her off immediately, but sang with her for a long time before dragging her away"). Charlotte Brontë does something similar to *salon* art in the passage quoted here from *Villette*.

Villette is the fictional name of Brussels, where the heroine and narrator, Lucy Snowe, is obliged to earn her bread as teacher in a girls' boarding-school. She is secretly and hopelessly in love with an English doctor, John Bretton, who escorts her to art galleries but leaves her to explore them alone – an arrangement which suits her independent spirit.

The painting under observation here belongs to a recognizable type in which the lavish depiction of the female nude is, as it were, rendered respectable by its attachment to a mythical or historical source, by the intimidating grandeur of its scale, and by various other coded signs that it belongs to high culture. The contradictions in such a spectacle were, of course, much more marked in Charlotte Brontë's own day, when women were obliged to keep almost every inch of their bodies covered at all times, than they are in ours. Through her heroine, Charlotte Brontë exposes these contradictions, and the essential falsity (as she saw it) of this kind of art, by describing the painting literally and truthfully, putting it in the context of the real life of women, and ignoring the discourse of art history and connoisseurship within which it is "habitually" perceived.

Thus the monumental size of the female figure and the superfluity of drapery about her, facts ignored or suppressed in conventional art appreciation, are brought into the open by an empirical, quasi-scientific calculation of weight and quantity: "from fourteen to sixteen stone ... seven-and-twenty yards, I should say, of drapery." We have become so familiar with the use of drapery in classical paintings of the nude, billowing round the figure in convoluted folds without covering anything except perhaps a few inches of pubic flesh, that we no longer perceive its essential artificiality. The same applies to the picturesque arrangement of various objects and utensils in the foreground of such paintings – why *are* those goblets invariably overturned on the floor, when the personages depicted would have had plenty of opportunity, or servants, to pick them up? Lucy's unblinking scrutiny raises questions habitually repressed in the ritual of gallery-visiting. The languorous reclining pose of the woman, with its tacit erotic invitation, is ridiculed by remarking on its incongruity with the time of day depicted, and the lack of any evidence of the subject's physical debility. And by holding back the title, "Cleopatra", till the end of her description, Lucy implies the arbitrariness and spuriousness of the historical/mythological justification claimed by the painting, which could just as well have been called "Dido" or "Delilah", or (more honestly) "Odalisque".

In itself, the description of the painting has no narrative content; the story "pauses" so that it may be delivered. But it does have a narrative *function*. Firstly, it contributes to the characterization of Lucy Snowe, a young woman of strong, independent and unconventional views, though her lack of beauty, status or wealth oblige her to keep them to herself most of the time. Secondly, it provokes an interesting scene with M. Paul Emmanuel, the testy, unprepossessing, but vital schoolmaster at Lucy's school, whom she in due course recognizes as a much more fulfilling mate than the super-ficially eligible Dr John. Paul Emmanuel discovers her in front of the "Cleopatra" and is shocked – a reaction which shows him as immune to the cant of connoisseurship (he is not impressed by the painting's high cultural pretensions), but in thrall to gender stereotyping (he does not think it suitable for contemplation by a young lady). He drags Lucy off to look at another painting, of three sentimental scenes in the life of a virtuous woman, which she finds as absurd and irrelevant as the Cleopatra.

Villette was the last novel Charlotte Brontë wrote before her untimely death, and her most mature. It has become a key text in contemporary feminist criticism, for reasons that are very obvious in this passage. But in defamiliarizing the representation of women in historical painting Charlotte Brontë was making a point about art as well as about sexual politics, and specifically about her own art, which had gradually and painfully emancipated itself from the falsifications and wish-fulfilments of melodrama and romance. "It seemed to me," says Lucy Snowe just before this passage, "that an original and good picture was just as scarce as an original and good book." *Villette* is such a book.

What do we mean – it is a common term of praise – when we say that a book is "original"? Not, usually, that the writer has invented something without precedent, but that she has made us "perceive" what we already, in a conceptual sense, "know", by deviating from the conventional, habitual ways of representing reality. Defamiliarization, in short, is another word for "originality". I shall have recourse to it again in these glances at the art of fiction.

55

12 The Sense of Place

In LA, you can't do anything unless you drive. Now I can't do anything unless I drink. And the drink-drive combination, it really isn't possible out there. If you so much as loosen your seatbelt or drop your ash or pick your nose, then it's an Alcatraz autopsy with the questions asked later. Any indiscipline, you feel, any variation, and there's a bullhorn, a set of scope sights, and a coptered pig drawing a bead on your rug.

So what can a poor boy do? You come out of the hotel, the Vraimont. Over boiling Watts the downtown skyline carries a smear of God's green snot. You walk left, you walk right, you are a bank rat on a busy river. This restaurant serves no drink, this one serves no meat, this one serves no heterosexuals. You can get your chimp shampooed, you can get your dick tattooed, twenty-four hour, but can you get lunch? And should you see a sign on the far side of the street flashing BEEF – BOOZE – NO STRINGS, then you can forget it. The only way to get across the road is to be born there. All the ped-xing signs say DON'T WALK, all of them, all the time. That is the message, the content of Los Angeles: don't walk. Stay inside. Don't walk. Drive. Don't walk. Run! I tried the cabs. No use. The cabbies are all Saturnians who aren't even sure whether this is a right planet or a left planet. The first thing you have to do, every trip, is teach them how to drive.

MARTIN AMIS *Money* (1984)

As will be evident to the reader by now, my division of the art of fiction into various "aspects" is somewhat artificial. Effects in fiction are plural and interconnected, each drawing on and contributing to all the others. The passage I have selected from Martin

56

Amis's *Money* as an example of the description of place could have served equally well to illustrate *Skaz* or Defamiliarization, as well as several topics not yet broached. Which is another way of saying that description in a good novel is never *just* description.

The sense of place was a fairly late development in the history of prose fiction. As Mikhail Bakhtin observed, the cities of classical romance are interchangeable backcloths for the plot: Ephesus might as well be Corinth or Syracuse, for all we are told about them. The early English novelists were scarcely more specific about place. London in Defoe's or Fielding's novels, for instance, lacks the vivid visual detail of Dickens's London. When Tom Jones arrives at the capital in search of his beloved Sophia, the narrator tells us that he

> was an entire stranger in London; and as he happened to arrive first in a quarter of the town, the inhabitants of which have very little intercourse with the householders of Hanover or Grosvenor Square (for he entered through Gray's Inn Lane) so he rambled about for some time, before he could even find his way to those happy mansions, where Fortune segregates from the vulgar those . . . whose ancestors being born in better days, by sundry kinds of merit, have entailed riches and honour on their posterity.

London is described entirely in terms of the variations of class and status in its inhabitants, as interpreted by the author's ironical vision. There is no attempt to make the reader "see" the city, or to describe its sensory impact on a young man up from the country for the first time. Compare Dickens's description of Jacob's Island in *Oliver Twist*:

> To reach this place, the visitor has to penetrate through a maze of close, narrow, and muddy streets, thronged by the roughest and poorest of the waterside people . . . The cheapest and least delicate provisions are heaped in the shops; the coarsest and commonest articles of wearing apparel dangle at the salesman's door, and stream from the house-parapet and windows . . . he walks beneath tottering housefronts projecting over the pavement, dismantled walls that seem to totter as he passes, chimneys half-crushed, half-hesitating to fall, windows guarded by rusty

iron bars that time and dirt have almost eaten away, every imaginable sign of desolation and neglect.

Tom Jones was published in 1749; *Oliver Twist* in 1838. What intervened was the Romantic movement, which pondered the effect of *milieu* on man, opened people's eyes to the sublime beauty of landscape and, in due course, to the grim symbolism of cityscapes in the Industrial Age.

Martin Amis is a late exponent of the Dickensian tradition of urban Gothic. His fascinated and appalled gaze at the post-industrial city mediates an apocalyptic vision of culture and society in a terminal state of decay. As with Dickens, his settings often seem more animated than his characters, as if the life has been drained out of people to re-emerge in a demonic, destructive form in things: streets, machines, gadgets.

The narrator of *Money*, John Self (Amis also cultivates a Dickensian playfulness with names) is not exactly a complex or sympathetic character. A scrofulous yuppie, addicted to fast food and fast cars, junk food and pornography, he commutes between England and America in his efforts to tie up a film deal that will make him rich. London and New York are the chief locations of the action, with the latter having the edge in physical and moral squalor, but the nature of his business inevitably takes Self to Los Angeles, the capital of the movie industry.

The challenge of the novel's chosen form is to make the style both eloquently descriptive of the urban wasteland *and* expressive of the narrator's slobbish, tunnel-visioned, philistine character. Amis manages this difficult trick by disguising his literary skills behind a barrage of streetwise slang, profanity, obscenities and jokes. The narrator speaks in a mid-Atlantic lingo that is partly derived from popular culture and the mass media and partly Amis's plausible invention. To decipher the first paragraph of this passage, for instance, you have to know that Alcatraz is a famous Californian prison, that "pig" is a term of abuse for policeman, that "drawing a bead" means taking aim, that "rug" is American slang for toupee (though Self uses it to refer to real hair), and guess that "coptered" is a participle derived from "helicopter". The metaphor for the

city's polluted sky, "a smear of God's green snot", suggesting the
deity of the Old Testament glowering over this latterday Sodom, is
as startling as T. S. Eliot's evening "spread out against the sky/
Like a patient etherized upon a table" in "The Love Song of J.
Alfred Prufrock", and owes something to Stephen Dedalus's
description of the sea as "snot-green", in the first episode of
Ulysses. But whereas Prufrock has high-cultural pretensions and
Stephen is consciously travestying Homer's favourite epithet for
the sea, "wine-dark", John Self seems to be merely indulging in
schoolboy nastiness, and this distracts us from the literary sophistication of the image.

The key trope of this description of Los Angeles is hyperbole,
or overstatement. In that respect it resembles another *skaz* narrative
we looked at earlier, *The Catcher in the Rye*. But Amis's passage is
much more of a rhetorical set-piece than anything to be found in
Salinger's novel. It performs a series of comically exaggerated
variations on the commonplace theme that Los Angeles is a city
dedicated to and dominated by the motor car ("The only way to
get across the road is to be born there"); and on the slightly less
commonplace observations that America favours highly specialized
retail outlets, and that American taxi-drivers are often recent
immigrants who don't know the way to anywhere.

On arriving in Boston recently, I took a cab whose driver had to
make three attempts, assisted by radio-telephone consultation in
Russian with his control, before he could find his way out of the
airport. It's difficult to exaggerate that kind of incompetence, but
Amis found a way: "The cabbies are all Saturnians who aren't even
sure whether this is a right planet or a left planet. The first thing
you have to do, every trip, is teach them how to drive." An echo of
the homely seat-belt safety slogan, "Clunk Click, every trip",
follows fast on the flip allusion to science fiction – Amis's prose
delights in such juxtapositions, culled from the *dreck* of contemporary urban consciousness. The echo also contributes to the jaunty,
finger-snapping rhythm of the whole passage, which threatens at
one particularly cherishable moment to break into rhyming coup-
lets ("You can get your chimp shampooed, you can get your dick
tattooed").

The danger of most set-piece descriptions of place (the novels of Sir Walter Scott provide plenty of examples) is that a succession of well-formed declarative sentences, combined with the suspension of narrative interest, will send the reader to sleep. No risk of that here. The present tense describes both the place and the narrator's movement through it. The shifts in verbal mood – from indicative ("You come out of the hotel") to interrogative ("but can you get lunch?") to imperative ("Don't walk. Drive. Don't walk. Run!") and the generalizing second-person pronoun ("You walk left, you walk right") – involve the reader in the process. After many pages of this sort of thing you might fall asleep from exhaustion, but not from boredom.

13 Lists

With Nicole's help Rosemary bought two dresses and two hats and four pairs of shoes with her money. Nicole bought from a great list that ran two pages, and bought the things in the windows besides. Everything she liked that she couldn't possibly use herself, she bought as a present for a friend. She bought coloured beads, folding beach cushions, artificial flowers, honey, a guest bed, bags, scarfs, love birds, miniatures for a doll's house, and three yards of some new cloth the colour of prawns. She bought a dozen bathing suits, a rubber alligator, a travelling chess set of gold and ivory, big linen handkerchiefs for Abe, two chamois leather jackets of kingfisher blue and burning bush from Hermes – bought all these things not a bit like a high-class courtesan buying underwear and jewels, which were after all professional equipment and insurance, but with an entirely different point of view. Nicole was the product of much ingenuity and toil. For her sake trains began their run at Chicago and traversed the round belly of the continent to California; chicle factories fumed and link belts grew link by link in factories; men mixed toothpaste in vats and drew mouthwash out of copper hogsheads; girls canned tomatoes quickly in August or worked rudely at the Five-and-Tens on Christmas Eve; half-breed Indians toiled on Brazilian coffee plantations and dreamers were muscled out of patent rights in new tractors – these were some of the people who gave a tithe to Nicole and, as the whole system swayed and thundered onward, it lent a feverish bloom to such processes of hers as wholesale buying, like the flush of a fireman's face holding his post before a spreading blaze. She illustrated very simple principles, containing in herself her own doom, but illustrated them so accurately that there was grace in the procedure, and presently Rosemary would try to imitate it.

F. SCOTT FITZGERALD *Tender is the Night* (1934)

"THE RICH are different from us," F. Scott Fitzgerald once said to Ernest Hemingway, who replied, "Yes, they have more money." This anecdote, recorded by Fitzgerald, is usually told against him. But Hemingway's positivist putdown surely missed the point: that in money, as in other matters, quantity sooner or later becomes quality, for good or ill. Fitzgerald's description of Nicole Diver's Paris shopping expedition eloquently illustrates the difference of the rich.

It also illustrates the expressive potential of the list in fictional discourse. On the face of it, a mere catalogue of discrete items would seem to be out of place in a story focused on character and action. But fictional prose is wonderfully omnivorous, capable of assimilating all kinds of nonfictional discourse – letters, diaries, depositions, even lists – and adapting them to its own purposes. Sometimes the list is reproduced in its own characteristically vertical form, contrasting with the surrounding discourse. In *Murphy*, for instance, Samuel Beckett mocks conventional novelistic description by listing the physical attributes of his heroine, Celia, in a flat, statistical fashion:

Head	Small and round
Eyes	Green
Complexion	White
Hair	Yellow
Features	Mobile
Neck	13″
Upper arm	11″
Forearm	9″

And so on.

The contemporary American writer, Lorrie Moore, has an amusing story called "How To Be an Other Woman" (*Self-Help*, 1985) based on two non-fictional types of discourse, the do-it-yourself manual, and the list. The narrator's insecurity in the role of mistress is aggravated by her lover's praise of his wife:

"She's just incredibly organized. She makes lists for everything. It's pretty impressive."
. . .

"That she makes lists? You like that?"

"Well, yes. You know, what she's going to do, what she has to buy, names of clients she has to see, et cetera."

"Lists?" you murmur hopelessly, listlessly, your expensive beige raincoat still on.

Soon, of course, the narrator is making her own lists:

CLIENTS TO SEE
Birthday snapshots
Scotch tape
Letters to TD and Mom

In fact she doesn't have any clients to see, being a humble secretary. The lists are a way of competing with the image of the absent wife. When her lover hints that his wife has had an adventurous sexual life, the narrator responds:

Make a list of all the lovers you've ever had.
Warren Lasher
Ed "Rubberhead" Catapano
Charles Deats or Keats
Alfonse
Tuck it in your pocket. Leave it lying around, conspicuously. Somehow you lose it. Make "mislaid" jokes to yourself. Make another list.

There is a kind of popular contemporary fiction about the lives of the rich, aimed mainly at women readers, which is known in the publishing trade as the "Sex and Shopping" (or less politely as the "S and F") novel. Such novels incorporate detailed descriptions of their heroines' purchases of luxury goods, down to the last designer label. Erotic and consumerist wish-fulfilment are simultaneously indulged. Scott Fitzgerald is also concerned with the connections between sexual allure and conspicuous consumption, but he handles it much more subtly, and critically. He doesn't reproduce Nicole's two-page shopping list in this passage from *Tender is the Night*, nor try to make brand names do his work for him. He creates the impression of prodigality with, in fact, remarkably few items, and invokes only one brand name, "Hermes" (which, interestingly, hasn't dated). But he emphasizes the *miscellaneousness* of the list to convey the completely non-utilitarian nature of Nicole's shopping. Cheap, trivial things like coloured beads, and homely things like honey, are mixed up promiscuously with large functional objects like the bed, expensive toys like the gold-and-ivory chess set, and frivolities like the rubber alligator. There is no logical order in the list, no hierarchy of price, or importance, or grouping of the items according to any other principle. That is the point.

Nicole quickly exceeds the parameters of the list she brought with her, and buys whatever takes her fancy. By exercising her taste and gratifying her whims without regard to economy or commonsense, she conveys a sense of a personality and temperament that is generous, impulsive, amusing and aesthetically sensitive, if out of touch with reality in some important respects. It's impossible not to respond to the fun and the sensual pleasure of this spending spree. How covetable those two chamois-leather jackets sound, kingfisher blue and burning bush (but the key word is "two": where lesser mortals might hesitate between two identical jackets of different, equally attractive colours, Nicole solves the problem by buying both). No wonder her young protégée, and future rival, Rosemary, will try to imitate her style.

Balancing the shopping list, however, is another list, of the human beings, or groups, on whose exploitation Nicole's inherited wealth depends, a list which throws our response into reverse. The whole passage turns on the sentence, "Nicole was the product of much ingenuity and toil," which suddenly makes us see her not as the consumer and collector of commodities, objects, things, but as herself a kind of commodity – the final, exquisite, disproportionately expensive and extravagantly wasteful product of industrial capitalism.

Whereas the first list was a sequence of nouns, the second is a series of verbal phrases: "trains began their run . . . chicle factories fumed . . . men mixed toothpaste . . . girls canned tomatoes . . ." At first sight these processes seem as mutually incongruous and randomly selected as the items of Nicole's shopping, but there is a connection between the men in the toothpaste factories and the girls in the dime stores and the Indian workers in Brazil: the profits made from their labour indirectly fund Nicole's shopping.

The second list is written in a more metaphorical style than the first one. It begins with a striking image, suggestive of both eroticism and gluttony, of the trains traversing the "round belly of the continent", and returns to the metaphor of the railway engine at the end to evoke the dangerous and potentially self-destructive energy of industrial capitalism. "As the whole system swayed and thundered onward" reminds one of the railway symbolism used to similar effect in Dickens' *Dombey and Son* ("The power that forced itself upon its iron way – its own – defiant of all paths and roads, piercing through the heart of every obstacle, and dragging living creatures of all classes, ages, and degrees behind it, was a type of the triumphant monster, Death.")

Typically of Fitzgerald, however, the image is developed in an unexpected and rather elusive way. The analogy shifts from that of a railway engine's furnace to that of a conflagration, and Nicole stands now in the position not of someone stoking a fire, but of someone trying to extinguish it, or at least defying it. The word "fireman" can bear either of these contradictory meanings, and Fitzgerald's use of it perhaps reveals the ambivalence of his own attitude to people like Nicole: a mixture of envy and admiration and disapproval. The words, "She illustrated very simple principles, containing in herself her own doom, but illustrated them so accurately that there was grace in the procedure" sounds like an echo, conscious or unconscious, of Hemingway's definition of courage: "grace under pressure."

65

14 Introducing a Character

A few minutes later, Sally herself arrived.

"Am I terribly late, Fritz darling?"

"Only half of an hour, I suppose," Fritz drawled, beaming with proprietary pleasure. "May I introduce Mr Isherwood – Miss Bowles? Mr Isherwood is commonly known as Chris."

"I'm not," I said. "Fritz is about the only person who's ever called me Chris in my life."

Sally laughed. She was dressed in black silk, with a small cape over her shoulders and a little cap like a page-boy's stuck jauntily on one side of her head:

"Do you mind if I use your telephone, sweet?"

"Sure. Go right ahead." Fritz caught my eye. "Come into the other room, Chris. I want to show you something." He was evidently longing to hear my first impressions of Sally, his new acquisition.

"For heaven's sake, don't leave me alone with this man!" she exclaimed. "Or he'll seduce me down the telephone. He's most terribly passionate."

As she dialled the number, I noticed that her finger-nails were painted emerald green, a colour unfortunately chosen, for it called attention to her hands, which were much stained by cigarette-smoking and as dirty as a little girl's. She was dark enough to be Fritz's sister. Her face was long and thin, powdered dead white. She had very large brown eyes which should have been darker, to match her hair and the pencil she used for her eyebrows.

"Hilloo," she cooed, pursing her brilliant cherry lips as though she were going to kiss the mouthpiece: "Ist dass Du, mein Liebling?" Her mouth opened in a fatuously sweet smile. Fritz and I sat watching her, like a performance at the theatre.

CHRISTOPHER ISHERWOOD *Goodbye to Berlin* (1939)

CHARACTER is arguably the most important single component of the novel. Other narrative forms, such as epic, and other media, such as film, can tell a story just as well, but nothing can equal the great tradition of the European novel in the richness, variety and psychological depth of its portrayal of human nature. Yet character is probably the most difficult aspect of the art of fiction to discuss in technical terms. This is partly because there are so many different types of character and so many different ways of representing them: major characters and minor characters, flat characters and round characters, characters rendered from inside their minds, like Virginia Woolf's Mrs Dalloway, and characters viewed from outside by others, like Christopher Isherwood's Sally Bowles.

Originally the subject of one of the lightly fictionalized stories and sketches that make up *Goodbye to Berlin*, Sally Bowles has enjoyed a remarkably long life in the public imagination of our time, thanks to the successful adaption of Isherwood's text first as a stage play and film (*I Am A Camera*), then as a stage and film musical (*Cabaret*). At first glance, it's hard to understand why she should have achieved this almost mythical status. She is not particularly beautiful, not particularly intelligent, and not particularly gifted as an artiste. She is vain, feckless, and mercenary in her sexual relationships. But she retains an endearing air of innocence and vulnerability in spite of it all, and there is something irresistibly comic about the gap between her pretensions and the facts of her life. Her story gains enormously in interest and significance from being set in Weimar Berlin, just before the Nazi takeover. Dreaming vainly of fame and riches in seedy lodging houses, bouncing from one *louche* protector to another, flattering, exploiting and lying, in the most transparent fashion, she is an emblem of the self-deception and folly of that doomed society.

The simplest way to introduce a character, common in older fiction, is to give a physical description and biographical summary. The portrait of Dorothea Brooke in the first chapter of George Eliot's *Middlemarch* is a consummate example of this method:

> Miss Brooke had that kind of beauty which seems to be thrown into relief by poor dress. Her hand and wrist were so finely

formed that she could wear sleeves not less bare of style than those in which the Blessed Virgin appeared to Italian painters; and her profile as well as her stature and bearing seemed to gain the more dignity from her plain garments, which by the side of provincial fashion gave her the impressiveness of a fine quotation from the Bible – or from one of our elder poets – in a paragraph of today's newspaper. She was usually spoken of as being remarkably clever, but with the addition that her sister Celia had more common sense.

And so on, for several pages. It is magnificent, but it belongs to a more patient and leisurely culture than ours. Modern novelists usually prefer to let the facts about a character emerge gradually, diversified, or actually conveyed, by action and speech. In any case, all description in fiction is highly selective; its basic rhetorical technique is synecdoche, the part standing for the whole. Both George Eliot and Christopher Isherwood evoke the physical appearance of their heroines by focusing on the hands and the face, leaving the reader to imagine the rest. An exhaustive description of Dorothea's or Sally Bowles's physical and psychological attributes would take many pages, perhaps an entire book.

Clothes are always a useful index of character, class, life-style, but especially in the case of an exhibitionist like Sally. Her black silk get-up (worn for a casual afternoon visit) signals desire-to-impress, theatricality (the cape), and sexual provocativeness (the page-boy's hat acquires connotations from the many references to sexual ambivalence and deviation, including transvestism, that run through the book). These traits are immediately reinforced by her speech and behaviour – asking to use the telephone in order to impress the two men with her latest erotic conquest – which then gives the narrator the opportunity for a description of Sally's hands and face.

This is what Henry James meant by the "scenic method", what he aimed to achieve when he exhorted himself to "Dramatize! dramatize!" James was thinking of the stage play, but Isherwood belonged to the first generation of novelists to grow up with the cinema, and its influence shows. When the narrator of *Goodbye to Berlin* says "I am a camera," he is thinking of a movie camera. Whereas Dorothea is posed statically, as if sitting for a verbal portrait, and is actually compared to a figure in a painting, Sally is shown to us *in action*. It is easy to break down this passage into a sequence of cinematic shots: Sally posing in her black silk outfit – a quick exchange of glances between the two men – a close-up of Sally's green fingernails as she dials the number – another close-up of her ill-coordinated, clown-like makeup and affected expression as she greets her lover – and a two-shot of the male spectators, riveted by the sheer ham of the performance.

No doubt this partly explains the ease with which Sally Bowles's story has transferred to the screen. But there are nuances in the passage which are purely literary. Those green fingernails on grubby hands are what I first think of when her name is mentioned. You could show the green nail-polish in a film, but not the narrator's ironic comment, "a colour unfortunately chosen". "Unfortunately chosen" is the story of Sally Bowles's life. And you could show the cigarette stains and the dirt, but only a narrator could observe, "dirty as a little girl's". The childlike quality beneath the surface sophistication is precisely what makes Sally Bowles a memorable character.

15 Surprise

"I say agin, I want you," Sir Pitt said, thumping the table. "*I* can't git on without you. I didn't see what it was till you went away. The house all goes wrong. It's not the same place. All my accounts has got muddled agin. You *must* come back. Do come back. Dear Becky, do come."

"Come – as what, sir?" Rebecca gasped out.

"Come as Lady Crawley, if you like," the Baronet said, grasping his crape hat. "There! will that zatusfy you? Come back and be my wife. Your vit vor't. Birth be hanged. You're as good a lady as ever I see. You've got more brains in your little vinger than any baronet's wife in the county. Will you come? Yes or no?"

"Oh, Sir Pitt!" Rebecca said, very much moved.

"Say yes, Becky," Sir Pitt continued. "I'm an old man, but a good'n. I'm good for twenty years. I'll make you happy, zee if I don't. You shall do what you like; spend what you like; and 'av it all your own way. I'll make you a zettlement. I'll do everything reg'lar. Look year!" and the old man fell down on his knees and leered at her like a satyr.

Rebecca started back a picture of consternation. In the course of this history we have never seen her lose her presence of mind; but she did now, and wept some of the most genuine tears that ever fell from her eyes.

"Oh, Sir Pitt!" she said. "Oh, sir – I – I'm *married already.*"

WILLIAM MAKEPEACE THACKERAY *Vanity Fair* (1848)

MOST NARRATIVES contain an element of surprise. If we can predict every twist in a plot, we are unlikely to be gripped by it. But the twists must be convincing as well as unexpected. Aristotle called this effect *peripeteia*, or reversal, the sudden shift from one state of affairs to its opposite, often combined with "discovery", the transformation of a character's ignorance into knowledge. Aristotle's example was the scene in *Oedipus Rex* when the messenger who has come to reassure the hero about his origins in fact reveals to him that he has killed his father and married his mother.

In the retelling of a well-known story like that of Oedipus, the surprise is experienced by the characters rather than the audience, for whom the primary effect is one of irony (see Section 39, below). The novel, however, differs from all previous narrative forms in undertaking (or pretending) to tell wholly new stories. On a first reading, therefore, most novels are likely to provide surprises, though some contain more than others.

Thackeray managed to pack several into this scene in *Vanity Fair*. Becky Sharp, a penniless and orphaned governess, is surprised to be offered marriage by a baronet; Sir Pitt Crawley and the reader are surprised to discover that she is married already. Thackeray gets still more mileage out of the situation. As Kathleen Tillotson observed in her *Novels of the 1840s*, this passage, which concludes Chapter XIV of the novel, also came at the end of the fourth number of the original serial publication. The first readers would therefore have been left in suspense for some time (rather like viewers of a modern TV soap) about the identity of Becky's husband. An analogy that might have occurred to Thackeray's contemporaries would be the end of an Act in a play. The tableau of the old roué on his knees before the beautiful and distraught young woman is inherently theatrical, and Becky's "Oh, sir – I – I'm *married already*" is a classic curtain-line, guaranteed to keep an audience buzzing through the interval.

The next chapter takes up the question of whom Becky has married without answering it immediately. Sir Pitt's half-sister, Miss Crawley, bursts into the room to find her brother on his knees before Becky, and *she* is surprised, especially to learn that the proposal had been declined. Not till the end of the chapter

71

does Thackeray reveal that Becky is secretly married to Miss Crawley's nephew, the spendthrift cavalry officer, Rawdon Crawley.

An effect like this needs careful preparation. As in a pyrotechnic set-piece, a slow-burning fuse eventually ignites a quick succession of spectacular explosions. Enough information must be fed to the reader to make the revelation convincing when it comes, but not so much that the reader will easily anticipate it. Thackeray witholds information, but he doesn't cheat. He uses letters a good deal in this part of his narrative to make his uncharacteristic reticence as narrator seem more natural.

Having been foiled in an attempt to catch the brother of her friend Amelia as a husband earlier in the story, the penniless Becky was obliged to take the position of governess to Sir Pitt's two daughters by his ailing second wife. She sets about making herself invaluable to the miserly and uncouth old baronet at his country seat, Queen's Crawley, and also to his rich spinster half-sister. Miss Crawley takes such a fancy to Becky that she insists on being nursed by her while indisposed at her London home. Sir Pitt reluctantly agrees to release Becky because he doesn't want to jeopardize his daughters' expectations of a bequest from Miss Crawley; but when his wife dies (an event to which all the characters are callously indifferent) he is impelled to get Becky back to Queen's Crawley at any price, even marriage. Miss Crawley has already spotted this danger – much as she enjoys Becky's company, she has no wish to welcome her into the family – and has tacitly encouraged her nephew to seduce Becky, to render her ineligible as the third Lady Crawley. In marrying her instead, Rawdon at least acts honourably, if recklessly. The rest of the characters act wholly out of calculation and self-interest, love and death being mere counters in the pursuit of wealth and status.

Thackeray's irony is remorseless. Becky is "very much moved", her tears are, for once, genuine – but why? She has married the stupid Rawdon hoping that he will inherit his aunt's wealth, only to find that she has missed a much bigger and more certain prize: to be the wife of a baronet and, in the nature of things, a rich dowager before long (his claim that he is "good for twenty years" is over-optimistic, and certainly the least of his attractions for Becky). The scene gains enormously from the comic characterization of Sir Pitt, of whom the narrator says earlier, "the whole baronetage, peerage, commonage of England did not contain a more cunning, mean, selfish, foolish, disreputable old man." In the image of his leering at Becky like a satyr, Thackeray goes as far as Victorian reticence would allow in hinting that Sir Pitt is not beyond taking a crude sexual interest in Becky. That she should weep at the loss of such a husband is a devastating comment not only on her but on the whole milieu of *Vanity Fair*.

16 Time-Shift

Monica's anger was rising in her face. "It was Mr Lloyd with his one arm round her," she said. "I saw them. I'm sorry I ever told you. Rose is the only one that believes me."

Rose Stanley believed her, but this was because she was indifferent. She was the least of all the Brodie set to be excited by Miss Brodie's love affairs, or by anyone else's sex. And it was always to be the same. Later, when she was famous for sex, her magnificently appealing qualities lay in the fact that she had no curiosity about sex at all, she never reflected upon it. As Miss Brodie was to say, she had instinct.

"Rose is the only one who believes me," said Monica Douglas.

When she visited Sandy at the nunnery in the late nineteen-fifties, Monica said, "I really did see Teddy Lloyd kiss Miss Brodie in the art room one day."

"I know you did," said Sandy.

She knew it even before Miss Brodie had told her so one day after the end of the war, when they sat in the Braid Hills Hotel eating sandwiches and drinking tea which Miss Brodie's rations at home would not run to. Miss Brodie sat shrivelled and betrayed in her long-preserved dark musquash coat. She had been retired before time. She said, "I am past my prime."

"It was a good prime," said Sandy.

MURIEL SPARK *The Prime of Miss Jean Brodie* (1961)

THE SIMPLEST WAY to tell a story, equally favoured by tribal bards and parents at bedtime, is to begin at the beginning, and go on until you reach the end, or your audience falls asleep. But even in antiquity, storytellers perceived the interesting effects that could be obtained by deviating from chronological order. The classical epic began *in medias res*, in the midst of the story. For example, the narrative of the *Odyssey* begins halfway through the hero's hazardous voyage home from the Trojan War, loops back to describe his earlier adventures, then follows the story to its conclusion in Ithaca.

Through time-shift, narrative avoids presenting life as just one damn thing after another, and allows us to make connections of causality and irony between widely separated events. A shift of narrative focus back in time may change our interpretation of something which happened much later in the chronology of the story, but which we have already experienced as readers of the text. This is a familiar device of cinema, the flashback. Film has more difficulty in accommodating the effect of "flashforward" – the anticipatory glimpse of what is going to happen in the future of the narrative, known to classical rhetoricians as "prolepsis". This is because such information implies the existence of a narrator who knows the whole story, and films do not normally have narrators. It is significant that in this respect the film of *The Prime of Miss Jean Brodie* was much less complex and innovative than the novel on which it was based. The film told the story in straightforward chronological order, whereas the novel is remarkable for its fluid handling of time, ranging rapidly back and forward over the span of the action.

The story concerns Jean Brodie, an eccentric and charismatic teacher at an Edinburgh girls' school between the Wars, and a group of pupils who were under her spell, including Monica who was famous for her skill in maths, Rose who was famous for sex, and Sandy Stranger, who was famous for her vowel sounds and "merely notorious for her small, almost non-existent eyes." These eyes, however, miss nothing and Sandy is the main point-of-view character of the novel. It begins when the girls are Seniors, quickly moves back to describe their time as Juniors when Miss Brodie's influence was at its most potent, and frequently jumps forward to give glimpses of them as adult women, still teased and haunted by memories of their extraordinary teacher.

In Junior School they speculate obsessively about Miss Brodie's sexual life, particularly whether she is having an affair with Mr

Lloyd, the handsome art-master who "had lost the contents" of one of his sleeves in the Great War. Monica claims to have seen them embracing in the art room, and is vexed that only Rose believes her. Her remark to Sandy years later implies that this incredulity still rankles. Sandy, who has in the meantime become a nun in an enclosed order, acknowledges that Monica was right. She knew this, says the narrator, even before Miss Brodie told her one day soon after the end of the war.

In this short passage the reader is whisked backwards and forwards with breathtaking rapidity between a great many different points in time. There is the time of the main narrative, probably the late 1920s, when the Junior schoolgirls are discussing Miss Brodie's amorous life. There is the time in Senior School, in the 1930s, when Rose became famous for sex. There is the time, in the late 1950s, when Monica visits Sandy in her convent. There is the time in the late 1940s when Sandy had tea with the compulsorily retired Miss Brodie. And there is the unspecified time when Sandy discovered that Miss Brodie had indeed been kissed by Mr Lloyd in the art room.

She discovered it, we learn much later in the book, in Senior School. The occasion is a conversation in which Miss Brodie declares that Rose will be Mr Lloyd's mistress as surrogate for herself, because she has dedicated herself to her girls. Sandy decides that there is something dangerous as well as exhilarating about her teacher's rampant egotism. "She thinks she is Providence, thought Sandy, she thinks she is the God of Calvin, she sees the beginning and the end." Of course novelists also see the beginning and the end of their stories, but there is a difference, Muriel Spark implies, between useful fictions and dangerous delusions – also, perhaps, between the Catholic God who allows for free will and the Calvinistic one who doesn't. There is a telling description elsewhere in the novel of Calvin's doctrine of predestination, the belief that "God had planned for practically everybody before they were born a nasty surprise when they died."

Sandy falsifies Miss Brodie's prediction, and thus challenges her claim to control the destinies of others, by becoming Lloyd's mistress herself. Later she shops Miss Brodie to the school authorities for sending another pupil off on a fatal adventure in fascist Spain. That is why Miss Brodie is described as "betrayed" in this extract, and Sandy never seems to be free from guilt on this account, in spite of her religious vocation. Miss Brodie is described as "shrivelled" because she is dying of cancer, so it's a sad scene. But it is placed less than halfway through the novel, and its pathos is countered by many still to come of Miss Brodie in her prime.

Time-shift is a very common effect in modern fiction, but usually it is "naturalized" as the operation of memory, either in the representation of a character's stream of consciousness (Molly Bloom's interior monologue is constantly shifting from one phase of her life to another, like a gramophone pickup skating backwards and forwards between tracks on an LP disc) or, more formally, as the memoir or reminiscence of a character–narrator (for instance, Dowell in Ford's *The Good Soldier*). Graham Greene's *The End of the Affair* (1951) is a virtuoso performance of this latter type. The narrator is a professional writer, Bendrix, who at the beginning of his narrative meets Henry, the husband of Sarah, with whom Bendrix had an affair years before, which Sarah broke off abruptly. Bendrix, who presumed that she had found another lover, is still bitter and jealous, and, when Henry confides his own suspicions of Sarah's infidelity, Bendrix perversely hires a detective to discover her secret. What the detective discovers is a journal kept by Sarah, which describes the affair with Bendrix from her point of view, revealing a completely unexpected motive for her breaking it off, and an unsuspected religious conversion. These developments are the more plausible and dramatic for being narrated out of their proper chronological place.

Muriel Spark's combination of frequent time-shift with authorial third-person narrative is a typical postmodernist strategy, calling attention to the artificial construction of the text, and preventing us from "losing ourselves" in the temporal continuum of the fictional story or in the psychological depth of the central character. Kurt Vonnegut's *Slaughterhouse Five* (1969) is another striking example. The author tells us at the outset that the story of his hero, Billy Pilgrim, is a fiction based on his own real experience of being a prisoner of war in Dresden when it was destroyed by Allied bombers in 1945, one of the most horrific air-raids of World War II. The story proper begins: "*Listen. Billy Pilgrim has come unstuck in time,*" and it shifts frequently and abruptly between various episodes in Billy's civilian life as an optometrist, husband and father in the American midwest, and episodes of his war-service culminating in the horror of Dresden. This is more than just the operation of memory. Billy is "time-tripping". With other traumatized veterans he seeks to escape the intolerable facts of modern history by means of the science-fiction myth of effortless travel through time and intergalactic space (which is measured in time – "light-years"). He claims to have been abducted for a period to the planet Tralfamadore, which is inhabited by little creatures who look like plumber's friends with an eye on top. These passages are both amusingly parodic of science fiction and philosophically serious. To the Tralfamadorians, all times are simultaneously present, and one can choose where to locate oneself. It is the inexorable, unidirectional movement of time that makes life tragic in our human perspective, unless one believes in an eternity in which time is redeemed, and its effects reversed. *Slaughterhouse Five* is a wistful, thought-provoking meditation on these matters, post-Christian as well as postmodernist. One of its most striking and poignant images is of a war-film which Billy Pilgrim watches in reverse:

> American planes, full of holes and wounded men and corpses took off backwards from an airfield in England. Over France, a few German fighter planes flew at them backwards, sucked bullets and shell fragments from some of the planes and crewmen. They did the same for wrecked American bombers on the ground, and those planes flew up backwards to join the formation.

Martin Amis has (with due acknowledgment to Vonnegut) recently developed this conceit into a whole book, *Time's Arrow*, narrating the life of a Nazi war criminal backwards from the moment of his death to his birth, with an effect that is comically grotesque at first, and then increasingly disturbed and disturbing as the story approaches the horrors of the Holocaust. It is possible to interpret the story as a kind of purgatory in which the central character's soul is compelled to relive his appalling past, and as a myth of cancelled evil whose impossibility is all too evident. Most examples of radical experiment with narrative chronology that come to mind seem to be concerned with crimes, misdemeanours and sins.

17 The Reader in the Text

How could you, Madam, be so inattentive in reading the last chapter? I told you in it, *That my mother was not a papist.* – Papist! You told me no such thing, Sir. Madam, I beg leave to repeat it over again, That I told you as plain, at least as words, by direct inference, could tell you such a thing. – Then, Sir, I must have miss'd a page. – No, Madam, – you have not missed a word. – Then I was asleep, Sir. – My pride, Madam, cannot allow you that refuge. – Then, I declare, I know nothing at all about the matter. – That, Madam, is the very fault I lay to your charge; and as a punishment for it, I do insist upon it, that you immediately turn back, that is, as soon as you get to the next full stop, and read the whole chapter over again.

I have imposed this penance upon the lady, neither out of wantonness or cruelty, but from the best of motives; and therefore shall make her no apology for it when she returns back: – 'Tis to rebuke a vicious taste which has crept into thousands besides herself, – of reading straight forwards, more in quest of the adventures, than of the deep erudition and knowledge which a book of this cast, if read over as it should be, would infallibly impart with them.

LAURENCE STERNE *The Life and Opinions of
Tristram Shandy, Gent.* (1759–67)

EVERY NOVEL must have a narrator, however impersonal, but not necessarily a narratee. The narratee is any evocation of, or surrogate for, the reader of the novel within the text itself. This can be as casual as the Victorian novelist's familiar apostrophe, "Dear reader," or as elaborate as the frame of Kipling's "Mrs

Bathurst", discussed earlier (Section 7), in which the "I" narrator is also the narratee of a story told by three other characters who themselves are constantly swapping the two roles. Italo Calvino begins his *If on a winter's night a traveller* by exhorting his reader to get into a receptive mood: "Relax. Concentrate. Dispel every other thought. Let the world around you fade. Best to close the door; the TV is always on in the next room." But a narratee, however constituted, is always a rhetorical device, a means of controlling and complicating the responses of the real reader who remains outside the text.

Laurence Sterne, narrating under the light disguise of Tristram Shandy, plays all kinds of games with the narrator–narratee relationship. Rather like a music-hall comedian who plants stooges in the audience, and integrates their heckling into his act, he sometimes personifies his reader as a Lady or a Gentleman whom he interrogates, teases, criticizes and flatters, for the entertainment and instruction of the rest of us.

Tristram Shandy is a highly idiosyncratic novel whose eponymous narrator undertakes to relate his life from the moment of his conception to adulthood, but never gets beyond his fifth year because the attempt to describe and explain every incident faithfully and exhaustively leads him into endless digression. Everything is connected with other things that occurred before or after or in another place. Gamely, but hopelessly, Tristram struggles to preserve chronological order. In Chapter XIX, still hopelessly bogged down in his pre-natal history, he alludes to the ironic fate of his father, who abominated the name "Tristram" above all others, but lived to see his son inadvertently christened with it, and declares: "if it was not necessary I should be born before I was christened, I would this moment give the reader an account of it."

This is the sentence (he reveals after the passage I have extracted) that should have given his Lady reader the clue to his mother's religious allegiance, for "Had my mother, Madam, been a Papist, that consequence did not follow." The reason being that, according to a document which Tristram reprints (in the original French) in his text, some learned theologians of the Sorbonne had recently approved the idea of conditionally baptizing infants endangered by a difficult birth, *in utero*, by means of a "squirt". In a Roman Catholic country, therefore, it is possible to be christened before one is born.

Baiting Roman Catholics (he was himself an Anglican vicar) and indulging in nudge-nudge humour about the private parts are features of Sterne's writing that are sometimes held against him, but you would have to be a very dour reader not to be disarmed by the wit and elegance of his repartee with "Madam" (its liveliness much enhanced by Sterne's free and idiosyncratic punctuation) and his aside to "the reader". For the real function of this digression is to define and defend his own art. The Lady is sent off to re-read the preceding chapter, "to rebuke a vicious taste . . . of reading straight forwards, more in quest of the adventures, than of the deep erudition and knowledge which a book of this cast, if read over as it should be, would infallibly impart . . ."

No wonder *Tristram Shandy* has been a favourite book of experimental novelists and theorists of the novel in our own century. As I indicated in the preceding section, modernist and postmodernist novelists have also sought to wean readers from the simple pleasures of story by disrupting and rearranging the chain of temporality and causality on which it traditionally depended. Sterne anticipated Joyce and Virginia Woolf in letting the vagaries of the human mind determine the shape and direction of the narrative. And one of the slogans of modernist poetics is "Spatial Form", which means giving unity to a literary work by a pattern of interconnected motifs that can only be perceived by "reading over" (i.e., re-reading) the text in the manner recommended by Tristram.

His dialogue with his readers spatializes the temporal nature of the reading experience in a still more radical way. The novel is figured as a room in which we, as readers, are closeted with the narrator. Before giving the intimate details of his conception, for instance, he declares that "'tis wrote only for the curious and inquisitive," and invites those readers not interested in such descriptions to skip over it, saying:

"—— —— Shut the door —— ——"

slyly confident that we will choose to remain with him.

In the passage cited, one of our number, the Lady, is sent off to re-read the preceding chapter "as soon as you get to the next full stop" (a neat, and characteristic, reminder of the nature of the reading process). We who, as it were, remain with the author are made to feel privileged by his confidence, and tacitly invited to distance ourselves from the imperceptive reader and the "vicious taste which has crept into thousands besides herself", of reading a novel just for the story. Being at this point as much in the dark as she is about the reference to Roman Catholicism, we cannot put up much resistance to the author's defence of his method.

18 Weather

The evening of this day was very long, and melancholy, at Hartfield. The weather added what it could of gloom. A cold stormy rain set in, and nothing of July appeared but in the trees and shrubs, which the wind was despoiling, and the length of the day, which only made such cruel sights the longer visible.

JANE AUSTEN *Emma* (1816)

London. Michaelmas term lately over, and the Lord Chancellor sitting in Lincoln's Inn Hall. Implacable November weather. As much mud in the streets, as if the waters had but newly retired from the face of the earth, and it would not be wonderful to meet a Megalosaurus, forty feet long or so, waddling like an elephantine lizard up Holborn Hill. Smoke lowering down from chimney-pots, making a soft black drizzle with flakes of soot in it as big as full-grown snowflakes – gone into mourning, one might imagine, for the death of the sun. Dogs, undistinguishable in mire. Horses, scarcely better; splashed to their very blinkers. Foot passengers, jostling one another's umbrellas, in a general infection of ill temper, and losing their foot-hold at street-corners, where tens of thousands of other foot passengers have been slipping and sliding since the day broke (if this day ever broke), adding new deposits to the crust upon crust of mud, sticking at those points tenaciously to the pavement, and accumulating at compound interest.

CHARLES DICKENS *Bleak House* (1853)

APART FROM THE ODD STORM at sea, weather was given scant attention in prose fiction until the late eighteenth century. In the nineteenth, novelists always seem to be talking about it. This was the consequence partly of the heightened appreciation of Nature engendered by Romantic poetry and painting, partly of a growing literary interest in the individual self, in states of feeling that affect and are affected by our perceptions of the external world. As Coleridge put it in his ode on "Dejection":

> O Lady! We receive but what we give
> And in our life alone does Nature live.

We all know that the weather affects our moods. The novelist is in the happy position of being able to invent whatever weather is appropriate to the mood he or she wants to evoke.

Weather is therefore frequently a trigger for the effect John Ruskin called the pathetic fallacy, the projection of human emotions onto phenomena in the natural world. "All violent feelings . . . produce in us a falseness in our impressions of external things, which I would generally characterize as the pathetic fallacy," he wrote. As the name implies, Ruskin thought it was a bad thing, a symptom of the decadence of modern (as compared to classical) art and literature, and it is indeed often the occasion of overblown, self-indulgent writing. But used with intelligence and discretion it is a rhetorical device capable of moving and powerful effects, without which fiction would be much the poorer.

Jane Austen retained an Augustan suspicion of the Romantic imagination, and satirized it in the characterization of Marianne in *Sense and Sensibility*. "It is not everyone who has your passion for dead leaves," her sister Elinor comments drily after Marianne's autumn rhapsody, "How have I delighted, as I walked, to see them driven in showers about me by the wind. What feelings have they, the season, the air altogether inspired!" Weather in Jane Austen's novels is usually something that has an important practical bearing on the social life of her characters, rather than a metaphorical index of their inner lives. The snow in Chapters 15 and 16 of *Emma* is representative in this respect. The first mention comes in

85

the middle of Mr Weston's pre-Christmas dinner party, when Mr John Knightley, who never wanted to attend it in the first place, comes into the drawing-room and announces with ill-concealed *Schadenfreude* that it is "snowing hard with a strong drifting wind", striking terror into the heart of Emma's valetudinarian father, Mr Woodhouse. There follows a discussion in which everybody has something to say, more self-revealing than to the point, until Mr George Knightley returns from his own examination of the weather, and gives a typically reasonable and reassuring report of it. He and Emma, concluding that Mr Woodhouse will nevertheless fret for the rest of the evening, decide to call for the carriages. Mr Elton takes advantage of this sudden departure to get unaccompanied into Emma's carriage, and makes a declaration of love which is both unexpected and deeply embarrassing to her, since she has been under the illusion that he was courting her protégée, Harriet. Fortunately, the weather over the next few days gives her a welcome alibi to avoid meeting either of the other two parties:

> The weather was most favourable to her . . . The ground covered with snow, and the atmosphere in that unsettled state between frost and thaw, which is of all the others the most unfriendly for exercise, every morning beginning in rain or snow, and every evening setting in to freeze, she was for many days a most honourable prisoner.

The weather is described because it is relevant to the story, but the description is quite literal.

Even Jane Austen, however, makes discreet use of the pathetic fallacy on occasion. When Emma's fortunes are at their lowest ebb, when she has discovered the truth, with all its embarrassing implications for her own conduct, about Jane Fairfax, when she belatedly realizes that she loves Mr Knightley but has reason to believe he is going to marry Harriet – on this, the worst day of her life, "the weather added what it could of gloom." Ruskin would point out that the weather is incapable of any such intention. But the summer storm is a precise analogy for the heroine's feelings about her future, because her very fixed and prominent position in the small and enclosed society of Highbury will only make such

"cruel sights" as Harriet's marriage to Knightley "the longer visible". Being unseasonable, however, it is an unreliable portent: next day, the sun comes out again and George Knightley turns up to propose to Emma.

Where Jane Austen slips the pathetic fallacy past us so stealthily that we hardly notice, Dickens hits us over the head with it in the famous opening paragraph of *Bleak House*. "Implacable November weather." The personification of the weather as "implacable" is a commonplace colloquialism, but here it carries suggestions of divine displeasure, being in close conjunction with allusions to the Old Testament. "As if the waters had but newly retired from the face of the earth," echoes both the description of the Creation in Genesis and the story of the Flood. These Biblical allusions are mixed up in a very Victorian way with a more modern, post-Darwinian cosmology in the references to the Megalosaurus and the running down of the solar system from entropy. The total effect is a startling feat of defamiliarization.

On one level this is a realistic picture of nineteenth-century London streets in bad weather, a montage of typical details quite simply and literally described: smoke lowering down from chimney-pots . . . dogs undistinguishable in mire . . . horses splashed to their very blinkers . . . jostling umbrellas. But Dickens's metaphoric imagination transforms this commonplace scene into an apocalyptic vision of the proud capital of the British Empire reverting to primitive swamp, or anticipating the final extinction of all life on earth. The metaphorical double somersault from soot flake, to snowflake in mourning, to the death of the sun, is particularly stunning.

It is a scenario of a kind we meet later in science fiction (the vision of the Megalosaurus waddling up Holborn Hill anticipates King Kong scaling the Empire State Building, the "death of the sun" the chilling finale of H. G. Wells's *The Time Machine*) and in postmodernist prophets of doom like Martin Amis. It sets up for denunciation the idea of a society that has denatured itself by greed and corruption, which Dickens is about to examine in his many-stranded plot centering on a disputed estate. Wittily, the mud

87

accumulates at compound interest here in the City of London, reminding us of the Biblical condemnation of money as filthy lucre. The Lord Chancellor described at the beginning of the passage (in a series of terse statements like headlines from "News at Ten") presiding over the court of Chancery, seems also to preside over the weather, and the equation is clinched some paragraphs later: "Never can there come fog too thick, never can there come mud and mire too deep, to assort with the groping and floundering condition which this High Court of Chancery, most pestilent of hoary sinners, holds, this day, in the sight of heaven and earth."

19 Repetition

In the fall the war was always there, but we did not go to it any more. It was cold in the fall in Milan and the dark came very early. Then the electric lights came on, and it was pleasant along the streets looking in the windows. There was much game hanging outside the shops, and the snow powdered in the fur of the foxes and the wind blew their tails. The deer hung stiff and heavy and empty, and small birds blew in the wind and the wind turned their feathers. It was a cold fall and the wind came down from the mountains.

We were all at the hospital every afternoon, and there were different ways of walking across the town through the dusk to the hospital. Two of the ways were alongside canals, but they were long. Always, though, you crossed a bridge across a canal to enter the hospital. There was a choice of three bridges. On one of them a woman sold roasted chestnuts. It was warm, standing in front of her charcoal fire, and the chestnuts were warm afterward in your pocket. The hospital was very old and very beautiful, and you entered through a gate and walked across a courtyard and out a gate on the other side. There were usually funerals starting from the courtyard. Beyond the old hospital were the new brick pavilions, and there we met every afternoon and were all very polite and interested in what was the matter, and sat in the machines that were to make so much difference.

ERNEST HEMINGWAY "In Another Country" (1927)

IF YOU HAVE the time and inclination, get some coloured pens or pencils and draw a ring round the words that occur more than once in the first paragraph of Hemingway's story, a different colour for each word, and join them up. You will reveal a complex pattern of verbal chains linking words of two kinds: those with referential meaning, *fall, cold, dark, wind, blew,* which we can call lexical words, and articles, prepositions and conjunctions like *the, of, in, and,* which we can call grammatical words.

It is almost impossible to write English without the repetition of grammatical words, so normally we don't notice it as such, but you can't fail to notice the extraordinary number of "*ands*" in this short paragraph. This is a symptom of its very repetitive syntax, stringing together declarative statements without subordinating one to another. The repetition of the lexical words is less evenly distributed, clustering at the beginning and end of the paragraph.

Lexical and grammatical repetition on this scale would probably receive a black mark in a school "composition", and quite rightly. The traditional model of good literary prose requires "elegant variation": if you have to refer to something more than once, you should try to find alternative ways of describing it; and you should give your syntax the same kind of variety. (The passage by Henry James discussed in Section 6 is rich in examples of both kinds of variation.)

Hemingway, however, rejected traditional rhetoric, for reasons that were partly literary and partly philosophical. He thought that "fine writing" falsified experience, and strove to "put down what really happened in action, what the actual things were which produced the emotion that you experienced" by using simple, denotative language purged of stylistic decoration.

It looks easy, but of course it isn't. The words are simple but their arrangement is not. There are many possible ways of arranging the words of the first sentence, but the one chosen by Hemingway splits the phrase "go to war" in two, implying an as yet unexplained tension in the persona of the narrator, a mixture of relief and irony. As we soon learn, he and his companions are soldiers wounded while fighting on the Italian side in World War I, now recuperating, but conscious that the war which nearly killed them may have made their lives not worth living anyway. It is a story about trauma, and how men cope with it, or fail to cope. The unspoken word which is a key to all the repeated words in the text is "death".

The American word for autumn, *fall*, carries in it a reminder of the death of vegetation, and echoes the conventional phrase for those who die in battle, "the fallen". Its juxtaposition with *cold* and *dark* in the second sentence strengthens these associations. The brightly lit shops seem to offer some distraction (an effect heightened by the fact that there is no lexical repetition in this sentence) but the narrator's attention quickly focuses on the game hanging outside the shops, further emblems of death. The description of the snow powdering in their fur, and the wind ruffling their feathers, is literal and exact, but tightens the association of *fall*, *cold*, *dark*, *wind*, *blew*, with death. Three of the repeated words come together for the first time in the last sentence with a poetic effect of closure: "It was a cold fall and the wind came down from the mountains." The mountains are where the war is going on. Wind, so often a symbol of life and spirit in religious and Romantic writing, is here associated with lifelessness. God is very dead in these early stories of Hemingway. The hero has learned from the trauma of combat to distrust metaphysics as well as rhetoric. He trusts only his senses, and sees experience in starkly polarized terms: cold/warm, light/dark, life/death.

The incantatory rhythms and repetitions persist in the second paragraph. It would have been easy to find elegant alternatives for "hospital", or simply to have used the pronoun "it" occasionally; but the hospital is the centre of the soldiers' lives, their daily place of pilgrimage, the repository of their hopes and fears, and the repetition of the word is therefore expressive. It is possible to vary the route by which the hospital is reached, but the terminus is always the same. There is a choice of bridges, but always you have to cross a canal (a faint suggestion of the river Styx in the underworld, perhaps). The narrator prefers the bridge where he can buy roasted chestnuts, warm in the pocket like the promise of life – except that Hemingway doesn't use that simile, he merely implies it; just as in the first paragraph he manages to make his description of the season as emotionally powerful as any example of the pathetic fallacy (see the preceding section) without using a metaphor. The line between charged simplicity and mannered monotony is a fine one, and Hemingway didn't always stay on the right side of it, but in his early work he forged an entirely original style for his times.

Needless to say, repetition is not necessarily linked to a bleakly positivist, anti-metaphysical representation of life such as we find in Hemingway. It is also a characteristic feature of religious and mystical writing, and is used by novelists whose work tends in that direction – D. H. Lawrence, for instance. The language of the opening chapter of *The Rainbow*, evoking a lost agrarian way of life, echoes the verbal repetition and syntactical parallelism of the Old Testament:

> The young corn waved and was silken, and the lustre slid along the limbs of the men who saw it. They took the udder of the cows, the cows yielded milk and pulsed against the hands of the men, the pulse of the blood of the teats of the cows beat into the pulse of the hands of the men.

Repetition is also a favourite device of orators and preachers, roles that Charles Dickens often adopted in his authorial persona. This, for instance, is the conclusion to his chapter describing the death of Jo, the destitute crossing-sweeper, in *Bleak House*:

> Dead, your Majesty. Dead, my lords and gentlemen. Dead, Right Reverends and Wrong Reverends of every order. Dead, men and women, born with Heavenly compassion in your hearts. And dying thus around us every day.

And of course repetition can be funny, as in this passage from Martin Amis's *Money*:

> Intriguingly enough, the only way I can make Selina actually *want* to go to bed with me is by not wanting to go to bed with her. It never fails. It really puts her in the mood. The trouble is, when I don't want to go to bed with her (and it does happen), I don't

want to go to bed with her. When does it happen? When don't I want to go to bed with her? When she wants to go to bed with me. I like going to bed with her when going to bed with me is the last thing she wants. She nearly always does go to bed with me, if I shout at her a lot or threaten her or give her enough money.

It hardly needs to be pointed out that the frustrations and contradictions of the narrator's sexual relationship with Selina are rendered all the more comic and ironic by the repetition of the phrase "go to bed with" for which any number of alternatives were available. (If you doubt that, try rewriting the passage using elegant variation.) The final sentence also illustrates another important type of repetition: the recurrence of a thematic keyword throughout an entire novel – in this case, "money". It is "money" not "go to bed" that occupies the crucially important last-word space in the paragraph I have just quoted. Thus one kind of repetition, belonging to the macro-level of the text, functions as variation on the micro-level.

20 Fancy Prose

Lolita, light of my life, fire of my loins. My sin, my soul. Lo-lee-ta: the tip of the tongue taking a trip of three steps down the palate to tap, at three, on the teeth. Lo. Lee. Ta.

She was Lo, plain Lo, in the morning, standing four feet ten in one sock. She was Lola in slacks. She was Dolly at school. She was Dolores on the dotted line. But in my arms she was always Lolita.

Did she have a precursor? She did, indeed she did. In point of fact, there might have been no Lolita at all had I not loved, one summer, a certain initial girl-child. In a princedom by the sea. Oh when? About as many years before Lolita was born as my age was that summer. You can always count on a murderer for a fancy prose style.

Ladies and gentlemen of the jury, exhibit number one is what the seraphs, the misinformed, simple, noble-winged seraphs, envied. Look at this tangle of thorns.

VLADIMIR NABOKOV *Lolita* (1955)

THE GOLDEN RULE of fictional prose is that there are no rules – except the ones that each writer sets for him or herself. Repetition and simplicity worked (usually) for Hemingway's artistic purposes. Variation and decoration worked for Nabokov's, especially in *Lolita*. This novel takes the form of a brilliant piece of special pleading by a man whose attraction to a certain type of pubescent girl, whom he calls a "nymphet", leads him to commit evil deeds. The book aroused controversy on its first publication, and still disturbs, because it gives a seductive eloquence to a child-abuser and murderer. As Humbert Humbert himself says, "You can always count on a murderer for a fancy prose style."

There is of course plenty of repetition in the opening passage of the novel, but it isn't lexical repetition, such as we encountered in the Hemingway passage discussed in the previous section. It is a matter of parallel syntactical structures and similar sounds – just the kind of repetition, in fact, that you expect to find in poetry. (Another term for fancy prose is poetic prose.) There's a veritable firework display of alliteration, for instance, in the first paragraph, "*l*"s and "*t*"s exploding brilliantly in rapturous celebration of the beloved's name: *light, life, loins, tip, tongue, trip. Lo. Lee. Ta.*

Each of the four paragraphs exhibits a different type of discourse. This first one is a lyrical outburst, a series of exclamations, without finite verbs. Its opening salvo of metaphors is extravagant and faintly archaic in diction: *light of my life, fire of my loins, my sin, my soul* (more alliteration there). The next metaphor, of the tongue tripping down the palate to tap on the teeth, is more homely and humorous, but it draws attention to an organ used in the service of both eloquence and lust, never far apart in this character.

The second paragraph is tenderly reminiscent. A series of identically structured clauses lists the variant names of the beloved like a profane litany: *She was Lo . . . She was Lola . . . She was Dolly . . . She was Dolores . . . But in my arms she was always Lolita.* You could set it to music. (There was in fact an ill-fated stage musical of *Lolita*: "a nice little flop," Nabokov drily noted in his diary.) And of course, if we didn't know already, this paragraph gives us the first inkling that Lolita was an under-age object of desire, in the references to her height, sock and school.

The third paragraph takes yet another tack. It is more conversational, answering implied questions from an unspecified interlocutor, in the manner of a dramatic monologue: "Did she have a precursor?" The affirmative answer is given with poetic redundancy: "She did, she did." The forensic phrase, "In point of fact," prepares us for the explicit evocation of a court-room context in the last paragraph. (Humbert is supposed to be writing his apologia while awaiting trial.) "Oh when?" The riddling, roundabout answer

95

to that question foregrounds the disparity of age between Humbert and Lolita.

In this paragraph narrative interest begins, with the raising of questions about cause-and-effect ("there might have been . . . had I not . . .") and about the identity of the "initial girl-child". Heightening the poetic quality of this prose is an allusion to a well-known poem, Edgar Allan Poe's "Annabel Lee":

> *I* was a child and *she* was a child,
>   In this kingdom by the sea,
> But we loved with a love that was more than love –
>   I and my ANNABEL LEE –
> With a love that the winged seraphs of heaven
>   Coveted her and me.

Humbert's explanation of, and excuse for, his erotic fixation on young girls is that an adolescent sweetheart called Annabel died before they could consummate their love. Poe's poem is a morbidly sentimental threnody on the same theme: the speaker blames the envious angels for taking his beloved from this world, and finds solace in lying beside her grave. Humbert, however, unscrupulously seeks nymphet surrogates for his Annabel. There is a diabolic sneer in the epithets he applies to the seraphs, "misinformed, simple, noble-winged," and a blasphemous hint that his own suffering is to be compared to the crown of thorns. (This kind of gesturing of one text to another is known as intertextuality, and deserves a section to itself – see p. 98.)

Nabokov's virtuosity in a language that was not his mother-tongue never ceases to amaze; but perhaps it was this very fact that allowed him to discover the full resources of English prose, and to use them with uninhibited delight.

One of the earliest exponents of "fancy prose" in English fiction – indeed, one might risk calling him the first – was the Elizabethan writer John Lyly, whose *Euphues: the Anatomy of Wit* (1578) was a very fashionable book in its day, and gave to the language the word "euphuism" and the adjective "euphuistic" (not to be confused with euphemism/euphemistic). Here is a specimen:

The freshest colors soonest fade, the keenest razor soonest turneth his edge, the finest cloth is soonest eaten with moths, and the cambric sooner stained than the coarse canvas. Which appeared well in this Euphues, whose wit being, like wax, apt to receive any impression, and bearing the head in his own hand, either to use the rein or the spur, disdaining counsel, leaving his country, loathing his old acquaintance, thought either by wit to obtain some conquest or by shame to abide some conflict; who, preferring fancy before friends and his present humour before honor to come, laid reason in water, being too salt for his taste, and followed unbridled affection, most pleasant for his tooth.

It's clever, and amusing in short extracts, but after a few pages it is apt to weary the modern reader by the *sameness* of its stylistic exhibitionism. The same patterns of syntax and sound are used again and again, and used by all the characters as well as the authorial voice. It is a kind of prose that is exclusively literary, belonging entirely to the written word. What is missing, what entered into the prose of English fiction between *Euphues* and *Lolita*, is the sound of the human voice, or many voices, speaking in a variety of accents, rhythms and registers, animating and modifying the formal patterns of literary rhetoric. More will be said about this under the heading of "Telling in Different Voices" (Section 27). But first: intertextuality.

21 Intertextuality

"We must try to haul this mainsail close up," I said. The
shadows swayed away from me without a word. Those men
were the ghosts of themselves, and their weight on a rope could
be no more than the weight of a bunch of ghosts. Indeed, if ever
a sail was hauled up by sheer spiritual strength it must have
been that sail; for, properly speaking, there was not muscle
enough for the task in the whole ship, let alone the miserable
lot of us on deck. Of course, I took the lead in the work myself.
They wandered feebly after me from rope to rope, stumbling
and panting. They toiled like Titans. We were an hour at it at
least, and all the time the black universe made no sound. When
the last leech-line was made fast, my eyes, accustomed to the
darkness, made out the shapes of exhausted men dropping over
the rails, collapsed on hatches. One hung over the after-capstan,
sobbing for breath; and I stood amongst them like a tower of
strength, impervious to disease and feeling only the sickness of
my soul. I waited for some time, fighting against the weight of
my sins, against my sense of unworthiness, and then I said:

"Now, men, we'll go aft and square the mainyard. That's
about all we can do for the ship; and for the rest she must take
her chance."

JOSEPH CONRAD *The Shadow-Line* (1917)

THERE ARE MANY WAYS by which one text can refer to another:
parody, pastiche, echo, allusion, direct quotation, structural parallelism. Some theorists believe that intertextuality is the very
condition of literature, that all texts are woven from the tissues of

98

other texts, whether their authors know it or not. Writers committed to documentary-style realism will tend to deny or suppress this principle. Samuel Richardson, for instance, thought he had invented an entirely new kind of fiction which was quite independent of earlier literature, but it is easy to see in *Pamela* (1740), his story of a virtuous maidservant who marries her master after many trials and tribulations, a fairy-tale archetype. The next important English novel was Henry Fielding's *Joseph Andrews* (1742), which starts out as a parody of *Pamela*, and incorporates a reworking of the parable of the Good Samaritan and many passages written in mock-heroic style. Intertextuality, in short, is entwined in the roots of the English novel, while at the other end of the chronological spectrum novelists have tended to exploit rather than resist it, freely recycling old myths and earlier works of literature to shape, or add resonance to, their presentation of contemporary life.

Some writers signpost such references more explicitly than others. James Joyce tipped off his readers by entitling his epic of modern Dublin life *Ulysses*, Nabokov by giving Lolita's precursor the name of Poe's Annabel. Conrad may have been conveying a subtler hint in the subtitle of *The Shadow-Line*: "A Confession."

This novella, autobiographical in origin, is the account of a young merchant naval officer who, while waiting in a Far Eastern port for a passage home, is unexpectedly offered his first command, a sailing ship whose captain has died at sea. Setting out into the Gulf of Siam, he soon discovers that the deceased captain was deranged, and his own first mate believes that the old man has put a curse on the ship. This fear seems confirmed when the vessel is becalmed, the crew fall sick with fever, and the young captain discovers that his predecessor has destroyed all the stocks of quinine. Then, in the middle of a pitch-black night, there are signs of a change in the weather.

The description of the sick and enfeebled sailors obeying their captain's command to haul up the mainsail, so that the ship can run with the wind when it comes, shows in its technical detail ("leech-line", "after-capstan", "square the mainyard") that Conrad knew what he was talking about – he was of course a master mariner with twenty years experience at sea. But it also recalls a passage in one of the most famous poems in English literature, Samuel Taylor Coleridge's "The Rime of the Ancient Mariner", where the dead sailors rise from the decks of the enchanted ship and man the rigging:

> The mariners all gan work the ropes,
> Where they were wont to do;
> They raised their limbs like lifeless tools –
> We were a ghastly crew.

The Mariner kills an albatross, brings a curse on his ship in the form of calm and pestilence, is released from it when he blesses the watersnakes unawares, and wafted back home by supernatural agencies; he alone survives the ordeal, but feels guilt and responsibility for his shipmates' fate. In Conrad's story the evil deed which curses the ship is transferred to the dead captain, but for the narrator the sequel is a quasi-religious experience not unlike the Mariner's. What might have been merely a ripping yarn becomes a rite of passage across the "shadow-line" that divides innocence from experience, youth from maturity, arrogance from humility. Unaccountably spared the fever (like the Mariner) the young captain feels "the sickness of my soul . . . the weight of my sins . . . my sense of unworthiness." He is haunted by the "vision of a ship drifting in calm and swinging in light airs, with all the crew dying slowly about her decks." After the mainsail is raised and the wind springs up, he reflects, "the malicious spectre had been laid, the evil spell broken, the curse removed. We were now in the hands of a kind and energetic providence. It was rushing us on . . ." Compare:

> Swiftly, swiftly flew the ship,
> Yet she sailed softly too:
> Sweetly, sweetly blew the breeze –
> On me alone it blew.

When the ship in Conrad's story finally arrives in port, flying the signal requesting medical assistance, the naval surgeons who board her are as astonished to find the decks deserted as the Pilot and the Hermit are, in Coleridge's poem, at the return of the Mariner in sole charge of his ship. Like the Ancient Mariner, the captain cannot rid himself of a sense of responsibility for the sufferings of his crew. As they are removed from the ship, he says, "They passed under my eyes one after another – each of them an embodied reproach of the bitterest kind . . ." Compare:

> The pang, the curse, with which they died,
> Had never passed away:
> I could not draw my eyes from theirs,
> Nor turn them up to pray.

Like the Mariner, who "stoppeth one in three" to unburden himself, the captain is impelled to make a "confession" of his experience.

Whether Conrad consciously intended these allusions cannot be proved from the text, and though it might be interesting to try and find out, the answer wouldn't make much difference. The echoes are evidence that he knew Coleridge's poem, but he might have reproduced them unconsciously (though I personally doubt it), just as they may have a subliminal effect on readers who have read the poem and forgotten it, or know it only through selective quotation. It was certainly not the first or only occasion on which Conrad employed literary allusion in this way. Marlow's journey up the Congo in *Heart of Darkness* is explicitly compared to Dante's descent into the circles of hell in the *Inferno*, and his late novel *Victory* is modelled on Shakespeare's *The Tempest*.

James Joyce's *Ulysses* is probably the most celebrated and influential example of intertextuality in modern literature. When it appeared in 1922, T. S. Eliot hailed Joyce's use of the *Odyssey* as a structural device, "manipulating a continuous parallel between contemporaneity and antiquity", as an exciting technical breakthrough, "a step towards making the modern world possible for art." Since Eliot had been reading Joyce's novel in serial form over the preceding years, while working on his own great poem "The Waste Land", also published in 1922, in which he manipulated a continuous parallel between contemporaneity and the Grail legend, we may interpret his praise of *Ulysses* as part acknowledgment, and part manifesto. But in neither work is intertextuality limited to one source, or to structural parallelism. "The Waste Land" echoes many different sources; *Ulysses* is full of parody, pastiche, quotations from and allusions to all kinds of texts. There is, for instance, a chapter set in a newspaper office, divided into sections with headlines that mimic the development of journalistic style, a chapter written largely in a pastiche of cheap women's magazines, and another, set in a maternity hospital, that parodies the historical development of English prose from the Anglo-Saxon period to the twentieth century.

Since I combined writing fiction with an academic career for nearly thirty years it is not surprising that my own novels became increasingly intertextual; and, as it happens, both Joyce and Eliot were significant influences in this respect, especially the former. The parodies in *The British Museum is Falling Down* were inspired by the example of *Ulysses*, as was its one-day action, and the last chapter is a rather cheeky *hommage* to Molly Bloom's monologue. The "break-through" point in the genesis of *Small World* came when I perceived the possibility of basing a comic-satiric novel about the academic jet-set, zooming round the world to international conferences where they competed with each other both professionally and erotically, on the story of King Arthur and his knights of the Round Table and their quest for the Grail, especially as interpreted by Jessie L. Weston in a book that T. S. Eliot had raided for "The Waste Land". I have written elsewhere about the genesis of these novels (in the Afterword to *The British Museum* and in *Write On*) and mention them here to make the point that intertextuality is not, or not necessarily, a merely decorative addition to a text, but sometimes a crucial factor in its conception and composition.

There is however another aspect of the art of fiction, known only to writers, which often involves intertextuality, and that is the Missed Opportunity. Inevitably, in the course of reading, one sometimes comes across echoes, anticipations and analogues of one's own work long after the latter is finished and done with, too late to take advantage of the discovery. Towards the end of *Small World* there is a scene set in New York during the MLA Convention, which is always held in the last days of December. Following the triumph of the hero, Persse McGarrigle, at the session on the Function of Criticism, there is an astonishing change in the weather, a warm southerly airstream raising the temperature in Manhattan to a level unprecedented at that season. In the mythic scheme of the book, this is equivalent to the fertilization of the Fisher King's barren kingdom in the Grail Legend, as a result of the Grail Knight asking the necessary question. Arthur Kingfisher, the *doyen* of modern academic criticism presiding over the Convention, feels the curse of sexual impotence miraculously lifted from him. He tells his Korean mistress, Song-mi:

> "It's like the halcyon days ... A period of calm weather in the middle of winter. The ancients used to call them the halcyon days, when the kingfisher was supposed to hatch its eggs. Remember Milton – *'The bird sits brooding on the charmèd wave'*? The bird was a kingfisher. That's what 'halcyon' means in Greek, Song-mi: kingfisher. The halcyon days were kingfisher days. My days. Our days."

He might have gone on to quote another, wonderfully apposite snatch of verse:

> Kingfisher weather, with a light fair breeze,
> Full canvas, and the eight sails drawing well.

And he might have added: "They were the best lines in 'The Waste Land', but Ezra Pound persuaded Tom Eliot to cut them out." Unfortunately I didn't come across these lines, in Valerie Eliot's edition of *The Waste Land: a facsimile and transcript of the original drafts including the annotations of Ezra Pound*, until some time after *Small World* had been published.

22 The Experimental Novel

Bridesley, Birmingham.

Two o'clock. Thousands came back from dinner along streets.

"What we want is go, push," said works manager to son of Mr Dupret. "What I say to them is – let's get on with it, let's get the stuff out."

Thousands came back to factories they worked in from their dinners.

"I'm always at them but they know me. They know I'm a father and mother to them. If they're in trouble they've but to come to me. And they turn out beautiful work, beautiful work. I'd do anything for 'em and they know it."

Noise of lathes working began again in this factory. Hundreds went along road outside, men and girls. Some turned in to Dupret factory.

Some had stayed in iron foundry shop in this factory for dinner. They sat round brazier in a circle.

"And I was standing by the stores in the doorway with me back to the door into the pipe shop with a false nose on and green whiskers. Albert inside was laughin' and laughin' again when 'Tis 'im comes in through the pipe shop and I sees Albert draw up but I didn't take much notice till I heard, 'Ain't you got nothin' better to do Gates but make a fool of yourself?' And 'e says to Albert, 'What would you be standin' there for Milligan?' And I was too surprised to take the nose off, it was so sudden. I shan't ever forget that."

HENRY GREEN Living (1929)

"THE EXPERIMENTAL NOVEL" was a phrase coined by Zola to claim some equivalence between his sociologically oriented fiction and scientific investigation of the natural world, but this comparison will not stand up to scrutiny. A work of fiction is not a reliable method of verifying or falsifying a hypothesis about society, and "experiment" in literature, as in other arts, is more usefully regarded as a radical approach to the perennial task of "defamiliarization" (see Section 11). An experimental novel is one that ostentatiously deviates from the received ways of representing reality – either in narrative organization or in style, or in both – to heighten or change our perception of that reality.

The second and third decades of the twentieth century, the heyday of modernism, were notable for experimental fiction – Dorothy Richardson, James Joyce, Gertrude Stein and Virginia Woolf are just a few names that come to mind. One writer's experiments, however, are quickly appropriated and put to different uses by others, so it is usually difficult to attribute the discovery of a particular technique to a single author. The opening of Henry Green's *Living* is unmistakably of its period in method. The abrupt shifting of the discourse from narrative to dialogue and back to narrative, without smooth transitions or explanatory links, is analogous to, and perhaps directly influenced by, the cubist compositions of Picasso, the cinematic jump-cuts of Eisenstein, the fragments T. S. Eliot shored against his ruins in "The Waste Land". Fragmentation, discontinuity, montage, are pervasive in the experimental art of the nineteen-twenties.

But there is one feature of *Living* that was an original innovation of Henry Green's, and that is the systematic omission of articles (*a, the*) from the narrative discourse. It is not absolutely consistent (in this passage the men "sat round brazier in *a* circle"), but it is sufficiently thoroughgoing to arrest the reader's attention, reinforcing the effect of other, more familiar types of condensation (the omission of finite verbs, for instance, and of nouns and adjectives with sensuous or emotive weight). Where a conventionally smooth, elegant narrative prose would read, "*It was two o'clock. Thousands of workers came back from their dinners along the streets,*" or even, in a more old-fashioned literary style, "*Thousands of factory hands wearing cloth caps and headscarves hurried back through the drab streets from their hastily consumed mid-day meals,"* Henry Green writes: "Two o'clock. Thousands came back from dinner along streets."

Henry Green was the pen-name of Henry Yorke, whose family owned an engineering firm in Birmingham. Henry trained to become its managing director by working his way up through the various departments from the shop floor, acquiring in the process a priceless understanding of the nature of industrial work, and a deep affection and respect for the men and women who laboured at it. *Living* is a wonderful celebration, tender without being sentimental, of English working-class life at a particular moment in time.

One of the difficulties of writing truthfully about working-class life in fiction, especially evident in the well-intentioned industrial novels of the Victorian age, is that the novel itself is an inherently middle-class form, and its narrative voice is apt to betray this bias in every turn of phrase. It is hard for the novel not to seem condescending to the experience it depicts in the contrast between the polite, well-formed, educated discourse of the narrator and the rough, colloquial, dialect speech of the characters. Consider, for example, Dickens's handling of the scene in *Hard Times* where Stephen Blackpool refuses to join in a Trade Union strike on conscientious grounds:

"Stephen Blackpool," said the chairman, rising, "think on't agen. Think on't once agen lad, afore thour't shunned by aw owd friends."

There was a universal murmur to the same effect, though no man articulated a word. Every eye was fixed on Stephen's face. To repent of his determination, would be to take a load from all their minds. He looked around him, and knew that it was so. Not a grain of anger with them was in his heart; he knew them, far below their surface weaknesses and misconceptions, as no-one but their fellow labourer could.

"I ha thowt on't, above a bit, sir. I simply canna come in. I mun go th' way as lays afore me. I mun tak my leave o'aw heer."

Green tried to close such a painfully obvious gap between authorial speech and characters' speech in *Living* by deliberately deforming the narrative discourse – giving it, as he said himself, something of the compactness of Midland dialect and avoiding "easy elegance". Not that the narrative sentences are in the same register as the characters' dialogue. There is a bleak, functional economy about the former, expressive of the mechanical, repetitive routines that industry imposes on its workers, to which the speech of the characters offers a kind of resistance in its poetic redundancies ("beautiful work, beautiful work") proverbial phrases ("a father and mother to them") and private codes (the works manager is known by the phrase used to warn of his approach, "'Tis 'im"). By such experiments with style an old Etonian, improbably enough, produced what is arguably the best novel ever written about factories and factory workers.

It is easy to accept and appreciate experiments like Green's that have some discoverable mimetic or expressive purpose. More problematical are stylistic deviations which set an arbitrary, artificial obstacle between the language of prose and its normal functions, such as the "lipogram", in which a letter of the alphabet is systematically omitted. The late Georges Perec, a French novelist best known for his *Life: A User's Manual*, wrote a novel called *La Disparition* which excludes use of the letter "e", for instance, a feat even more astonishing in French than it would be in English (though one does not envy Gilbert Adair, currently reported to be engaged in translating it). The contemporary American writer, Walter Abish, wrote a novel called *Alphabetical Africa*, the chapters of which conform to the following fiendishly difficult rule: the first chapter contains only words beginning with "A" ("Africa again: Albert arrives, alive and arguing about African art, about African angst and also, alas, attacking Ashanti architecture . . ."); chapter two contains only words beginning with B and A, the third only words beginning with C, B, A; and so on, each succeeding chapter being allowed to draw on words beginning with an additional letter of the alphabet, until Z is reached; upon which the novel reverses itself and the range of available words shrinks, chapter by chapter, initial letter by initial letter, until A is reached again.

These works are probably more fun to read about than to read. Such drastic and all-embracing constraints obviously preclude the composition of a novel according to normal procedures – starting with a thematic and/or narrative kernel, which is expanded by the invention of actions and actants according to some kind of narrative logic. The challenge is to tell any kind of coherent story at all within the self-imposed constraints of the form; and the motive, presumably (apart from the writer's satisfaction in testing his own ingenuity) is the hope that the constraints will yield the kind of pleasure that comes from the achievement of formal symmetry against odds, and also lead to the generation of meanings that would not otherwise have occurred to the author. In this respect such experiments in prose resemble very ordinary features of poetry, such as rhyme and stanzaic form. They seem to constitute a deliberate transgression of the boundary that normally separates these two forms of discourse, and, astonishingly clever as they are, to be "marginal" to the art of fiction.

23 The Comic Novel

"Let's see now; what's the exact title you've given it?" Dixon looked out of the window at the fields wheeling past, bright green after a wet April. It wasn't the double-exposure effect of the last half-minute's talk that had dumbfounded him, for such incidents formed the staple material of Welch colloquies; it was the prospect of reciting the title of the article he'd written. It was a perfect title, in that it crystallized the article's niggling mindlessness, its funereal parade of yawn-enforcing facts, the pseudo-light it threw upon non-problems. Dixon had read, or begun to read, dozens like it, but his own seemed worse than most in its air of being convinced of its own usefulness and significance. "In considering this strangely neglected topic," it began. This what neglected topic? This strangely what topic? This strangely neglected what? His thinking all this without having defiled and set fire to the typescript only made him appear to himself as more of a hypocrite and fool. "Let's see," he echoed Welch in a pretended effort of memory: "oh yes; *The Economic Influence of the Developments in Shipbuilding Techniques, 1450 to 1485.* After all, that's what it's . . ."

Unable to finish his sentence, he looked to his left again to find a man's face staring into his own from about nine inches away. The face, which filled with alarm as he gazed, belonged to the driver of a van which Welch had elected to pass on a sharp bend between two stone walls. A huge bus now swung into view from further round the bend. Welch slowed slightly, thus ensuring that they would still be next to the van when the bus reached them, and said with decision: "Well, that ought to do it nicely, I should say."

KINGSLEY AMIS *Lucky Jim* (1954)

THE COMIC NOVEL is a very English, or at least British and Irish, kind of fiction, that does not always travel well. Reviewing one of Kingsley Amis's later novels, *Jake's Thing*, John Updike said rather condescendingly, "his ambition and reputation alike remain in thrall to the 'comic novel'," adding: "There is no need to write 'funny novels' when life's actual juxtapositions, set down attentively, are comedy enough." Enough for whom, one has to ask. Certainly the English novel tradition is remarkable for the number of comic novels among its classics, from the work of Fielding, and Sterne and Smollett in the eighteenth century, through Jane Austen and Dickens in the nineteenth, to Evelyn Waugh in the twentieth. Even novelists whose primary intention is not to write funny novels, such as George Eliot, Thomas Hardy and E. M. Forster, have scenes in their fiction which make us laugh aloud, even on repeated acquaintance.

Comedy in fiction would appear to have two primary sources, though they are intimately connected: situation (which entails character – a situation that is comic for one character wouldn't necessarily be so for another) and style. Both depend crucially upon timing, that is to say, the order in which the words, and the information they carry, are arranged. The principle can be illustrated by a single sentence from Evelyn Waugh's *Decline and Fall*. At the beginning of the novel, the shy, unassuming hero, Paul Pennyfeather, an Oxford undergraduate, is divested of his trousers by a party of drunken aristocratic hearties, and with monstrous injustice is sent down from the University for indecent behaviour. The first chapter concludes:

> "God damn and blast them all to hell," said Paul Pennyfeather meekly to himself as he drove to the station, and then he felt rather ashamed, because he rarely swore.

If we laugh at this, and I think most readers do, it is because of the delayed appearance of the word "meekly": what appears, as the sentence begins, to be a long-overdue explosion of righteous anger by the victimized hero turns out to be no such thing, but a further exemplification of his timidity and passiveness. The effect would be destroyed if the sentence ran: "Paul Pennyfeather said meekly to himself, as he drove to the station, 'God damn and blast them all to hell . . .'" This suggests another characteristic of comedy in fiction: a combination of surprise (Paul is at last expressing his feelings) and conformity to pattern (no he isn't after all).

Humour is a notoriously subjective matter, but it would be a very stony-hearted reader who did not crack a smile at the passage from *Lucky Jim*, which exhibits all these properties of comic fiction in a highly polished form. As a temporary assistant lecturer at a provincial university, Jim Dixon is totally dependent for the continuance of his employment on his absent-minded professor's patronage, which itself requires that Jim should demonstrate his professional competence by publishing a scholarly article. Jim despises both his professor and the rituals of academic scholarship, but cannot afford to say so. His resentment is therefore interiorized, sometimes in fantasies of violence (e.g. "to tie Welch up in his chair and beat him about the head and shoulders with a bottle until he disclosed why, without being French himself, he'd given his sons French names") and at other times, as here, in satirical mental commentary upon the behaviour, discourses and institutional codes which oppress him.

The style of *Lucky Jim* introduced a new tone of voice into English fiction. It was educated but classless, eloquent but not conventionally elegant. In its scrupulous, sceptical precision it owed something to the "ordinary language" philosophy that dominated Oxford when Amis was a student (an influence particularly evident in "the pseudo-light it threw upon non-problems"). It is full of little surprises, qualifications and reversals, which satirically deconstruct clichés and stock responses.

Dixon doesn't immediately answer Welch's question about the title of his article, though "it wasn't the double-exposure effect of the last half-minute's talk that had dumbfounded him." If it wasn't, why tell us? There are two reasons: (1) it makes an amusing metaphorical comment on Welch's irritating habit of saying, as if he had just thought of it, something Jim has just said himself, and (2) it creates a delay, a tiny moment of comic suspense, that enhances the revelation of the real reason for Jim's silence: his embarrassment at having to recite the title of his article. It is a "perfect" title only in the ironical sense that it distils every feature of academic discourse that Jim despises. "Dixon had read, *or begun to read*, dozens like it . . ." The phrase I have italicized tells us much about Jim's bored and impatient perusal of academic journals. His superbly destructive analysis of the article's opening sentence, in which each word of a conventional scholarly formula is subjected in turn to derisive interrogation, needs no further comment. There follows a characteristic condemnation by Jim of his own intellectual bad faith, a condition from which he will eventually release himself involuntarily by his drunken lecture on Merrie England. Then, at long last, we get the title of the article, an epitome of dryasdust scholarship that many academic readers of my acquaintance have committed to memory. This utterance could have followed immediately upon Welch's question without detriment to narrative cohesion, but with a huge loss of comic effect.

Jim's powerlessness is physically epitomized by his being a passenger in Welch's car, and a helpless victim of his appalling driving. The banal and apparently superfluous earlier sentence about Dixon looking out of the car at the green fields now proves to have a function. Looking through the same window moments later, Jim is startled to find "a man's face staring into his from about nine inches away." Surprise is combined with conformity to pattern (Welch's incompetence). A slow-motion effect is created by the leisurely precision of the language ("about nine inches away", "filled with alarm", "had elected to pass") contrasting comically with the speed with which the imminent collision approaches. The reader is not told immediately what is happening, but made to infer it, re-enacting the character's surprise and alarm. It's all in the timing.

24 Magic Realism

And then suddenly they were all singing the three or four simple notes again, speeding up the steps of their dance, fleeing rest and sleep, outstripping time, and filling their innocence with strength. Everyone was smiling, and Eluard leaned down to a girl he had his arm around and said,

A man possessed by peace never stops smiling.

And she laughed and stamped the ground a little harder and rose a few inches above the pavement, pulling the others along with her, and before long not one of them was touching the ground, they were taking two steps in place and one step forward without touching the ground, yes, they were rising up over Wenceslaus Square, their ring the very image of a giant wreath taking flight, and I ran off after them down on the ground, I kept looking up at them, and they floated on, lifting first one leg, then the other, and down below – Prague with its cafés full of poets and its jails full of traitors, and in the crematorium they were just finishing off one Socialist representative and one surrealist, and the smoke climbed to the heavens like a good omen, and I heard Eluard's metallic voice intoning,

Love is at work it is tireless,

and I ran after that voice through the streets in the hope of keeping up with that wonderful wreath of bodies rising above the city, and I realized with anguish in my heart that they were flying like birds and I was falling like a stone, that they had wings and I would never have any.

MILAN KUNDERA The Book of Laughter and
Forgetting (1978)

MAGIC REALISM – when marvellous and impossible events occur in what otherwise purports to be a realistic narrative – is an effect especially associated with contemporary Latin-American fiction (for example the work of the Colombian novelist, Gabriel García Márquez) but it is also encountered in novels from other continents, such as those of Günter Grass, Salman Rushdie and Milan Kundera. All these writers have lived through great historical convulsions and wrenching personal upheavals, which they feel cannot be adequately represented in a discourse of undisturbed realism. Perhaps Britain's relatively untraumatic modern history has encouraged its writers to persevere with traditional realism. The magic variety has been imported into our fiction from outside rather than springing up spontaneously, though it has been enthusiastically embraced by a few native English novelists, especially women novelists with strong views about gender, such as Fay Weldon, Angela Carter and Jeannette Winterson.

Since defiance of gravity has always been a human dream of the impossible, it is perhaps not surprising that images of flight, levitation and free fall often occur in this kind of fiction. In Márquez's *One Hundred Years of Solitude* a character ascends to heaven while hanging out the washing. At the beginning of Salman Rushdie's *The Satanic Verses* the two chief characters fall from an exploded jumbo-jet, clinging to each other and singing rival songs, to alight unharmed on a snow-covered English beach. The heroine of Angela Carter's *Nights at the Circus* is a trapeze artist called Fevvers, whose gorgeous plumage is not mere stage-costume, but wings that enable her to fly. Jeannette Winterson's *Sexing the Cherry* has a floating city with floating inhabitants – "After a few simple experiments it became certain that for the people who had abandoned gravity, gravity had abandoned them." And in this passage from *The Book of Laughter and Forgetting* the author claims to have seen a circle of dancers rise into the air and float away.

Milan Kundera was one of many young Czechs who welcomed the Communist coup of 1948, hopeful that it would usher in a brave new world of freedom and justice. He was soon disillusioned, "said something that would have been better left unsaid," and was expelled from the Party. His subsequent experiences formed the basis of his fine first novel, *The Joke* (1967). In *The Book of Laughter and Forgetting* (1978) he explored the public ironies and private tragedies of post-war Czech history in a looser, more fragmentary narrative that moves freely between documentary, autobiography and fantasy.

The narrator's sense of being expelled from human fellowship as well as from the Party, of being made an "unperson", is symbolized by his exclusion from the rings of dancing students that routinely celebrate Party-approved anniversaries. He recalls a particular day in June 1950 when "the streets of Prague were once again crowded with young people dancing in rings. I wandered from one to the next, stood as close as I could to them, but I was forbidden entrance." The day before, a Socialist politician and a surrealist artist were hanged as "enemies of the state". The surrealist, Zavis Kalandra, had been a friend of Paul Eluard, at that time probably the most celebrated Communist poet in the Western world, who might have saved him. But Eluard refused to intervene: he was "too busy dancing in the gigantic ring encircling . . . all the socialist countries and all the Communist parties of the world; too busy reciting his beautiful poems about joy and brotherhood."

Wandering through the streets, Kundera suddenly comes across Eluard himself dancing in a ring of young people. "Yes, there was no doubt about it. The toast of Prague. Paul Eluard!" Eluard begins to recite one of his high-minded poems about joy and brotherhood, and the narrative "takes off", both literally and metaphorically. The ring of dancers rises from the ground and begins to float into the sky. This is an impossible event. Yet we suspend our disbelief, because it so powerfully and poignantly expresses the emotion that has been built up over the preceding pages. The image of the dancers rising into the air, still lifting their feet in unison, as the smoke of two cremated victims of the State climbs into the same sky, epitomizes the fatuous self-deception of the comrades, their anxiety to declare their own purity and innocence, their determination not to see the terror and injustice of the political system they serve. But it also expresses the envy and loneliness of the authorial persona, banished for ever from the euphoria and security of the collective dance. One of Kundera's most appealing characteristics is that he never claims a heroic martyr's status for himself, and never underestimates the ordinary human cost of being a dissident.

I don't know how this passage reads in the original Czech, but it works remarkably well in translation, perhaps because it is so brilliantly visualized. Kundera taught film in Prague for a period, and this description shows a cinematic sense of composition in the way its perspective shifts between the aerial panorama of Prague and the longing upward gaze of the narrator as he runs through the streets. The floating ring of dancers itself is like a filmic "special effect". Grammatically this extract consists mostly of one immensely long sentence; its clauses are the equivalents of "shots", joined together by the simple conjunction *and* in a flowing sequence that refuses to give priority to either the narrator's sense of irony or his sense of loss. They are inseparably intertwined.

25 Staying on the Surface

And there is much to talk over. "What do you fear from her?" asks Flora, her big weight lying on top of Howard, her breasts before his face. "I think," says Howard, "we compete too closely in the same area. It makes sense. Her role's still bound too tightly to mine; that traps her growth, so she feels compelled to undermine me. Destroy me from within." "Are you comfortable there?" says Flora, "I'm not squashing you?" "No," says Howard. "Destroy you how?" asks Flora. "She has to find a weak core in me," says Howard. "She wants to convince herself that I'm false and fake." "You have a lovely chest, Howard," says Flora. "So do you, Flora," says Howard. "Are you false and fake?" asks Flora. "I don't think so," says Howard, "not more than anyone else. I just have a passion to make things happen. To get some order into the chaos. Which she sees as a trendy radicalism." "Oh, Howard," says Flora, "she's cleverer than I thought. Is she having affairs?" "I think so," says Howard. "Can you move, you're hurting me?" Flora tumbles off him and lies by his side; they rest there, faces upward toward the ceiling, in her white apartment. "Don't you know?" asks Flora. "Don't you bother to find out?" "No," says Howard. "You have no proper curiosity," says Flora. "There's a living psychology there, and you're not interested. No wonder she wants to destroy you." "We believe in going our own way," says Howard. "Cover yourself up with the sheet," says Flora, "you're sweating. That's how people catch colds. Anyway, you stay together." "Yes, we stay together, but we distrust one another." "Ah, yes," says Flora, turning on her side to look at him, so that her big right breast dips against his body, and wearing a puzzled expression on her face, "but isn't that a definition of marriage?"

MALCOLM BRADBURY *The History Man* (1975)

I SUGGESTED earlier (Section 9) that the novel is supreme among the forms of narrative literature in rendering subjectivity. The earliest English novels – Defoe's *Robinson Crusoe*, Richardson's *Pamela* – used journals and letters to portray the inner thoughts of their characters with unprecedented realism; and the subsequent development of the genre, at least up to Joyce and Proust, can be seen in terms of a progressively deeper and subtler exploration of consciousness. So when a novelist chooses to stay on the surface of human behaviour we register the absence of psychological depth with a surprised attentiveness, and perhaps uneasiness, even if we cannot immediately put our finger on the reason.

Malcolm Bradbury's *The History Man* is such a novel. It concerns a sociology lecturer who has just written a book called *The Defeat of Privacy*, dedicated to the proposition that "there are no more private selves." Howard Kirk believes that the self is an outmoded bourgeois concept, that individual human beings are mere bundles of conditioned reflexes; and that the only way to be free is to identify the plot of History (with the aid of Marxist sociology) and co-operate with it. By staying on the surface of behaviour and environment, the discourse of the novel imitates this bleak, anti-humanist philosophy of life in a way which seems to satirize it, yet gives the reader no privileged vantage-point from which to condemn or dismiss it. Although the story is told mainly from Howard's point of view, in the sense that he is present at most of the events it describes, the narrative does not enable us to judge his motives by giving us access to his private thoughts. The same goes for the other characters, including Kirk's antagonists.

The novel consists of description and dialogue. The description focuses obsessively on the surfaces of things – the décor of the Kirks' house, the bleak, dehumanizing architecture of the campus, the outward behaviour of staff and students in seminars, committees and parties. The dialogue is presented flatly, objectively, without introspective interpretation by the characters, without authorial commentary, without any variation on the simple, adverb-less speech tags *he/she asks/says*, without even breaks between the lines of speech. The "depthlessness" of the discourse is further emphasized by its preference for the present tense. The past tense of conventional narrative implies that the story is known to and has been assessed by the narrator in its entirety. In this novel the narrative discourse impassively tracks the characters as they move from moment to moment towards an unknown future.

The effect, at once comic and chilling, of this technique is particularly striking in scenes of sexual intercourse, where one would normally expect to find an internalized account of the emotions and sensations of at least one of the participants. In the passage quoted here, Howard Kirk is in bed with his colleague Flora Beniform, "who likes going to bed with men who have troubled marriages; they have so much more to talk about, hot as they are from the intricate politics of families which are Flora's specialist field of study," and they are talking about Howard's relationship with his wife Barbara.

There is of course comedy inherent in the idea of having sex in order to talk, especially about one's lover's marriage, and in the contrast drawn here between the intimate physical contact of the couple's bodies and the abstract intellectualism of their conversation. But there is more than comic incongruity in the way the dialogue zig-zags between the physical and cerebral, the trivial and the portentous. When Howard says his wife wants to convince herself that he is false and fake, he articulates the central issue of the novel. Flora at first seems to evade it with a gesture towards eros: "You have a lovely chest, Howard." His rejoinder, "So do you, Flora," is funny, but the joke is at whose expense? We have to make up our own minds, just as we do on the more momentous question. Is Howard false and fake? Or is his "passion to make things happen" a kind of integrity, a manifestation of energy in a world of moral entropy? The absence of interiority, which would help to decide such questions, throws the burden of interpretation back onto the reader.

Many found the text's refusal to comment, to give unambiguous guidance as to how its characters should be evaluated, disturbing, but this is undoubtedly the source of its power and fascination. It is interesting in this connection to compare the BBC Television adaptation of the novel. The script, by Christopher Hampton, was very faithful to the original novel, and the production was extremely well cast, directed and acted. Anthony Sher was stunning in the role of Howard Kirk – but, as an actor, he had to give an interpretation of the role, and, probably inevitably, chose to portray him unambiguously as a despicable manipulator and exploiter of other people for his own gratification. In this way the television version took back much of the burden of interpretation which the novel had planted firmly in the audience's lap, and to that extent it was, though hugely enjoyable, a less challenging piece of work. (It has to be said, too, that in the rendering of the scene quoted here, one's attention was somewhat distracted from the witty dialogue by the visible evidence of Flora Beniform's beautiful chest.)

26 Showing and Telling

"You are too much inclined to passion, child, and have set your affections so absolutely on this young woman, that, if G – required her at your hands, I fear you would reluctantly part with her. Now, believe me, no Christian ought so to set his heart on any person or thing in this world, but that, whenever it shall be required or taken from him in any manner by Divine Providence, he may be able, peaceably, quietly, and contentedly, to resign it." At which words one came hastily in, and acquainted Mr Adams that his youngest son was drowned. He stood silent a moment, and soon began to stamp about the room and deplore his loss with the bitterest agony. Joseph, who was overwhelmed with concern likewise, recovered himself sufficiently to endeavour to comfort the parson; in which attempt he used many arguments that he had at several times remembered out of his own discourses, both in private and public (for he was a great enemy to the passions, and preached nothing more than the conquest of them by reason and grace), but he was not at leisure now to hearken to his advice. "Child, child," said he, "do not go about impossibilities. Had it been any other of my children, I could have borne it with patience; but my little prattler, the darling and comfort of my old age – the little wretch to be snatched out of life just at his entrance into it; the sweetest, best-tempered boy, who never did a thing to offend me. It was but this morning I gave him his first lesson in *Quae Genus*. This was the very book he learnt; poor child! it is of no further use to thee now. He would have made the best scholar, and have been an ornament to the Church; – such parts and such goodness never met in one so young." "And the handsomest lad too," says Mrs Adams, recovering from a swoon in Fanny's arms. – 'My poor Jacky, shall I never see thee more?" cries the parson. – "Yes, surely," says Joseph, "and in a better place; you will meet again, never to part more." – I believe the

121

parson did not hear these words, for he paid little regard to them, but went on lamenting, whilst the tears trickled down into his bosom. At last he cried out, "Where is my little darling?" and was sallying out, when, to his great surprise and joy, in which I hope the reader will sympathize, he met his son in a wet condition indeed, but alive and running towards him.

HENRY FIELDING *Joseph Andrews* (1742)

FICTIONAL DISCOURSE constantly alternates between *showing* us what happened and *telling* us what happened. The purest form of showing is the quoted speech of characters, in which language exactly mirrors the event (because the event is linguistic). The purest form of telling is authorial summary, in which the conciseness and abstraction of the narrator's language effaces the particularity and individuality of the characters and their actions. A novel written entirely in the mode of summary would, for this reason, be almost unreadable. But summary has its uses: it can, for instance, accelerate the tempo of a narrative, hurrying us through events which would be uninteresting, or *too* interesting – therefore distracting, if lingered over. It is easy to examine this effect in the work of Henry Fielding, because he was writing before the technique of free indirect style, in which authorial speech and characters' speech are fused together, had been discovered (see Section 9). In his novels the boundary between these two kinds of discourse is clear and unambiguous.

Parson Abraham Adams is a benevolent, generous, unworldly man, but he is also a great comic character – one of the most memorable in English fiction – because he is constantly entrammelled in contradiction. There is always a disparity between what he believes the world to be (full of people as altruistic as himself) and what it is really like (full of selfish opportunists); between what he preaches (a rather austere dogmatic Christianity) and what he practices (ordinary instinctive human decency). This contrast between illusion and reality (which Fielding borrowed, with

acknowledgment, from Cervantes's characterization of Don Quix-
ote) makes him a constant figure of fun – but a sympathetic one,
because his heart is in the right place even if his judgment is
unreliable.

In this excerpt, Parson Adams is lecturing the hero, Joseph,
about his impatience to marry his sweetheart Fanny, with whom he
has just been reunited after a long and hazardous separation.
Adams subjects the young man to a lengthy sermon, warning him
against lust, and lack of trust in Providence. He invokes the
example of Abraham in the Old Testament, who was ready to
sacrifice his son, Isaac, to God if required. This homily is quoted
verbatim, "shown". Just as Adams has declared that we should
always serenely accept the sacrifices God demands of us, his
principles are put cruelly to the test: "At which words one came
hastily in, and acquainted Mr Adams that his youngest son was
drowned." This is the baldest kind of summary. "Acquainted"
seems a coldly formal word in the context, and we are not even
told who "one" is. The lamentations of the bereaved father and
Joseph's attempts to comfort him are also summarized – but
Adams's rejection of Joseph's counsel is "shown", quoted in full,
"Child, child, do not go about impossibilities . . .", to emphasize
the contradiction between his practice and his preaching.

Fielding is playing a risky game here. On the one hand we
register the contradiction as the comic confirmation of a familiar
character trait; on the other hand there is nothing funny about the
death of a child. Our inclination to smile at Abraham Adams's
failure to live up to the sacrificial piety of his biblical namesake is
checked by the pathos of his situation, and the naturalness of his
grief. We hesitate, uncertain how to respond.

Fielding has, however, prepared a way out of the impasse, for
the characters and for the reader. After a few more lines of
lamentation from Mr and Mrs Adams, and vain attempts to console
them by Joseph, Adams discovers that his son has not been
drowned after all. And it is not long, of course, before Adams
blithely resumes his sermon to Joseph about Christian resignation.

The narrator's explanation for the child's survival is that "The
person who brought the news of his misfortune had been a little

too eager, as people sometimes are, from, I believe, no very good principle, to relate ill news, and having seen him fall into the river, instead of running to his assistance, directly ran to acquaint his father of a fate which he had concluded to be inevitable," leaving him to be rescued by somebody else. This explanation is acceptable partly because it belongs to a series of examples of human folly and spitefulness that run through the novel; and partly because *it comes very quickly after the event*. If the character of the messenger had been filled in in more detail, and his speech describing the incident given in direct form, the whole tempo of the scene would have been more "lifelike" and its emotive effect quite different. The circumstances of the drowning of the little boy would have acquired a distressing particularity, and the comic mood of the novel would have been destroyed irretrievably. When the report was shown to be false we might, as readers, have felt that we had been exploited. Fielding avoids these unwanted effects by a judicious use of summary.

27 Telling in Different Voices

Christie is that year's Bachelor Catch. While the winter snow lies impacted month after month, and half Europe starves, and the bombers overhead carry food for Germany instead of bombs, and the gas dwindles to a flicker and the electric lights waver, and strangers stand close to each other for comfort – Christie shines before Grace like a beacon of hope and promise. He is all clear-cut, up-standing (but only in marriage) masculinity. Christie is Grace's ambition. Not a diploma, not a career, nor the world's recognition, not any more. Just Christie.

She loves him. Oh, indeed she does. Her heart quickens at the sight of him, her bowels dissolve with longing. But she will not, she cannot, succumb to his embraces. He takes her on his boat, well chaperoned (yes, he sails) and up mountains, rather less chaperoned (yes, he climbs). He offers to buy her a flat (yes, he can afford to) but no she will not. No diamonds, thank you, Christie. No wrist watches. No gifts, no bribes, my dearest. Chocolates, yes, oh thank you! And orchids, and invitations to dinner and a taxi ride home, and yes, a kiss, and yes, you may touch my breast (how wicked we are!) and quickly, quickly, goodnight, Christie. My own, my love, my dearest dear. I would die for you but I will not sleep with you.

Christie stops off at Soho on the way home and spends an hour with a tart. How else will he survive?

She loves him. She means to marry him. How else will she survive?

FAY WELDON *Female Friends* (1975)

125

IN THE PRECEDING SECTION, discussing the balanced alternation of telling and showing in Henry Fielding's *Joseph Andrews*, I suggested that a novel written entirely in summary form would be almost unreadable. But a number of contemporary novelists have deliberately gone a long way in that direction, without paying such a heavy price. The summary narrative method seems to suit our modern taste for irony, pace and pithiness. It's a particularly effective way of handling a large cast of characters and a story that spreads itself over a long period of time, without getting bogged down in the slow temporal rhythms and dense detail of the classic novel. (I used it myself, for those reasons, in a novel called *How Far Can You Go?*) Care must be taken, however, to ensure that the summary style doesn't become monotonously uniform in vocabulary and syntax. Fay Weldon's novels, which use summary extensively, are notable for both their hectic narrative tempo and their stylistic vivacity.

Female Friends traces the fortunes of three women through the nineteen-forties, fifties and sixties, focusing on their sexual and marital experiences, against a background of rapidly changing social *mores*. It portrays women as on the whole helpless victims of their wombs and hearts, craving husbands and lovers even while being abused and betrayed by them. Men are portrayed as equally helpless victims of their own egotism and sexual appetites; but being naturally promiscuous, they get more fun out of the advent of the Permissive Society than do the female characters. The passage quoted here, however, deals with an earlier period, the nineteen-forties, when Nice Girls Didn't, and could use this assumption as a bargaining counter in the war between the sexes. Grace is not in fact a virgin, but pretends that she is, knowing that Christie "feels virginity to be essential in the woman he loves, while doing his damnedest to dispose of it." Thus both characters are comically compromised by contradiction and hypocrisy.

The first paragraph evokes the period context – austerity, shortages, the Cold War – in a brisk sequence of images, like a cinematic montage, then ironically juxtaposes Grace's private emotional obsession with these public miseries and anxieties. While half Europe starves, Grace can think only of how to persuade

126

Christie to marry her. Her ambitions to be a painter (she is a student at the Slade at this point in the story) are forgotten. "Christie is Grace's ambition. Not a diploma, not a career, nor the world's recognition. Just Christie." The discourse here begins to shift from a précis of events to a précis of Grace's thoughts, an effect that becomes still more marked towards the end of the next paragraph.

In fact what we have here is not a single uniform style, like Fielding's authorial voice in the passage from *Joseph Andrews*, but a polyphonic medley of styles, or voices, through which the serio-comic skirmishing of Grace and Christie's courtship is vividly but concisely evoked. "She loves him. Oh, indeed she does. Her heart quickens at the sight of him, her bowels dissolve with longing." Here the narrator seems to borrow the traditional literary discourse of "love" – love letters, love poetry, love stories. "She cannot succumb to his embraces" is a cliché straight out of Mills & Boon romance – its parodic quality underlines the inauthenticity of Grace's behaviour. The parentheses in the next sentence, ("Yes, he sails . . . yes, he climbs . . . yes, he can afford to") might be the narrator anticipating the reader's questions, acknowledging, but not apologizing for the belatedness of this information. Or they might be echoes of Grace's boasting about Christie to her female friends. (A further complication is that the narrator is in fact one of those friends, Chloe, who writes about herself in the third person and claims a novelist's knowledge of the secret thoughts of the other characters.)

"No diamonds, thank you, Christie. No wrist watches. No gifts, no bribes, my dearest. Chocolates, yes, oh thank you!" Grammatically this, and all the rest of the paragraph, is Grace's direct speech, but it has no quotation marks round it in the text, and obviously it isn't the record of a single speech act. It's speech functioning as summary, a condensation of what Grace said on several different occasions – or thought, or implied. She would have said "goodnight" and conceivably "My own, my love, my dearest dear," but almost certainly not, "I would die for you but I will not sleep with you," another line that seems to come from some half-remembered literary source. Two short, symmetrical paragraphs sum up the sexual deadlock in a narrative voice that drily echoes each character's special pleading.

This passage exemplifies in a striking but by no means unrepresentative way a property of novelistic prose which the Russian critic Mikhail Bakhtin called "polyphony" or, alternatively, "dialogism". (Readers antipathetic to literary theory may wish to skip the remainder of this section; though the subject is of more than theoretical interest – it is at the very heart of the novel's representation of life.) According to Bakhtin, the language of traditional epic and lyric poetry, or the language of expository prose, is "monologic", striving to impose a single vision, or interpretation, on the world by means of a single unitary style. The novel in contrast is "dialogic", incorporating many different styles, or voices, which as it were talk to each other, and to other voices outside the text, the discourses of culture and society at large. The novel does this in various ways. At the simplest level there is the alternation of the narrator's voice with the voices of the characters, rendered in their own specific accents and idioms of class, region, occupation, gender etc. We take this for granted in the novel, but it was a relatively rare phenomenon in narrative literature before the Renaissance. There is a foundling in Charles Dickens's *Our Mutual Friend* called Sloppy, who is adopted by an old woman called Betty Higden, in whose eyes he is especially gifted. "You mightn't think it, but Sloppy is a beautiful reader of a newspaper," she says. "He do the Police in different voices." Novelists do the Police in different voices.

"For the prose artist the world is full of other people's words," wrote Bakhtin, "among which he must orient himself and whose speech characteristics he must be able to perceive with a very keen ear. He must introduce them into the plane of his own discourse, but in such a way that this plane is not destroyed." Novelists can do this in various ways. By the technique of free indirect style (see Section 9) they can combine their own voice with the voices of their characters in order to render thought and emotion. Or they can give their own narrative voice a different kind of colouring that has nothing to do with character. Henry Fielding, for instance, often narrates in a mock-heroic style, applying the language of classical and neoclassical epic poetry to vulgar brawls or amorous encounters. This is how he describes the efforts of Mrs Waters to seduce the eponymous hero of *Tom Jones* over the supper table:

> First, from two lovely blue eyes, whose bright orbs flashed lightning at their discharge, flew forth two pointed ogles. But happily for our heroe, hit only a vast piece of beef which he was then conveying onto his plate, and harmless spent their force.

And so on. Bakhtin called this kind of writing "doubly-oriented discourse": the language simultaneously describes an action, and imitates a particular style of speech or writing. In this case an effect of parody is created because the style is incongruous with the subject matter, and thus its mannerisms seem absurd and artificial. The gap between subject matter and style is less obvious in the passage from Fay Weldon's novel, because the language it borrows from romantic literary fiction and glossy women's magazines is not inappropriate to the subject matter, merely exaggerated and cliché-ridden. Probably one should describe this kind of writing as "pastiche" rather than parody, or use Bakhtin's own term, "stylization". His categorization of the various levels of speech in novelistic discourse is complex, but the basic point is simple: the language of the novel is not *a* language, but a medley of styles and voices, and it is this which makes it a supremely democratic, anti-totalitarian literary form, in which no ideological or moral position is immune from challenge and contradiction.

28 A Sense of the Past

The great mole was far from isolated that day. There were fishermen tarring, mending their nets, tinkering with crab- and lobster-pots. There were better-class people, early visitors, local residents, strolling beside the still swelling but now mild sea. Of the woman who stared, Charles noted, there was no sign. But he did not give her – or the Cobb – a second thought and set out, with a quick and elastic step very different from his usual languid town stroll, along the beach under Ware Cleeves for his destination.

He would have made you smile, for he was carefully equipped for his role. He wore stout nailed boots and canvas gaiters that rose to encase Norfolk breeches of heavy flannel. There was a tight and absurdly long coat to match; a canvas wideawake hat of an indeterminate beige; a massive ashplant, which he had bought on his way to the Cobb; and a voluminous rucksack, from which you might have shaken out an already heavy array of hammers, wrappings, notebooks, pillboxes, adzes and heaven knows what else. Nothing is more incomprehensible to us than the methodicality of the Victorians; one sees it best (at its most ludicrous) in the advice so liberally handed out to travellers in the early editions of Baedeker. Where, one wonders, can any pleasure have been left? How, in the case of Charles, can he not have seen that light clothes would have been more comfortable? That a hat was not necessary? That stout nailed boots on a boulder-strewn beach are as suitable as ice-skates?

JOHN FOWLES *The French Lieutenant's Woman* (1969)

THE FIRST WRITER to use the novel to evoke a sense of the past with convincing specificity was Sir Walter Scott, in his novels about seventeenth- and eighteenth-century Scotland, like *Waverley* (1814) and *The Heart of Midlothian* (1816). These were "historical" novels in that they dealt with historical personages and events; but they also evoked the past in terms of culture, ideology, manners and morals — by describing the whole "way of life" of ordinary people. In so doing Scott had a profound effect on the subsequent development of prose fiction. It has been said that the Victorian novel was a kind of historical novel about the present. Many of them (e.g. *Middlemarch*, *Vanity Fair*) were in fact set back in time from the point of composition, in the period of their authors' childhood and youth, in order to highlight the phenomenon of social and cultural change. This effect is easily lost on the modern reader. Take, for example, the opening sentence of *Vanity Fair*:

> While the present century was in its teens, and on one sunshiny morning in June, there drove up to the great iron gate of Miss Pinkerton's academy for young ladies, on Chiswick Mall, a large family coach, with two fat horses in blazing harness, driven by a fat coachman in a three-cornered hat and wig, at the rate of four miles an hour.

The time when Thackeray wrote this, the late eighteen-forties, seems almost as distant to us as the time about which he was writing, but Thackeray was clearly aiming to evoke a mood of humorous and perhaps slightly condescending nostalgia. For him and his readers the Railway Age had intervened between the teens and the forties of the century, and the reference to the slow speed of the coach draws attention to the more leisurely pace of life in the earlier period. The description of the coachman's hat and wig would also have been more precisely coded indicators of period for the original readers than for us.

The recent past has remained a favourite subject for novelists up to the present day. Fay Weldon's *Female Friends* is one of countless examples. But there is a great difference between doing that, and writing about life in a previous century, especially when that life has already been memorably described by its own contemporaries. How can a novelist of the late twentieth century compete with Charles Dickens, or Thomas Hardy, in the representation of nineteenth-century men and women? The answer, of course, is that he can't. What he can do is bring a twentieth-century perspective to bear upon nineteenth-century behaviour, perhaps revealing things about the Victorians that they did not know themselves, or preferred to suppress, or simply took for granted.

If we encountered the first paragraph of the extract from *The French Lieutenant's Woman* out of context, we should be hard put to say when it was written. This is because it focuses on "timeless" properties of the novel's seaside setting, Lyme Regis (the fishermen, their nets and lobster-pots, the strollers by the sea), and because it is written according to the conventions of a kind of fictional realism that has been going strong for the last two hundred years. The description of the scene from Charles's point of view, as he sets out on a fossil-hunting expedition, deftly recapitulates the main question of narrative interest in the novel so far – the identity of the mysterious woman he encountered on the Cobb in stormier weather. Only the slightly archaic use of the word "elastic" would suggest that this is either a Victorian novel or a modern imitation of one.

The second paragraph, however, makes overt the author's, and the reader's, temporal distance from the action of the novel, which takes place in 1867, exactly one hundred years before Fowles was writing it. Clothes are prime indicators of period in fiction (especially in popular forms, witness the terms "costume drama" and "bodice-ripper"), and information about the kind of clothing people wore in the past can be recuperated by historical research, such as Fowles has obviously carried out. But what Charles's clothes, and supplementary equipment, would have signified to himself and his contemporaries (namely that he was a gentleman, who knew the correct way to do things) is different from what they signify to us: their excessiveness, inconvenience and unsuitability to the activity for which they were employed, and what that reveals about Victorian values.

The shift in perspective between the two paragraphs, from the imaginative recreation of the past in the first, to the open acknowledgment of separation from it in the second, is characteristic of Fowles's method in this novel. The passage I have quoted continues: "Well, we laugh. But perhaps there is something admirable in this dissociation between what is most comfortable and what is most recommended. We meet here, once again, this bone of contention between the two centuries: is duty to drive us or not?" The word "duty" has an asterisk against it, directing our attention to a footnote, quoting a genuine Victorian novelist, George Eliot, on the subject of duty. The most striking reminder that Fowles is a twentieth-century novelist writing a nineteenth-century novel comes when Charles finally consummates his desire for the mysterious Sarah, and his state of mind is described, with deliberate anachronism, as "like a city struck out of a quiet sky by an atom bomb." But exposing the gap between the date of the story and the date of its composition inevitably reveals not just the artificiality of historical fiction, but the artificiality of *all* fiction. It is not long before Fowles is writing: "This story I am telling is all imagination. These characters I create never existed outside my own mind." *The French Lieutenant's Woman* is a novel as much about novel-writing as about the past. There is a word for this kind of fiction, "Metafiction" – which will be discussed in due course (see Section 45).

29 Imagining the Future

It was a bright cold day in April, and the clocks were striking thirteen. Winston Smith, his chin nuzzled into his breast in an effort to escape the vile wind, slipped quickly through the glass doors of Victory Mansions, though not quickly enough to prevent a swirl of gritty dust from entering along with him.

The hallway smelt of boiled cabbage and old rag mats. At one end of it a coloured poster, too large for indoor display, had been tacked to the wall. It depicted simply an enormous face, more than a metre wide: the face of a man of about forty-five, with a heavy black moustache and ruggedly handsome features. Winston made for the stairs. It was no use trying the lift. Even at the best of times it was seldom working, and at present the electric current was cut off during daylight hours. It was part of the economy drive in preparation for Hate Week. The flat was seven flights up, and Winston, who was thirty-nine and had a varicose ulcer above his right ankle, went slowly, resting several times on the way. On each landing, opposite the lift-shaft, the poster with the enormous face gazed from the wall. It was one of those pictures which are so contrived that the eyes follow you about when you move. BIG BROTHER IS WATCHING YOU, the caption beneath it ran.

Inside the flat a fruity voice was reading out a list of figures which had something to do with the production of pig-iron. The voice came from an oblong metal plaque like a dulled mirror which formed part of the surface of the right-hand wall. Winston turned a switch and the voice sank somewhat, though the words were still distinguishable. The instrument (the tele-screen, it was called) could be dimmed, but there was no way of shutting it off completely.

GEORGE ORWELL *Nineteen Eighty-Four* (1949)

IT IS ONLY SUPERFICIALLY paradoxical that most novels about the future are narrated in the past tense. Michael Frayn's *A Very Private Life* (1968) starts in the future tense ("Once upon a time there will be a little girl called Uncumber") but he can't keep it up for long, and soon shifts into the present tense. To enter into the imagined world of a novel we have to orientate ourselves in space and time with the characters, and the future tense makes that impossible. The past tense is "natural" for narrative; even the use of the present tense is somewhat paradoxical, since anything that has been written down has by inference already happened.

Of course, for us, today, 1984 *has* already happened. But when Orwell wrote the novel he was imagining the future, and to make sense of it we have to read it as a prophetic, not a historical novel. He used the narrative past tense to give his picture of the future a novelistic illusion of reality. By setting his story only thirty-odd years ahead he was perhaps aiming to impress his readers with the imminence of the political tyranny he envisaged. But there is also a grim humour in the anagrammatic mirroring of the date of the novel's completion (1948) in its title. Orwell drew on many recognizable features of life in "austerity" post-war Britain, as well as on reports of life in Eastern Europe, to create the depressing atmosphere of London in 1984: drabness, shortages, dilapidation. Science fiction usually tells us how different the material conditions of life will be in the future. Orwell suggested that they would be much the same, only worse.

The first sentence of the book is justly admired. "It was a bright cold day in April, and the clocks were striking thirteen." The sting is in the last word, though it is probably more powerful for readers who remember a time when there were no digital clocks or twenty-four-hour timetables. Until you reach it, the discourse sounds reassuringly familiar. It could be the beginning of an "ordinary" novel about an ordinary day in the contemporary world. It's the anomalous word "thirteen" that tells us with wonderful economy that a very different experience is in store. Clocks, time, and the calculations that go with them, are part of the rule of reason by which we order our lives in the ordinary, familiar world. So "thirteen" is like the moment in a nightmare when something tells

135

you you are dreaming and you wake up. But in this case the nightmare is only beginning, and the hero, at least, never wakes up – from a world in which power can decree that two and two make five.

In the next sentence only the proper names seem to stand out from the style of low-key realism. Winston Smith was obviously named for Winston Churchill, leader of the nation in World War II, and the mansion block he lives in would have been built shortly after the end of that war. The irony of these details becomes evident when we learn later in the text that the globe is embroiled in continuous intercontinental warfare thirty-six years on. The gritty dust that blows into the lobby suggests that the roads and pavements outside are not well cleaned, and this note of physical squalor and deprivation deepens in the following paragraph, with the references to boiled cabbage, the old rag mats on the floor, the power-cuts, and Winston's varicose ulcer.

The reference to "Hate Week", and the huge coloured poster with the caption, "BIG BROTHER IS WATCHING YOU," are the only unfamiliar details in what could otherwise be a description of a run-down block of council flats in 1948. They are equivalent in effect to the clock striking thirteen. They are enigmas, arousing our curiosity – and apprehension, since what they imply about the social context is not reassuring, and already we are beginning to identify with Winston Smith as a victim of this society. Hate Week and Big Brother are associated, by contiguity, with the physical squalor and deprivation of the environment – even with the vile wind in the first paragraph. The features of Big Brother resemble Stalin's, but they also recall a famous recruiting poster of World War I, depicting a heavily moustached military man (Lord Kitchener) pointing a finger, with the caption, "Your Country Needs You." Only in the two-way television screen (which keeps the viewer under permanent observation) does Orwell use the licence of science-fiction to imagine a gadget that did not exist in his own time. Its technological sophistication seems all the more sinister in the drab and poverty-stricken setting of Victory Mansions.

Orwell, in short, imagined the future by invoking, modifying and recombining images of what his readers, consciously or unconsciously, already knew. To some extent, this is always the case. Popular science fiction, for instance, is a curious mixture of invented gadgetry and archetypal narrative motifs very obviously derived from folk tale, fairy tale and Scripture, recycling the myths of Creation, Fall, Flood and a Divine Saviour, for a secular but still superstitious age. Orwell himself echoes the story of Adam and Eve in his treatment of the love affair between Winston and Julia, secretly monitored and finally punished by Big Brother, but with an effect that is the reverse of reassuring, and so subtly that the reader may not be conscious of the allusion. In that respect as in others his technique is indistinguishable from that of the traditional realist novel, though his purpose was different: not to reflect contemporary social reality, but to paint a daunting picture of a possible future.

30 Symbolism

"The fool!" cried Ursula loudly. "Why doesn't he ride away till it's gone by?"

Gudrun was looking at him with black-dilated, spellbound eyes. But he sat glistening and obstinate, forcing the wheeling mare, which spun and swerved like a wind, and yet could not get out of the grasp of his will, nor escape from the mad clamour of terror that resounded through her, as the trucks thumped slowly, heavily, horrifying, one after the other, one pursuing the other, over the rails of the crossing.

The locomotive, as if wanting to see what could be done, put on the brakes, and back came the trucks rebounding on the iron buffers, striking like horrible cymbals, clashing nearer and nearer in frightful strident concussions. The mare opened her mouth and rose slowly, as if lifted up on a wind of terror. Then suddenly her fore-feet struck out, as she convulsed herself utterly away from the horror. Back she went, and the two girls clung to each other, feeling she must fall backwards on top of him. But he leaned forward, his face shining with fixed amusement, and at last he brought her down, sank her down, and was bearing her back to the mark. But as strong as the pressure of his compulsion was the repulsion of her utter terror, throwing her back away from the railway, so that she spun round and round on two legs, as if she were in the centre of some whirlwind. It made Gudrun faint with poignant dizziness, which seemed to penetrate to her heart.

D. H. LAWRENCE *Women in Love* (1921)

ROUGHLY SPEAKING, anything that "stands for" something else is a symbol, but the process operates in many different ways. A cross may symbolize Christianity in one context, by association with the Crucifixion, and a road intersection in another, by diagrammatic resemblance. Literary symbolism is less easily decoded than these examples, because it tries to be original and tends towards a rich plurality, even ambiguity, of meaning (all qualities that would be undesirable in traffic signs and religious icons, especially the former). If a metaphor or simile consists of likening A to B, a literary symbol is a B that *suggests* an A, or a number of As. The poetic style known as Symbolism, which started in France in the late nineteenth century in the work of Baudelaire, Verlaine and Mallarmé, and exerted considerable influence on English writing in the twentieth, was characterized by a shimmering surface of suggested meanings without a denotative core.

Somebody once said, however, that the novelist should make his spade a spade before he makes it a symbol, and this would seem to be good advice for a writer who is aiming to create anything like the "illusion of life". If the spade is introduced all too obviously just for the sake of its symbolic meaning, it will tend to undermine the credibility of the narrative as human action. D. H. Lawrence was often prepared to take that risk to express a visionary insight – as when, in another episode of *Women in Love*, he has his hero rolling naked in the grass and throwing stones at the reflection of the moon. But in the passage quoted here he has kept a nice balance between realistic description and symbolic suggestion.

The "spade" in this case is a complex action: a man controlling a horse frightened by a colliery train passing at a level crossing, while being watched by two women. The man is Gerald Critch, the son of the local colliery owner, who manages the business and will eventually inherit it. The setting is the Nottinghamshire landscape in which Lawrence, a coalminer's son, was brought up: a pleasant countryside scarred and blackened in places by the pits and their railways. One might say that the train "symbolizes" the mining industry, which is a product of culture in the anthropological sense, and that the horse, a creature of Nature, symbolizes the countryside. Industry has been imposed on the countryside by the masculine power and will of capitalism, a process Gerald symbolically re-enacts by the way he dominates his mare, forcing the animal to accept the hideous mechanical noise of the train.

The two women in the scene are sisters, Ursula and Gudrun Brangwen, the former a teacher, the latter an artist. They are out on a country walk when they witness the scene at the level crossing. Both identify sympathetically with the terrified horse. Ursula is outraged by Gerald's behaviour, and speaks her mind. But the scene is described from Gudrun's point of view, and her response is more complex and ambivalent. There is sexual symbolism in the way Gerald controls his mount – "at last he brought her down, sank her down, and was bearing her back to the mark" – and there is certainly an element of macho exhibitionism in his display of strength in front of the two women. Whereas Ursula is simply disgusted by the spectacle, Gudrun is sexually aroused by it, almost in spite of herself. The mare "spun round and round on two legs, as if she were in the centre of some whirlwind. It made Gudrun faint with poignant dizziness, which seemed to penetrate to her heart." "Poignant" is a transferred epithet, which logically belongs to the suffering of the horse; its rather odd application to "dizziness" expresses the turmoil of Gudrun's emotions, and calls attention to the root meaning of *poignant* – pricking, piercing – which, with "penetrate" in the next clause, gives a powerfully phallic emphasis to the whole description. A couple of pages later, Gudrun is described as "numbed in her mind by the sense of indomitable soft weight of the man bearing down into the living body of the horse: the strong, indomitable thighs of the blond man clenching the palpitating body of the mare into pure control." The whole scene is indeed prophetic of the passionate but mutually destructive sexual relationship that will develop later in the story between Gudrun and Gerald.

This rich brew of symbolic suggestion would, however, be much less effective if Lawrence did not at the same time allow us to picture the scene in vivid, sensuous detail. The ugly noise and motion of trucks as the train brakes is rendered in onomatopoeic syntax and diction ("clashing nearer and nearer in frightful strident concussions"), followed by an eloquent image of the horse, graceful even in panic: "The mare opened her mouth and rose slowly, as if lifted up on a wind of terror." Whatever you think of Lawrence's men and women, he was always brilliant when describing animals.

It is worth noting that symbolism is generated in two different ways in this passage. The Nature/Culture symbolism is modelled on the rhetorical figures of speech known as metonymy and synecdoche. Metonymy substitutes cause for effect or vice versa (the locomotive stands for Industry because it is an effect of the Industrial Revolution) and synecdoche substitutes part for whole or vice versa (the horse stands for Nature because it is part of Nature). The sexual symbolism, on the other hand, is modelled on metaphor and simile, in which one thing is equated with another on the basis of some similarity between them: Gerald's domination of his mare is described in such a way as to suggest a human sexual act. This distinction, originally formulated by the Russian structuralist Roman Jakobson, operates on every level of a literary text, and indeed outside literature too, as my heroine Robyn Penrose demonstrated to a sceptical Vic Wilcox in *Nice Work*, by analysing cigarette advertisements. For more examples of how it operates in fictional symbolism, see the passage by Graham Greene, discussed under the heading of "The Exotic" in Section 35.

31 Allegory

So far, however, as I could collect anything certain, I gathered that they have two distinct currencies, each under the control of its own banks and mercantile codes. One of these (the one with the Musical Banks) was supposed to be *the* system, and to give out the currency in which all monetary transactions should be carried on; and as far as I could see, all who wished to be considered respectable, kept a larger or smaller balance at these banks. On the other hand, if there is one thing of which I am more sure than another, it is that the amount so kept had no direct commercial value in the outside world; I am sure that the managers and cashiers of the Musical Banks were not paid in their own currency. Mr Nosnibor used to go to these banks, or rather to the great mother bank of the city, sometimes but not very often. He was a pillar of one of the other kinds of banks, though he appeared to hold some minor office also in the musical ones. The ladies generally went alone; as indeed was the case in most families, except on state occasions.

I had long wanted to know more of this strange system, and had the greatest desire to accompany my hostess and her daughters. I had seen them go out almost every morning since my arrival and had noticed that they carried their purses in their hands, not exactly ostentatiously, yet just so as that those who met them should see whither they were going. I had never, however, yet been asked to go with them myself.

SAMUEL BUTLER *Erewhon* (1872)

ALLEGORY is a specialized form of symbolic narrative, which does not merely suggest something beyond its literal meaning, but insists on being decoded in terms of another meaning. The most famous allegory in the English language is John Bunyan's *The Pilgrim's Progress*, which allegorizes the Christian struggle to achieve salvation as a journey from the City of Destruction, through obstacles and distractions like the Slough of Despond and Vanity Fair, to the Celestial City. Virtues and vices are personified as people Christian encounters on his journey, e.g.:

> Now, when he was got up to the top of the hill, there came two men running to meet him amain; the name of the one was *Timorous*, and of the other, *Mistrust*; to whom *Christian* said, Sirs, what's the matter? You run the wrong way. *Timorous* answered, that they were going to the City of *Zion*, and had got up that difficult place; but, said he, the further we go, the more danger we meet with; wherefore we turned, and are going back again.

Since the development of an allegorical narrative is determined at every point by its one-to-one correspondence to the implied meaning, it tends to work against what Henry James called "the sense of felt life" in the novel. Allegory therefore appears in mainstream fiction, if at all, in interpolated narratives like dreams (*Pilgrim's Progress* is itself framed as a dream) or stories told by one character to another. Graham Greene's *A Burnt-out Case*, for instance, features a bed-time story told by the hero Querry to the childlike Marie Rycker. The story, about a successful but cynical jeweller, is a transparent allegory of Querry's professional career as a famous Catholic architect who has lost his religious faith; it also has a teasing relevance to Greene's own life and literary career:

> "Everyone said he was a master-technician, but he was highly praised too for the seriousness of his subject matter because on the top of each egg there was a gold cross set with chips of precious stones in honour of the King."

As an extended fictional device allegory is used mainly in didactic, satirical fables, such as *Gulliver's Travels*, *Animal Farm* and *Erewhon*. In these masterpieces a surface realism of presentation gives the fantastic events a kind of weird plausibility, and the game of correspondences is played with such wit and ingenuity that it never becomes boringly predictable. The title *Erewhon* is "nowhere" spelled backwards (almost). Butler thus places his book in the tradition of Thomas More's *Utopia* ("No Place"), the description of an imaginary country which has instructive resemblances to and differences from our own. A young Englishman crosses a range of mountains in some outpost of Empire (it sounds like New Zealand, where Butler spent several years) and stumbles upon a previously undiscovered country. Its inhabitants have reached approximately the same stage of development as Victorian England, but their values and beliefs seem bizarre and perverse to the narrator. For example, they regard illness as a crime, requiring punishment and segregation from respectable people, and crime as an illness, deserving of commiseration from friends and relatives, and requiring expensive treatment by sympathetic practitioners called "straighteners". We soon cotton on to the basic conceit – Erewhon exhibits Victorian *mores* in displaced or inverted forms – but it is important that the narrator does not. Part of the pleasure of this kind of fiction is that our intelligence is exercised and flattered by interpreting the allegory.

The Erewhonians do not have any religious belief, and they attribute the narrator's observance of the Sabbath as "a fit of sulkiness which they remarked as coming over me upon every seventh day." What they have instead are Musical Banks, thus called because in them "all mercantile transactions are accompanied with music . . . though the music was hideous to a European ear." These buildings are elaborately decorated with marble cladding, sculptures, stained-glass etc. Respectable people like the Nosnibors (Robinsons), who have befriended the narrator, go through the motions of conducting small financial transactions at these banks, and deplore the fact that so few people make full use of them, though everyone knows that their currency has no real value.

The implication that Victorian religion was largely a social ritual; that, while nominally subscribing to the tenets of Christianity, the

English bourgeoisie conducted their affairs on an entirely different, materialistic basis, is very clear. It is not for the sake of such a rather obvious message, however, that we read and enjoy *Erewhon*, but for the absurdist humour and thought-provoking felicity with which the analogies are developed. Banks, for example, especially large, important banks, *are* rather like churches or cathedrals in their architecture and décor; noting the neatness of the analogy we are made to think about the hypocrisy and false pretensions of financial as well as ecclesiastical institutions. And the discreetly self-righteous comportment of the ladies on their way to the Musical Bank, carrying their purses "not exactly ostentatiously, yet just so as that those who met them should see whither they were going", is much more amusing than it would be if they were characters in a realistic novel carrying prayerbooks. Allegory is yet another technique of defamiliarization.

32 Epiphany

They reach the tee, a platform of turf beside a hunchbacked fruit tree offering fists of taut pale buds. "I better go first," Rabbit says. "Till you calm down." His heart is hushed, held in mid-beat, by anger. He doesn't care about anything except getting out of this mess. He wishes it would rain. In avoiding looking at Eccles he looks at the ball, which sits high on the tee and already seems free of the ground. Very simply he brings the clubhead around his shoulder into it. The sound has a hollowness, a singleness he hasn't heard before. His arms force his head up and his ball is hung way out, lunarly pale against the beautiful black blue of storm clouds, his grandfather's colour stretched dense across the east. It recedes along a line straight as a ruler-edge. Stricken; sphere, star, speck. It hesitates, and Rabbit thinks it will die, but he's fooled, for the ball makes this hesitation the ground of a final leap: with a kind of visible sob takes a last bite of space before vanishing in falling. "That's it!" he cries and, turning to Eccles with a smile of aggrandizement, repeats, "That's it."

JOHN UPDIKE *Rabbit, Run* (1960)

AN EPIPHANY is, literally, a showing. In Christian terminology it denotes the showing of the infant Jesus to the three Magi. James Joyce, apostate Catholic, for whom the writer's vocation was a kind of profane priesthood, applied the word to the process by which a commonplace event or thought is transformed into a thing of timeless beauty by the exercise of the writer's craft: "when the soul of the commonest object seems to us radiant," as his fictional *alter ego*, Stephen Dedalus, says. The term is now loosely applied to any descriptive passage in which external reality is charged with a kind of transcendental significance for the perceiver. In modern fiction an epiphany often has the function performed by a decisive action in traditional narrative, providing a climax or resolution to a story or episode. Joyce himself showed the way in this respect. Many of the stories in *Dubliners* seem to end with an anticlimax – some defeat or frustration or trivial incident – but the language makes the anticlimax into a moment of truth for the protagonist, or the reader, or both. In *A Portrait of the Artist as a Young Man* the sight of a young girl wading in the sea with her skirts tucked up is elevated by the rhythms and repetitions of the style into a transcendent vision of profane beauty that confirms the hero in his commitment to an artistic rather than a religious vocation:

> Her slateblue skirts were kilted boldly about her waist and dovetailed behind her. Her bosom was as a bird's soft and slight, slight and soft as the breast of some darkplumaged dove. But her long fair hair was girlish: and girlish, and touched with the wonder of mortal beauty, her face.

The passage quoted from the first of John Updike's *Rabbit* novels describes an action in a contest, but it is the intensity of the moment, not its consequences, that are important (we never discover whether the hero won that particular hole). Harry "Rabbit" Angstrom is a young man stuck in a dead-end job in smalltown America, and stuck in a marriage that has gone erotically and emotionally dead after the birth of the couple's first child. He makes an ineffectual attempt to run away from his suffocating existence, getting no further than the arms of another woman. The local minister, Eccles, invites him to play a round of golf as a pretext for counselling him to return to his wife. Rabbit, who worked as a caddy in boyhood, knows the rudiments of the game, but under the stress of the situation his first drive "sputters away to one side, niggled by a perverse topspin that makes it fall from flight as dumpily as a blob of clay," and his play doesn't improve as Eccles nags at him. "Why have you left her?" "I *told* ya. There was this thing that wasn't there." "What thing? Have you ever seen it?

Are you sure it exists? . . . Is it hard or soft? Harry. Is it blue? Is it red? Does it have polka dots?" Badgered by Eccles' mockingly empirical questioning, Rabbit finds his answer by hitting, at last, the perfect drive.

In epiphanies, prose fiction comes closest to the verbal intensity of lyric poetry (most modern lyrics are in fact nothing but epiphanies); so epiphanic description is likely to be rich in figures of speech and sound. Updike is a writer prodigally gifted with the power of metaphoric speech. Even before he gets to the main subject of this paragraph he sets the scene with an effortlessly vivid description of the fruit tree, its "fists of taut pale buds" hinting at both the antagonism of the moment, and the promise of release. But the initial description of the drive is deliberately literal. "Very simply he brings the clubhead around his shoulder into it," is like a golf pro's description of a natural swing. "The sound has a hollowness, a singleness he hasn't heard before." The transformation of the epithets *hollow* and *single* into abstract nouns gives them a mysterious resonance. Then the language takes a metaphoric turn: "his ball is hung way out, lunarly pale against the beautiful black blue of storm clouds," and this cosmic, astronomical strain of imagery is extended later in "sphere, star, speck." The boldest trope is rightly reserved for the last: just as Rabbit thinks his ball is going to die, it "makes this hesitation the ground of a final leap: with a kind of visible sob takes a last bite of space before vanishing in falling." The synaesthesia (mixing of senses) of "visible sob" might seem a bit too rich to apply to a golf ball, if it didn't occupy the climactic position in the description. When Rabbit turns to Eccles and cries triumphantly, "That's it!" he is answering the minister's question about what is lacking in his marriage. But there is a suggestion of religious transcendence in the language applied to the golf ball ("the ground of a final leap" could be a phrase from modern existentialist theology) which comments obliquely on Eccles's own lack of real religious faith. Perhaps in Rabbit's cry of "That's it!" we also hear an echo of the writer's justifiable satisfaction at having revealed, through language, the radiant soul of a well-struck tee-shot.

33 Coincidence

For two very happy persons he found himself straightway taking them – a young man in shirt sleeves, a young woman easy and fair, who had pulled pleasantly up from some other place and, being acquainted with the neighbourhood, had known what this particular retreat could offer them. The air quite thickened, at their approach, with further intimations; the intimation that they were expert, familiar, frequent – that this wouldn't at all events be the first time. They knew how to do it, he vaguely felt – and it made them but the more idyllic, though at the very moment of the impression, as happened, their boat seemed to have begun to drift wide, the oarsman letting it go. It had by this time none the less come much nearer – near enough for Strether to fancy the lady in the stern had for some reason taken account of his being there to watch them. She had remarked on it sharply, yet her companion hadn't turned round; it was in fact almost as if our friend had felt her bid him keep still. She had taken in something as a result of which their course had wavered, and it continued to waver while they just stood off. This little effect was sudden and rapid, so rapid that Strether's sense of it was separate only for an instant from a sharp start of his own. He too had within the minute taken in something, taken in that he knew the lady whose parasol, shifting as if to hide her face, made so fine a pink point on the shining scene. It was too prodigious, a chance in a million, but, if he knew the lady, the gentleman, who still presented his back and kept off, the gentleman, the coatless hero of the idyll, who had responded to her start, was, to match the marvel, none other than Chad.

HENRY JAMES *The Ambassadors* (1903)

THERE IS ALWAYS a trade-off in the writing of fiction between the achievement of structure, pattern and closure on the one hand, and the imitation of life's randomness, inconsequentiality and openness on the other. Coincidence, which surprises us in real life with symmetries we don't expect to find there, is all too obviously a structural device in fiction, and an excessive reliance on it can jeopardize the verisimilitude of a narrative. Its acceptability varies, of course, from one period to another. Brian Inglis observes in his book *Coincidence* that "Novelists . . . provide an invaluable guide to their contemporaries' attitudes to coincidence through the ways in which they exploit it in their books."

Lord David Cecil's witticism that Charlotte Brontë "stretched the long arm of coincidence to the point of dislocation" could be applied to most of the great Victorian novelists, who wrote long, multi-stranded and heavily moralized stories involving numerous characters drawn from different levels of society. Through coincidence, intriguing and instructive connections could be contrived between people who would not normally have had anything to do with each other. Often this was linked with a Nemesis theme – the idea, dear to the Victorian heart, that wrongdoing will always be exposed in the end. Henry James was perhaps pointing the same moral in the coincidental meeting that forms the climax to *The Ambassadors*, but in a characteristically modern way the innocent party is as discomfited as the guilty ones.

The hero of the story, Lambert Strether, is an amiable, elderly American bachelor who is despatched to Paris by his formidable patroness, Mrs Newsome, to check out rumours that their son Chad is misbehaving himself with a Frenchwoman, and to bring him back to run the family business. Strether, enchanted with Paris, and with the much-improved Chad and his aristocratic friend, Mme de Vionnet, and trusting Chad's assurances that the relationship is entirely innocent, sides with the young man in the family struggle, at some cost to his own prospects. Then, in the course of a solitary excursion into the French countryside, while stopping at a riverside inn, he encounters Chad and Mme de Vionnet, who arrive unchaperoned at the same venue by rowing boat. For Strether the realization that they are, after all, lovers, is a bitter and humiliating disillusionment. The European culture whose beauty, style and elegance he has so enthusiastically embraced, turns out to be morally duplicitous, confirming the prejudices of puritanical and philistine New England.

This dénouement is contrived by means of coincidence, "a chance in a million," as the text itself boldly states. If it doesn't *seem* contrived, in the reading, that is partly because it is virtually the only twist in the entire plot (so that James has large reserves of credulity to draw on), and partly because the masterly narration of the event from Strether's point of view makes us experience it, rather than merely receive a report of it. Strether's perceptions have three stages, which are presented in, as it were, slow motion. First we share his benevolent observation of the couple in the boat on the assumption that they are strangers, whose appearance happily completes the idyllic scene he is contemplating. He constructs a little narrative around them, inferring from their comportment that they are "expert, familiar, frequent" visitors (which means that, when he identifies them as Chad and Mme de Vionnet, he must face the unpleasant fact that they are expert, familiar, frequent lovers, and have been deceiving him for some time). In the second stage he perceives various puzzling changes in the couple's behaviour: the boat drifts wide, the oarsman stops rowing, apparently at the behest of the lady who has taken note of Strether's presence. (Mme de Vionnet is wondering whether they can back off without being recognized.) Then, in the third and final stage Strether realizes that "he knew the lady whose parasol, shifting as if to hide her face, made so fine a pink point on the shining scene." Even now Strether's mind still clings to his aesthetic idyll; just as, in registering the presence of Chad, he tries to conceal his own dismay from himself by a hollow impersonation of pleased surprise. Having rendered the encounter so vividly, James can risk in the next paragraph terming it "as queer as fiction, as farce."

The frequency of coincidence in fictional plots varies with genre as well as period, and is related to how much the writer feels he can "get away with" in this respect. To cite my own experience, I felt much less inhibited about exploiting coincidence in *Small World* (the very title of which foregrounds the phenomenon) than in, say, *Nice Work*. *Small World* is a comic novel, and audiences of comedy will accept an improbable coincidence for the sake of the fun it generates. In associating coincidence with "farce", James was no doubt thinking of French boulevard comedies at the turn of the century, by writers like Georges Feydeau, which all turn on sexually compromising situations, and *Small World* belongs to this tradition. It is also a novel that consciously imitates the interlacing plots of chivalric romances, so there is an intertextual justification, too, for the multiplicity of coincidences in the story. One of the more outrageous examples in the story centres on Cheryl Summerbee, an airline employee at Heathrow airport who serves an improbable number of the novel's characters in the course of the book. At a late stage in the pursuit of the heroine, Angelica, by the hero, Persse McGarrigle, the former leaves the latter a message on the petition board of the chapel at Heathrow, coded as a reference to a stanza in Spenser's *Faerie Queene*. Having tried the Heathrow bookstalls in vain for a paperback edition of this work, Persse is just about to travel back to London when Cheryl, who is in charge of an Information desk, produces the very thing from under her counter. It transpires that she has substituted this for her usual reading of cheap romances as a result of having received a lecture on the nature of authentic literary romance from the relentlessly pedagogic Angelica, whom she recently checked in for a flight to Geneva. Thus Persse obtains both the means of decoding the message and information of Angelica's whereabouts. This is all highly implausible, but it seemed to me that by this stage of the novel it was almost a case of the more coincidences the merrier, providing they did not defy common sense, and the idea of someone wanting information about a classic Renaissance poem getting it from an airline Information desk was so piquant that the audience would be ready to suspend their disbelief.

Nice Work has its comic and intertextual elements, but it is a more serious, realistic novel, and I was conscious that coincidence must be used more sparingly as a plot device, and more carefully disguised or justified. Whether I succeeded is not for me to say, but I will give an example of what I mean. In Part Four of the novel, the hero Vic Wilcox is addressing a meeting of his workers when he is interrupted by a Kissogram, delivered by a girl dressed in sexy underwear, who sings a derisive message to him. This is a practical joke perpetrated by Vic's disaffected Sales Director. The meeting is about to collapse when the heroine Robyn Penrose comes to the rescue. The girl immediately obeys Robyn's command that she should leave because she is one of Robyn's students, Marion Russell. This is obviously a coincidence. If it works in narrative terms it is because certain clues have been planted earlier in the text which hinted that Marion might be doing this kind of job – not so obviously that the reader would guess that the Kissogram girl was Marion as soon as she appeared, but clearly enough in retrospect. Thus scepticism about a coincidence is, I hope, deflected by satisfactorily solving an enigma (what is Marion's part-time job?) and also by putting emphasis on Robyn's successful intervention rather than on her perception of the coincidence.

34 The Unreliable Narrator

"It is from Mrs Johnson, a companion of my aunt. She says my aunt died the day before yesterday." She paused a moment, then said: "The funeral is to take place tomorrow. I wonder if it might be possible for me to take the day off."

"I am sure that could be arranged, Miss Kenton."

"Thank you, Mr Stevens. Forgive me, but perhaps I may now have a few moments alone."

"Of course, Miss Kenton."

I made my exit, and it was not until after I had done so that it occurred to me I had not actually offered her my condolences. I could well imagine the blow the news would be to her, her aunt having been, to all intents and purposes, like a mother to her, and I paused out in the corridor, wondering if I should go back, knock and make good my omission. But then it occurred to me that if I were to do so, I might easily intrude upon her private grief. Indeed, it was not impossible that Miss Kenton, at that very moment, and only a few feet from me, was actually crying. The thought provoked a strange feeling to rise within me, causing me to stand there hovering in the corridor for some moments. But eventually I judged it best to await another opportunity to express my sympathy and went on my way.

KAZUO ISHIGURO *The Remains of the Day* (1989)

UNRELIABLE NARRATORS are invariably invented characters who are part of the stories they tell. An unreliable "omniscient" narrator is almost a contradiction in terms, and could only occur in a very deviant, experimental text. Even a character-narrator cannot be a hundred per cent unreliable. If everything he or she says is palpably false, that only tells us what we know already, namely that a novel is a work of fiction. There must be some possibility of discriminating between truth and falsehood within the imagined world of the novel, as there is in the real world, for the story to engage our interest.

The point of using an unreliable narrator is indeed to reveal in an interesting way the gap between appearance and reality, and to show how human beings distort or conceal the latter. This need not be a conscious, or mischievous, intention on their part. The narrator of Kazuo Ishiguro's novel is not an evil man, but his life has been based on the suppression and evasion of the truth, about himself and about others. His narrative is a kind of confession, but it is riddled with devious self-justification and special pleading, and only at the very end does he arrive at an understanding of himself – too late to profit by it.

The frame-story is set in 1956. The narrator is Stevens, the ageing butler of an English stately home, once the seat of Lord Darlington, now the property of a rich American. Encouraged by his new employer, Stevens takes a short holiday in the West Country. His private motive is to make contact with Miss Kenton, housekeeper at Darlington Hall in its great days between the Wars, when Lord Darlington hosted unofficial gatherings of high-ranking politicians to discuss the crisis in Europe. Stevens hopes to persuade Miss Kenton (he continues to refer to her thus, though she is married) to come out of retirement and help solve a staffing crisis at Darlington Hall. As he travels, he recalls the past.

Stevens speaks, or writes, in a fussily precise, stiffly formal style – butlerspeak, in a word. Viewed objectively, the style has no literary merit whatsoever. It is completely lacking in wit, sensuousness and originality. Its effectiveness as a medium for this novel resides precisely in our growing perception of its inadequacy for what it describes. Gradually we infer that Lord Darlington was a bungling amateur diplomat who believed in appeasing Hitler and gave support to fascism and antisemitism. Stevens has never admitted to himself or to others that his employer was totally discredited by subsequent historical events, and takes pride in the impeccable service he rendered his weak and unamiable master.

The same mystique of the perfect servant rendered him incapable of recognizing and responding to the love that Miss Kenton was ready to offer him when they worked together. But a dim, heavily censored memory of his treatment of her gradually surfaces in the course of his narrative – and we realize that his real motive for seeking her out again is a vain hope of undoing the past.

Stevens repeatedly gives a favourable account of himself which turns out to be flawed or deceptive. Having delivered to Miss Kenton a letter reporting the death of her aunt, he realizes that he has not "actually" offered his condolences. His hesitation about whether to return almost distracts us from his extraordinarily crass omission of any expression of regret in the preceding dialogue. His anxiety not to intrude on her grief seems to bespeak a sensitive personality, but in fact as soon as he finds another "opportunity to express my sympathy", he does no such thing, but instead rather spitefully criticises her supervision of two new maidservants. Typically, he has no word more expressive than "strange" for the feeling he experiences at the thought that Miss Kenton might be crying on the other side of the door. We may be surprised that he should suspect her of doing so, just after noting with approval her calm reception of the news. In fact many pages later he admits that he has attached this memory to the wrong episode:

> I am not at all certain now as to the actual circumstances which had led me to be standing thus in the back corridor. It occurs to me that elsewhere in attempting to gather such recollections, I may well have asserted that this memory derived from the minutes immediately after Miss Kenton's receiving news of her aunt's death . . . But now, having thought further, I believe I may have been a little confused about this matter; that in fact this fragment of memory derives from events that took place on an evening at least a few months after the death of Miss Kenton's aunt . . .

It was an evening, in fact, when he humiliated her by coldly rejecting her timid but unambiguous offer of love – *that* was why she was crying behind the closed door. But Stevens characteristically associates the occasion not with this private, intimate episode, but with one of Lord Darlington's most momentous conferences. The themes of political bad faith and emotional sterility are subtly interwoven in the sad story of Stevens's wasted life.

It is interesting to compare and contrast Ishiguro's novel with another virtuoso feat in the use of an unreliable narrator – Vladimir Nabokov's *Pale Fire*. This novel takes the unusual form of a long poem by a fictitious American poet called John Shade, with a detailed commentary upon it by an émigré European scholar, Shade's neighbour, called Charles Kinbote. The poem is an autobiographical work centering on the tragic suicide of the poet's daughter. Shade himself, we gather, had just been murdered when the manuscript of the poem came into Kinbote's hands. We soon realize that Kinbote is mad, believing himself to be the exiled king of some Ruritanian country resembling pre-Revolutionary Russia. He has convinced himself that Shade was writing a poem about his own history, and that he was shot in error by an assassin sent to murder Kinbote himself. The purpose of his commentary is to establish Kinbote's bizarre interpretation of the facts. One of the pleasures of reading it is to discern, by reference to the "reliable" narrative of Shade's poem, the degree of Kinbote's self-delusion. Compared with *The Remains of the Day*, *Pale Fire* is exuberantly comic at the expense of the unreliable narrator. Yet the effect is not totally reductive. Kinbote's evocation of his beloved kingdom, Zembla, is vivid, enchanting and haunting. Nabokov has invested his character with some of his own eloquence, and much of his own exile's poignant nostalgia. Ishiguro's novel in contrast accepts the limitations of a narrator quite without eloquence. If he had been reliable, the effect would, of course, have been incredibly boring.

35 The Exotic

Wilson sat on the balcony of the Bedford Hotel with his bald pink knees thrust against the ironwork. It was Sunday and the Cathedral bell clanged for matins. On the other side of Bond Street, in the windows of the High School, sat the young negresses in dark blue gym smocks engaged on the interminable task of trying to wave their wirespring hair. Wilson stroked his very young moustache and dreamed, waiting for his gin-and-bitters.

Sitting there, facing Bond Street, he had his face turned to the sea. His pallor showed how recently he had emerged from it into the port: so did his lack of interest in the schoolgirls opposite. He was like the lagging finger of the barometer, still pointing to Fair long after its companion had moved to Stormy. Below him the black clerks moved churchward, but their wives in brilliant afternoon dresses of blue and cerise aroused no interest in Wilson. He was alone on the balcony except for one bearded Indian in a turban who had already tried to tell his fortune: this was not the hour or the day for white men – they would be at the beach five miles away, but Wilson had no car. He felt almost intolerably lonely. On either side of the school the tin roofs sloped toward the sea, and the corrugated iron above his head clanged and clattered as a vulture alighted.

GRAHAM GREENE *The Heart of the Matter* (1948)

IMPERIALISM and its aftermath set off an extraordinary wave of travel, exploration and migration around the globe, in which writers, or potential writers, were inevitably caught up. One consequence was that many novels of the last hundred and fifty years, especially British novels, have had exotic settings. By "exotic" I mean foreign, but not necessarily glamorous or alluring. Indeed Graham Greene specialized in unprepossessing or, to use his own favourite epithet, "seedy" foreign locations for his novels. It has been said that they are all set in a country of the mind called Greeneland. They certainly have an atmospheric family resemblance (vultures, for instance, are more likely to inhabit his skies than doves or even sparrows) but the term does an injustice to the specificity of his settings.

The exotic in fiction is the mediation of an "abroad" to an audience assumed to be located at "home". Joseph Conrad, whose work is inextricably connected with the Age of Imperialism (he was a Polish émigré who joined the British Merchant Navy, and observed the workings of the British Empire, and its rivals, in many far-flung corners of the globe) understood this very well. At the beginning of *Heart of Darkness*, his classic study of the appalling effects of the Belgian colonization of the African Congo, both on the indigenous inhabitants, and on the Europeans who carried it out, Conrad frames his story by having the narrator, Marlow, tell it to a group of companions on a yawl moored in the Thames estuary. "'And this also,' said Marlow suddenly, 'has been one of the dark places of the earth.'" Marlow goes on to imagine how the banks of the Thames would have looked to a Roman trireme two millennia before –"'Sand-banks, marshes, forests, savages, – precious little to eat fit for a civilized man ... Here and there a military camp lost in a wilderness, like a needle in a bundle of hay – cold, fog, tempests, disease, exile and death, – death skulking in the air, in the water, in the bush.'" It's a neat reversal of the main story, in which an Englishman goes out from a busy, modern, "progressive" Europe to face the dangers and deprivations of darkest Africa, and it prepares us for the novella's radical questioning of the stereotypes of "savage" and "civilized" in the tale of Marlow's journey up the Congo.

Graham Greene often recorded his great admiration for Conrad, and confessed that he had to give up reading him for fear of being unduly influenced by the earlier writer's style. Whether the title of *The Heart of the Matter*, a novel that derived from Greene's war-

159

time service for MI6 in Sierra Leone, contains an allusion, or nod of homage, to Conrad's African tale, I do not know; but Greene's opening, like Conrad's, is particularly artful in the way it manipulates, juxtaposes and counterpoints signifiers of home and abroad. Wilson, newly arrived from England, is a minor character used specifically for the purpose of introducing the reader to the exotic setting. (Once this is achieved, the point of view of the narrative shifts to the hero, Scobie, a long-resident police officer.) Slyly, Greene abstains from telling us immediately where we are (Freetown) but makes us infer it, complicating the task by scattering some confusing clues. The Bedford Hotel, the Cathedral bell clanging for matins, Bond Street and the High School, all sound like features of an English city. In the first paragraph only the references to Wilson's exposed knees (implying that he is wearing shorts) and the young negresses suggest that the setting is probably tropical Africa. This double-take effect neatly encapsulates colonialism's tendency to impose its own culture on the indigenous one – partly as an instrument of ideological domination, and partly as a way of mitigating its own "home-sickness". There is irony and pathos too in the readiness with which the colonized collaborate in this process – the African girls in British-style gym-slips vainly trying to wave their hair, the black clerks and their wives dutifully attending the Anglican service. We tend to think of *The Heart of the Matter* as primarily a novel about the moral consequences of religious belief, but it is almost as importantly a novel about colonialism.

As I said earlier (in Section 14) description in fiction is necessarily selective, depending heavily on the rhetorical device of synecdoche, in which the part stands for the whole. Wilson is evoked for us by his knees, his pallor and his moustache, the young African girls by their gym smocks and wirespring hair, the Bedford Hotel by its ironwork balcony and corrugated-iron roof, and so on. These details of the scene constitute a minute proportion of all those that might have been noted. There is only one overtly metaphorical expression: the simile of the barometer, which actually seems a little strained, punning on "Fair" to maintain the antithesis between white and black that runs through the passage.

But some of the epithets applied to the literal details of the scene generate quasi-metaphorical connotations and cross-references. "Bald" (normally applied only to the head) emphasizes the hairlessness of Wilson's knees, and "young" (normally applied to the whole person) the feebleness of his moustache, contrasting with the luxuriance of the African girls' hair. There is equivalence as well as difference here. The way Wilson thrusts his knees against the ironwork symbolizes the repressiveness of his British public-school-and-civil-service mentality, still pristine, as his lack of sexual interest (twice noted) in the African women indicates. The girls' efforts to subdue their tightly curled hair is a still more obvious symbol of the natural subordinated to the cultural. The use of hair as an ethnic marker continues in the next paragraph with the bearded and turbaned Indian.

Although the scene is described from Wilson's position in space and time, it is not narrated from his subjective point of view, until we reach the sentence, "He felt almost intolerably lonely." Before that, Wilson is himself one of the objects in the scene, which is described by an omniscient but impersonal narrator, who knows things Wilson does not know, and sees things Wilson does not notice, and draws ironic connections between them that Wilson, waiting for his gin-and-bitters, dreaming (no doubt of home), is incapable of appreciating.

36 Chapters etc.

CHAPTER TWO

I grow up – Am hated by my relations – Sent to School –
Neglected by my Grandfather – Maltreated by my Master –
Seasoned to Adversity – I form Cabals against the Pedant – Am
debarred access to my Grandfather – Hunted by his Heir – I
demolish the Teeth of his Tutor.

> TOBIAS SMOLLETT *The Adventures of*
> *Roderick Random* (1748)

CHAPTER X

Is it not a shame to make two chapters of what passed in going
down one pair of stairs? for we are got no farther yet than to the
first landing, and there are fifteen more steps down to the
bottom; and for aught I know, as my father and my uncle Toby
are in a talking humour, there may be as many chapters as
steps: – let that be as it will, Sir, I can no more help it than my
destiny – A sudden impulse comes across me – drop the curtain,
Shandy – I drop it – Strike a line here across the paper, Tristram
– I strike it – and hey for a new chapter.

The deuce of any other rule have I to govern myself by in this
affair – and if I had one – as I do all things out of all rule – I
would twist it and tear it to pieces, and throw it into the fire
when I had done – Am I warm? I am, and the cause demands it
– a pretty story! is a man to follow rules – or rules to follow
him?

> LAURENCE STERNE *The Life and Opinions of*
> *Tristram Shandy, Gent.* (1759–67)

CHAPTER VIII

Arthur's Seat shall be my bed,
   The sheets shall ne'er be press'd by me;
St Anton's well shall be my drink,
   Sin' my true-love's forsaken me.
                              Old Song

SIR WALTER SCOTT *The Heart of Midlothian* (1818)

CHAPTER I

Since I can do no good because a woman,
Reach constantly at something that is near it.
   The Maid's Tragedy: BEAUMONT AND FLETCHER

GEORGE ELIOT *Middlemarch* (1871–2)

... She had a right to happiness. Frank would take her in his arms, fold her in his arms. He would save her.

*

She stood among the swaying crowd in the station at the North Wall. He held her hand and she knew that he was speaking to her, saying something about the passage over and over again.

JAMES JOYCE "Eveline" (1914)

WE TEND to take the division of novels into chapters for granted, as if it were as natural and inevitable as the division of the discourse into sentences and paragraphs. But of course it is not. The novels of Daniel Defoe, for instance, among the earliest English examples of the form, are continuous, uninterrupted streams of discourse. As usual with Defoe, it is hard to know whether this is a symptom of his own lack of literary sophistication, or a cunning imitation of naive, unprofessional narrators, pouring out their life-histories onto the page without a preconceived plan or structure. Whatever

163

the reason, it makes for a somewhat tiring reading experience, and a rather confused impression of the story being told (it is hard, for instance, to keep track of Moll Flanders's many journeys, partners and children, and difficult to refer back in the text to check up on them).

Breaking up a long text into smaller units has several possible effects. It gives the narrative, and the reader, time to take breath, as it were, in the intervening pauses. For this reason chapter breaks are useful for marking transitions between different times or places in the action. I have already noted, earlier, how Thackeray uses the concluding line of a chapter like the curtain line of a play, to heighten an effect of surprise and suspense (see Section 15). E. M. Forster does something very similar in the passage quoted from *Howards End* (see Section 2). Beginning a new chapter can also have a useful expressive or rhetorical effect, especially if it has a textual heading, in the form of a title, quotation or summary of contents. Smollett's chapter-headings, for instance, are like film trailers, enticing the reader with the promise of exciting action. In a sense they "give away" the development of the story in advance, but not in sufficient detail to kill our interest in it. These chapter-headings certainly convey the flavour of his fiction – racy, fast-moving and violent.

It is generally true to say that the more realistic a novelist is trying to be, the less likely he or she is to draw attention to this aspect of a novel's textual organization. Conversely, it is flaunted by self-consciously literary novelists. The very mention of the word "chapter" draws attention to the novel's compositional processes. We have already seen how Laurence Sterne uses such a reference to bring the idea of a narratee into play, having Tristram reproach his lady reader for being "so inattentive in reading the last chapter" (see Section 17). The quotation above is from Volume IV of *Tristram Shandy*, where the narrator is describing a conversation between his father and his Uncle Toby that took place on the day of his birth. In a more conventional novel, such a dialogue would not be broken up by chapter divisions, but Sterne typically makes the loquacity of his characters an excuse for defying the normal "rules" of composition, and starts a new chapter just because he feels like it. In fact this turns out to be "my chapter upon chapters, which I promised to write before I went to sleep." He summarizes the received wisdom on the subject, "that chapters relieve the mind – that they assist – or impose upon the imagination – and that in a work of this dramatic cast they are as necessary as the shifting of scenes," only to dismiss these statements as "cold conceits". He recommends the reader to study Longinus. "If you are not a jot the wiser by reading him the first time over – never fear – read him again." Like so much of *Tristram Shandy*, the chapter on chapters is an elaborate but instructive spoof.

Sir Walter Scott started a vogue for using quotations as epigraphs for chapters – a kind of overt intertextuality. Usually these quotations were culled from old ballads, of which he was a keen collector. They have several functions. One is thematic. The lines from "Old Song" at the head of Chapter VIII of *The Heart of Midlothian*, for instance, are relevant to one of the main components of the plot: Effie Deans, sister to the heroine Jeannie Deans, is accused of murdering the child she bore out of wedlock. The verse from "Old Song" connects her plight to the long narrative tradition of young women seduced and deserted by their lovers. The reference to "Arthur's Seat" (a hill overlooking Edinburgh) and St Anton's well ties this motif to a particular regional setting, the evocation of which was one of Scott's principal preoccupations, and a major source of his appeal to contemporary readers. The cumulative effect of these quotations from old songs and ballads is to establish the credentials of the authorial narrator as a well-informed and reliable guide to Scottish history, culture and topography.

It was a practice much imitated in the nineteenth century, by for instance George Eliot. Her epigraphs, however, tend to come from established, though often minor, literary figures like the Elizabethan playwrights Beaumont and Fletcher, from whom she quotes a couple of lines before introducing Dorothea Brooke in *Middlemarch*. The quotation highlights the frustration of Dorothea's idealism by her gender. It also reinforces the impression George Eliot wanted to give of a bookish, learned author who was the intellectual equal of any man.

When George Eliot quotes anonymous verses they are usually of her own composition. Kipling carried this practice of composing apocryphal sources for epigraphs to an extreme. "Mrs Bathurst", which I discussed earlier (see Section 7) is prefaced by a long extract from an "old play", written by Kipling himself in a pastiche of seventeenth-century dramatic prose, describing the death of a groom or clown at some royal court. Though fiendishly difficult to construe, it contains important clues to the meaning of the story. "She that damned him to death knew not that she did it, or would have died ere she had done it. For she loved him," seems, for instance, to rule out theories that the second corpse found beside Vickery's was that of Mrs Bathurst.

"Mrs Bathurst" doesn't have any chapters, of course. Short stories rarely do; though they sometimes have pauses or breaks in the text marked by a line space. James Joyce's "Eveline", for instance, consists mainly of a description of the principal character's thoughts as she sits at the window of her home, just before a planned elopement with her sailor lover. Then there is a break in the text marked by an asterisk, and the next section begins: "She stood among the swaying crowd in the station at the North Wall." The break in the text moves the action from the home to its climax on the dockside without describing how Eveline got there, which would be irrelevant to the story.

There are many different ways of dividing up a fictional text and of marking the divisions: "Books" or "Parts", numbered chapters, numbered or unnumbered sub-sections. Some authors have obviously given a great deal of thought to this matter, and taken pains to achieve a certain symmetry of form. Henry Fielding's *Tom Jones*, for example, has a hundred and ninety-eight Chapters, divided into eighteen Books, the first six of which are set in the country, the second six on the road, and the final six in London. The methods of publication and circulation of fiction at any given time affected this aspect of the novel. Throughout most of the nineteenth century, for instance, novels were commonly published in three volumes, mostly to suit the convenience of the circulating libraries, who were able to lend out one novel to three readers at once, but the practice may also have encouraged authors to see their novels in terms of a kind of three-act structure (it is possible to break down the action of Jane Austen's *Emma* in this way, for instance). Many Victorian novels were originally published in part or serial form, either as independent soft-cover publications or in magazines, and this too affected the shape of the eventual novel. The chapters of the novels Dickens wrote for weekly serial publication, like *Hard Times* and *Great Expectations*, are much shorter than those in novels like *Dombey and Son* or *Bleak House*, originally published in monthly parts. The magazine instalments often had also to meet a very precise and uniform length-requirement.

There would seem to be two dimensions to this topic: one is the purely spatial distribution and division of the text into smaller units. This is often a clue to the structure or architecture of the narrative as a whole, and it has some effect on the tempo of the reading experience. Insofar as it manifests a degree of symmetry it corresponds to stanzaic form in poetry. The other dimension is semantic: the addition of levels of meaning, implication, suggestion, through chapter headings, epigraphs and so on. Reviewing my own practice in this respect, I find considerable variation, according to the nature of the novel in question. I had forgotten, until I looked at it for this purpose, that my first novel, *The Picturegoers*, has no chapters. It is divided into three numbered Parts, each of which is concerned with the events of one weekend. Within each Part there are sections marked only by double line spaces or, more emphatically, asterisks, between them. I presume that this form was suggested by the nature of the narrative, which shifts frequently from scene to scene and from character to character situated in different places at the same time. The spaces between the sections function in fact like cinematic "cuts". My first novel to have numbered chapters was *The British Museum is Falling Down*, a comic and self-consciously literary novel containing a good deal of parody. Each chapter is headed by a (hopefully) amusing quotation from some printed source about the British Museum Reading Room, both imitating and mocking the procedures of literary scholarship. *Changing Places* is divided into numbered parts entitled "Flying", "Settling", "Corresponding", "Reading", "Changing" and "Ending"; and *How Far Can You Go?* is similarly divided into chapters, each of which begins with the word "How" – "How It Was", "How They Lost Their Virginities", "How They Lost the Fear of Hell" and so on. The verbal echoes were designed, I would say, to introduce an element of "symmetry" into the semantic level of chapter-headings, and perhaps to compensate for the fact that the chapters are very unequal in length. Symmetry, I believe, matters more to writers of fiction than readers consciously perceive.

37 The Telephone

He went to the telephone in the lobby outside. "Darling," he said.

"Is that Mr Last? I've got a message here, from Lady Brenda."

"Right, put me through to her."

"She can't speak herself, but she asked me to give you this message, that she's very sorry but she cannot join you tonight. She's very tired and has gone home to bed."

"Tell her I want to speak to her."

"I can't, I'm afraid, she's gone to bed. She's very tired."

"She's very tired and she's gone to bed?"

"That's right."

"Well, I want to speak to her."

"Good night," said the voice.

"The old boy's plastered," said Beaver as he rang off.

"Oh dear. I feel rather awful about him. But what *can* he expect, coming up suddenly like this? He's got to be taught not to make surprise visits."

"Is he often like that?"

"No, it's quite new."

The telephone bell rang. "D'you suppose that's him again? I'd better answer it."

"I want to speak to Lady Brenda Last."

"Tony, darling, this *is* me, Brenda."

"Some damn fool said I couldn't speak to you."

"I left a message from where I was dining. Are you having a lovely evening?"

EVELYN WAUGH *A Handful of Dust* (1934)

THE TELEPHONE is so familiar and ubiquitous a feature of modern life that we easily forget how unnatural it would have seemed, to previous ages, to speak and listen without being able to see or touch. In normal conversation, when the interlocutors are physically present to each other, they can add all kinds of meanings and nuances to their words by facial expression and body-language, or indeed communicate by such non-verbal means alone (a shrug, a squeeze of the hand, a lift of the eyebrow). Until the recent invention of the videophone (which is still in a very early stage of development) these channels of communication have not been available to the telephone user. By the same token, the "blindness" of telephonic communication lends itself to deception, and easily generates confusion, misunderstanding and alienation between the participants. It is therefore an instrument full of narrative potential.

Evelyn Waugh belonged to a generation of novelists – Henry Green, Christopher Isherwood and Ivy Compton-Burnett are other names that come to mind – who were particularly interested in the expressive possibilities of dialogue in fiction. Their work tends towards the effect I called "staying on the surface" (see Section 25): the characters revealing, or betraying, or condemning themselves by what they say, while the narrator maintains a dry detachment, abstaining from moral comment or psychological analysis. It is not surprising therefore that Evelyn Waugh was one of the first English novelists to recognize the importance of the telephone in modern social life, and its potential for comic and dramatic effect. It figures prominently in his second novel, *Vile Bodies* (1930), one chapter of which consists entirely of two telephone conversations between the hero and heroine, presented without comment and even without speech tags, in the course of which their engagement is broken off and the heroine announces her re-engagement to the hero's best friend. The language used is banal and formulaic – they keep saying "Well?" and "I see," when in fact nothing is well, and the one thing they can't do is see each other – and the effect is both funny and sad. The same is true of this passage from *A Handful of Dust*.

Brenda Last, bored with her husband Tony and life in his hideous stately home, starts an affair with the worthless and penniless young man-about-town, John Beaver, pretending that she needs to stay frequently in London to pursue a course in economics. One day Tony turns up in town unexpectedly, and finds she is dining out. He drowns his disappointment at his club in the company of an old chum, Jock Grant-Menzies. Then he is summoned to the telephone to receive a message from Brenda.

The first effect of the blindness of the telephone in the ensuing dialogue is a comic one: Tony's affectionate greeting, "Darling," meets with a very formal response from an unidentified third party. Tony doesn't seem to be able to grasp that this person is passing on a message, but keeps asking, with the drunk's persistence, to speak to his wife. There is pathos as well as comedy here, because the desperately lonely Tony does indeed yearn to communicate with his increasingly evasive and absent wife, and doesn't realize that she is turning away from him. The reader assumes that the third party is speaking from the place where Brenda dined – that is implied by "She ... has gone home to bed." But we discover that this speaker is in fact Beaver, and that he is with Brenda, possibly in that very bed, though of course Tony remains ignorant of this fact. "'The old boy's plastered,' said Beaver as he rang off" is a quite perfect sentence, simple though it may look. The revelation of how Tony is being tricked is all the more effective for being delayed as long as possible, casually implied in the speech-tag. The words spoken, which might seem affectionately familiar in another context, here express only contempt, callousness and complete lack of compunction. Brenda does "feel rather awful about" Tony, but in her next breath she turns normal ethics upside down (a recurrent motif of the novel) by implying that it is *he* who is at fault: "what *can* he expect, coming up suddenly like this?"

The telephone rings again, and again Tony asks to speak to Brenda. "Tony, darling, this *is* me, Brenda." Comedy and treachery are deftly blended here: another misunderstanding by Tony, a doubling of Brenda's betrayal in the insincere endearment, "darling". It is illogical of Tony to ask to speak to Brenda because he is telephoning her late at night at a flat so small he is not able to share it with her (he stays at his club); so if anyone answers it must be her. Fuddled with drink, he is confusing this conversation with the one he has just had with "some damn fool" supposedly calling from the place where Brenda had been earlier. But of course this "mistake" is no such thing. Brenda is quick to spot the danger and prop up the lie: "I left a message from where I was dining."

There is a sense in which all dialogue in prose fiction is like telephonic dialogue, because (unlike drama) it must make do without the physical presence of the speakers. Indeed, fictional dialogue is still more deprived, in being denied the expressive timbre and intonation of the human voice. Some novelists try to compensate by descriptive verbal phrases ("'No,' he whispered hoarsely," "'Yes!' she screamed ecstatically"), but Waugh has chosen to let the context comment on the speech acts of his characters, encouraging us to sound their words in our heads, and make our own assessment of their vanity, cruelty and pathos.

As I write this, a book has just been published which might reasonably be described as the Ultimate Telephone Novel. *Vox* (1992), by the American writer Nicholson Baker, author of three previous fictions of a highly original "minimalist" character, is accurately described on the cover of the British edition as "a novel about telephone sex." It consists of a long telephone conversation, rendered entirely in dialogue form apart from a few speech-tags, between a man and a woman on opposite coasts of North America, whose only connection is an adult contact line. They exchange detailed and mutually arousing information about their sexual preferences, fantasies and experiences, finally achieving simultaneous orgasm by masturbation. The unnaturalness of the telephone as a medium of communication could hardly be more strikingly epitomized than by using it as an instrument of sexual excitation and release, since it precludes what is normally considered essential to the sexual act: physical contact and penetration. Conversely one could say that telephone sex strikingly epitomizes the perversity of masturbation. Not surprisingly, *Vox* has proved a controversial novel, provoking sharply differing responses. Is it a piece of up-market pornography, or a devastating indictment of the sterility of sexual relations in the age of Aids, or a life-enhancing celebration of the ability of human beings to achieve harmless pleasure by co-operation? By writing the novel in dialogue form, the author has left the task of answering this question entirely to the reader – though not, of course, responsibility for having posed it.

38 Surrealism

I tried to nod and move away at the same time, but my knees were trembling so much that instead of going towards the staircase I shuffled crabwise nearer and nearer the pot. When I was well within range she suddenly jabbed the pointed knife into my backside and with a scream of pain I leapt right into the boiling soup and stiffened in a moment of intense agony with my companions in distress, one carrot and two onions.

A mighty rumbling followed by crashes and there I was standing outside the pot stirring the soup in which I could see my own meat, feet up, boiling away as merrily as any joint of beef. I added a pinch of salt and some peppercorns then ladled out a measure into my granite dish. The soup was not as good as a bouillabaisse but it was a good ordinary stew, very adequate for the cold weather.

From a speculative point of view I wondered which of us I was. Knowing that I had a piece of polished obsidian somewhere in the cavern I looked around, intending to use it as a mirror. Yes, there it was, hanging in its usual corner near the bat's nest. I looked into the mirror. First I saw the face of the Abbess of Santa Barbara de Tartarus grinning at me sardonically. She faded and then I saw the huge eyes and feelers of the Queen Bee who winked and transformed herself into my own face, which looked slightly less ravaged, owing probably to the dark surface of the obsidian.

LEONORA CARRINGTON *The Hearing Trumpet* (1976)

SURREALISM is better known and easier to define in the visual arts than in literature: Dali, Duchamp, Magritte and Ernst are well-established figures in the history of modern art. But there was a literary branch to the movement, which evolved in the nineteen-twenties and thirties out of earlier modernist and Dadaist experiments. Indeed, the chief theorist of Surrealism was a poet, André Breton, who declared that it was founded on "a belief in the supreme quality of certain forms of association heretofore neglected: in the omnipotence of dream, in the disinterested play of thought."

Leonora Carrington is a rare example of a Surrealist equally committed to visual and verbal art forms. A recent retrospective exhibition of her paintings at the Serpentine Gallery in London aroused much interest, and her novels and stories, published rather obscurely in several languages at long intervals over several decades, are beginning to attract critical attention, especially from feminists. Born in England, she was part of the heroic age of Surrealism in pre-war Paris, where she lived with Max Ernst for several years, before migrating to Mexico and the United States. Her work is now perceived as pioneering a good deal of postmodernist experimentation, especially by women artists and writers such as Angela Carter and Jeannette Winterson, who use surrealist effects to subvert patriarchal cultural assumptions.

Surrealism is not quite the same as magic realism, which I discussed earlier (Section 24), though there are obvious affinities between them. In magic realism there is always a tense connection between the real and the fantastic: the impossible event is a kind of metaphor for the extreme paradoxes of modern history. In surrealism, metaphors *become* the real, effacing the world of reason and common sense. The Surrealists' favourite analogy for their art, and often its source, was dreaming, in which, as Freud demonstrated, the unconscious reveals its secret desires and fears in vivid images and surprising narrative sequences unconstrained by the logic of our waking lives. The first great surrealist novel in the English language was arguably *Alice in Wonderland*, the story of a dream. Its influence is perceptible in this passage from Carrington's *The Hearing Trumpet*: in the jumbling together of the cruel and the grotesque with the domestic and the droll, in the matter-of-fact narration of fantastic events, and in the Cheshire-Cat-like visions of the faces in the obsidian mirror.

The narrator is a ninety-year-old Englishwoman called Marion Leatherby, apparently living in Mexico with her son Galahad and his wife Muriel. Marion is very deaf, but one day her friend Carmella gives her an ear-trumpet of amazing sensitivity, with the aid of which she overhears her son and his wife planning to put her away in a home for senile women. This early part of the novel is very amusingly written in a whimsical and eccentric style which it is possible to "naturalize" as the private thoughts of an intelligent but confused old lady:

> Time, as we all know, passes. Whether it returns in quite the same way is doubtful. A friend of mine who I did not mention up till now because of his absence told me that a pink and a blue universe cross each other in particles like two swarms of bees and when a pair of different coloured beads hit each other miracles happen. All this has something to do with time although I doubt if I could explain it coherently.

Once Marion crosses the threshold of the Home, however, events take an increasingly fantastic turn. In her living-quarters, for instance:

> The only real furniture was a wicker chair and a small table. All the rest was painted. What I mean is that the walls were painted with the furniture that wasn't there. It was so clever that I was almost taken in at first. I tried to open the painted wardrobe, a bookcase with books and their titles. An open window with a curtain fluttering in the breeze, or rather it would have fluttered if it were a real curtain ... All this one-dimensional furniture had a strangely depressing effect, like banging one's nose against a glass door.

The institution is run by an authoritarian born-again Christian, against whom the narrator and her friends eventually rebel, inspired by the portrait of a mysteriously winking nun on the dining-room wall. This nun is identified as an eighteenth-century

Abbess who was canonized as a saint, but was in fact a worshipper of the primal Mother or fertility goddess associated with the cult of Aphrodite, who appears to the narrator in the form of a queen bee. The story develops into a neo-pagan, feminist revision of the Grail legend, facilitated by apocalyptic natural events – a new Ice Age and an earthquake. A tower cracks open and reveals a staircase which the narrator follows into the underworld, where she meets her own double stirring a cauldron, and has the experience described in the extract. The splitting of the subject into observer and observed, both "meat" and cook, is a characteristically dream-like effect, as is the juxtaposition of the homely detail, "I added a pinch of salt and some peppercorns," with the violent and grotesque image of cannibalism. Such humorous touches are characteristic of the best Surrealist art, without which it is apt to become emptily portentous and tiresomely self-indulgent. Fortunately Leonora Carrington is as witty as she is imaginative.

39 Irony

Her face, viewed so close that he could see the almost imperceptible down on those fruit-like cheeks, was astonishingly beautiful; the dark eyes were exquisitely misted; and he could feel the secret loyalty of her soul ascending to him. She was very slightly taller than her lover; but somehow she hung from him, her body curved backwards, and her bosom pressed against his, so that instead of looking up at her gaze he looked down at it. He preferred that; perfectly proportioned though he was, his stature was a delicate point with him. His spirits rose by the uplift of his senses. His fears slipped away; he began to be very satisfied with himself. He was the inheritor of twelve thousand pounds, and he had won this unique creature. She was his capture; he held her close, permittedly scanning the minutiae of her skin, permittedly crushing her flimsy silks. Something in him had forced her to lay her modesty on the altar of his desire. And the sun brightly shone. So he kissed her yet more ardently, and with the slightest touch of a victor's condescension; and her burning response more than restored the self-confidence which he had been losing.

"I've got no one but you now," she murmured in a melting voice.

She fancied in her ignorance that the expression of this sentiment would please him. She was not aware that a man is usually rather chilled by it, because it proves to him that the other is thinking about his responsibilities and not about his privileges. Certainly it calmed Gerald, though without imparting to him her sense of his responsibilites. He smiled vaguely. To Sophia his smile was a miracle continually renewed; it mingled dashing gaiety with a hint of wistful appeal in a manner that never failed to bewitch her. A less innocent girl than Sophia might have divined from that adorable half-feminine smile that she could do anything with Gerald except rely on him. But Sophia had to learn.

ARNOLD BENNETT *The Old Wives' Tale* (1908)

178

IN RHETORIC, irony consists of saying the opposite of what you mean, or inviting an interpretation different from the surface meaning of your words. Unlike other figures of speech – metaphor, simile, metonymy, synecdoche etc. – irony is not distinguished from literal statement by any peculiarity of verbal form. An ironic statement is recognized as such in the act of interpretation. When, for example, the authorial narrator of *Pride and Prejudice* says, "It is a truth universally acknowledged, that a single man in possession of a fortune, must be in want of a wife," the reader, alerted by the false logic of the proposition about single men with fortunes, interprets the "universal" generalization as an ironic comment on a particular social group obsessed with matchmaking. The same rule applies to action in narrative. When the reader is made aware of a disparity between the facts of a situation and the characters' understanding of it, an effect called "dramatic irony" is generated. It has been said that all novels are essentially about the passage from innocence to experience, about discovering the reality that underlies appearances. It is not surprising, therefore, that stylistic and dramatic irony are all-pervasive in this form of literature. Most of the passages I have discussed in this book could have been analysed under the heading of Irony.

Arnold Bennett employs two different methods in this passage from *The Old Wives' Tale* to put his characters' behaviour in an ironic perspective. Sophia, the beautiful, passionate but inexperienced daughter of a draper in the Potteries, is sufficiently dazzled by Gerald Scales, a handsome commercial traveller who has inherited a small fortune, to elope with him. The embrace described here is their first in the privacy of their London lodgings. What should be a moment of erotic rapture and emotional unity is revealed as the physical conjunction of two people whose thoughts are running on quite different tracks.

Gerald in fact intends to seduce Sophia, though in the event he lacks the self-assurance to carry out his plan. Even in this embrace he is at first nervous and tentative, "perceiving that her ardour was exceeding his." But as the intimate contact continues, he becomes more confident and masterful. There is probably a sexual pun hidden in "His spirits rose by the uplift of his senses," for Bennett frequently hinted in this fashion at things he dared not describe explicitly. Gerald's sexual arousal has nothing to do with love, however, or even lust. It is a function of his vanity and self-esteem. "Something in him had forced her to lay her modesty on the altar of his desire." Like "the secret loyalty of her soul ascending to him" earlier, this florid metaphor mocks the complacent thought it expresses. The use of the word "altar" carries an extra ironic charge since at this point Gerald has no intention of leading Sophia to the altar of marriage.

Up to this point, Bennett keeps to Gerald's point of view, and uses the kind of language appropriate to that perspective, thus *implying* an ironic assessment of Gerald's character. The description of his timidity, vanity and complacency – so very different from what he *ought* to be feeling in this situation – and the slightly absurd, inflated rhetoric in which he represents his emotions to himself, are enough to condemn him in the reader's eyes. In the second paragraph, however, Bennett uses the convention of the omniscient intrusive author to switch to Sophia's point of view, and to comment explicitly on her misconceptions, adding to the layers of irony in the scene.

Sophia's thoughts are more creditable than Gerald's, but her words, "I've got no one but you now," are partly calculated to endear him to her. This merely reveals her naivety, however. As the "burning" Sophia utters this sentiment in a "melting" voice, Gerald is "chilled" by the reminder of his responsibilities. He responds with a non-committal smile, which the infatuated Sophia finds charming, but which, the narrator assures us, was an index of his unreliability and a portent of disillusionment to come. The authorial voice, dry, precise, urbane, overrides the "inner voice" of Sophia to expose the fallibility of her judgment.

The reader, privileged with knowledge denied to the participants in the scene, looks over the author's shoulder with pity for Sophia and contempt for Gerald. One of Bennett's *Notebook* entries reads, rather surprisingly, "Essential characteristic of the really great novelist: a Christ-like, all-embracing compassion"; his treatment of Gerald fell short of that high standard. This type of irony leaves us with little work of inference or interpretation to do; on the contrary, we are the passive recipients of the author's worldly wisdom. If the effect does not seem as heavy-handed as it easily might, that is because the acuteness of Bennett's psychological observation earns our respect, and because he allows characters like Sophia to "learn" from their mistakes, and survive them.

40 Motivation

On the eleventh day, however, Lydgate when leaving Stone Court was requested by Mrs Vincy to let her husband know that there was a marked change in Mr Featherstone's health, and that she wished him to come to Stone Court on that day. Now Lydgate might have called at the warehouse, or might have written a message on a leaf of his pocket-book and left it at the door. Yet these simple devices apparently did not occur to him, from which we may conclude that he had no strong objection to calling at the house at an hour when Mr Vincy was not at home, and leaving the message with Miss Vincy. A man may, from various motives, decline to give his company, but perhaps not even a sage would be gratified that nobody missed him. It would be a graceful, easy way of piecing on the new habits to the old, to have a few playful words with Rosamond about his resistance to dissipation, and his firm resolve to take long fasts even from sweet sounds. It must be confessed, also, that momentary speculations as to all the possible grounds for Mrs Bulstrode's hints had managed to get woven like slight clinging hairs into the more substantial web of his thoughts.

GEORGE ELIOT *Middlemarch* (1871–2)

WHAT KIND OF KNOWLEDGE do we hope to derive from reading novels, which tell us stories we know are not "true"? One traditional answer to that question is: knowledge of the human heart, or mind. The novelist has an intimate access to the secret thoughts of her characters denied to the historian, the biographer or even the psychoanalyst. The novel, therefore, can offer us more or less convincing models of how and why people act as they do.

Postmodernism and poststructuralism have deconstructed but not demolished the Christian or liberal humanist ideas of the self on which this project is based – the unique, autonomous individual responsible for his or her own acts. We continue to value novels, especially novels in the classic realist tradition, for the light they throw on human motivation.

Motivation in a novel like *Middlemarch* is a code of *causality*. It aims to convince us that the characters act as they do not simply because it suits the interests of the plot (though it usually does, of course: half the plot of *Middlemarch* would collapse if Lydgate did not call on Rosamond Vincy in Chapter 31) but because a combination of factors, some internal, some external, plausibly cause them to do so. Motivation in the realist novel tends to be, in Freudian language, "overdetermined", that is to say, any given action is the product of several drives or conflicts derived from more than one level of the personality; whereas in folk-tale or traditional romance a single cause suffices to explain behaviour – the hero is always courageous because he is the hero, the witch is always malevolent because she is a witch, etc. etc. Lydgate has several reasons for calling on Rosamond Vincy, some pragmatic, some ego-gratifying, some self-deceiving, some subconscious.

The context of this passage is as follows: Lydgate is a talented and ambitious young doctor with a promising medical career ahead of him when he comes to the provincial town of Middlemarch in the mid-1830s. There he meets and enjoys the company of Rosamond Vincy, the attractive but rather shallow-minded daughter of a prosperous merchant. To Rosamond, Lydgate is the most eligible man ever likely to appear on her horizons, and she soon considers herself to be in love with him. Her aunt, Mrs Bulstrode, warns Lydgate that his attentions to Rosamond may be interpreted as courtship. Lydgate, who has no wish to hamper his medical career with the responsibilities of marriage, immediately stops visiting the Vincys. But, after ten days' abstention, he calls to deliver a message.

George Eliot does not expose the secret motives of her characters with the ironic detachment of Arnold Bennett in the passage I discussed in the previous section, but in a more speculative and sympathetic fashion. At least, she is sympathetic to Lydgate. It has been often noted that George Eliot is rather less tolerant of beautiful, self-regarding women like Rosamond. In the paragraph immediately preceding the one I have quoted, Rosamond's anxiety about Lydgate's ten-day absence is rather dismissively summarized as follows:

> Any one who imagines ten days too short a time – not for falling into leanness, lightness, or other measurable effects of passion, but – for the whole spiritual circuit of alarmed conjecture and disappointment, is ignorant of what can go on in the elegant leisure of a young lady's mind.

"Elegant leisure" has a tone of tart disparagement that tends to devalue Rosamond's emotional stress. The analysis of Lydgate's motives is less summary, and more sympathetic, in style.

Instead of simply stating that Lydgate rejected other possible means of delivering his message because he wanted to see Rosamond, the authorial voice notes that "these simple devices apparently did not occur to him, from which we may conclude that he had no strong objections to calling at the house at an hour when Mr Vincy was not at home, and leaving the message with Miss Vincy." By this roundabout phrasing, George Eliot imitates both the way we have to infer motives from behaviour in real life, and the way we conceal our true motives even from ourselves. There is irony here, but it is humorous and humane. "Perhaps not even a sage would be gratified that nobody missed him," identifies Lydgate's vanity as a universal failing. The discourse then slips into free indirect style to show Lydgate's mental rehearsal of the note he intends to strike with Rosamond: a "graceful, easy . . . playful" signalling of his lack of serious intentions towards her. The last sentence of the paragraph is authorial, and plumbs the deepest level of Lydgate's motivation for calling on Rosamond: he is fascinated and flattered by the suggestion that she may have fallen in love with him, though he has hardly admitted this to himself. The image of the web which George Eliot uses to express this idea was a favourite one of hers, perhaps because it suggested the complexity and interconnectedness of human experience.

Lydgate's vanity and curiosity are his undoing. What happens is that Rosamond, normally so poised and self-controlled, reacts to Lydgate's sudden, unexpected reappearance with barely controlled emotion, and their meeting takes a quite different turn from the one he had planned. Both parties are surprised into natural, spontaneous behaviour which, in that society, at that time, has momentous consequences. Rosamond, in her perturbation, drops a "piece of trivial chain-work" which she has in her hands. Lydgate stoops to pick it up, and as he rises to his feet notices the tears welling irrepressibly in her eyes. "That moment of naturalness was the crystallizing feather touch: it shook flirtation into love," says the narrator. Within a few minutes Lydgate has taken Rosamond in his arms and is an engaged man. "He did not know where the chain went." Symbolically, it has gone round his neck: his professional future is mortgaged to a bourgeois marriage which will bring him little happiness and no fulfilment. It is one of the most brilliantly rendered "love-scenes" in English fiction; and it succeeds partly because Lydgate's motives for exposing himself to Rosamond's powerful sexual allure are so subtly and convincingly established beforehand.

41 Duration

Hubert gave Charles and Irene a nice baby for Christmas. The baby was a boy and its name was Paul. Charles and Irene who had not had a baby for many years were delighted. They stood around the crib and looked at Paul; they could not get enough of him. He was a handsome child with dark hair, dark eyes. Where did you get him Hubert? Charles and Irene asked. From the bank, Hubert said. It was a puzzling answer, Charles and Irene puzzled over it. Everyone drank mulled wine. Paul regarded them from the crib. Hubert was pleased to have been able to please Charles and Irene. They drank more wine.

Eric was born.

Hubert and Irene had a clandestine affair. It was important they felt that Charles not know. To this end they bought a bed which they installed in another house, a house some distance from the house in which Charles, Irene and Paul lived. The new bed was small but comfortable enough. Paul regarded Hubert and Irene thoughtfully. The affair lasted for twelve years and was considered very successful.

Hilda.

Charles watched Hilda growing from his window. To begin with, she was just a baby, then a four-year-old, then twelve years passed and she was Paul's age, sixteen. What a pretty young girl! Charles thought to himself. Paul agreed with Charles; he had already bitten the tips of Hilda's pretty breasts with his teeth.

DONALD BARTHELME "Will You Tell Me?"
Come Back, Dr Caligari (1964)

IN SECTION 16 I discussed chronology, and its possible rearrangement, in fiction. Another aspect of fictional time is duration, as measured by comparing the time events would have taken up in reality with the time taken to read about them. This factor affects narrative tempo, the sense we have that a novel is fast-moving or slow-moving. The adventure novel moves rapidly from one crisis to another – though the rendering of the critical situations may be artificially prolonged to increase suspense. The stream-of-consciousness novel lingers over every moment, however banal. A novel like *Middlemarch* seems to approximate to the rhythm of life itself, since so much of it consists of extended scenes in which the characters speak and interact as they would have done in real time; and for the original readers of that novel, buying it in bi-monthly instalments over a whole year, the correspondence in tempo between life and art would have seemed even closer. One of the disorienting features of Donald Barthelme's story is that it skims rapidly over the surface of emotional and sexual relationships that we are accustomed to seeing treated in fiction with detailed deliberation.

Barthelme, who died in 1989, was one of the key figures in American postmodernist fiction, whose stories continually tested the limits of fictional form. It is not, of course, only duration which is being handled rather unconventionally in the opening of this story: causality, continuity, cohesion, consistency in point of view – all the attributes that bind together the ingredients of realistic fiction into a smooth, easily assimilable discourse – are also discarded or disrupted. Motivation of the kind exemplified by the passage from *Middlemarch*, discussed in the preceding section, is not on offer. Barthelme implies that people do not act on rational motives, but in response to whim, chance and unconscious drives – that life is, in a word, "absurd". In this story he reports bizarre or alarming behaviour in a matter-of-fact, *faux-naif* style that owes something to primary-school reading books and children's "compositions" (an effect generated by the simple declarative sentences, absence of subordination, repetition of words in close proximity, and omission of quotation marks). The characters are hardly more defined than Janet and John and their parents, and sometimes seem as witless.

The first paragraph is technically a "scene", but a very laconic

187

account is given of it. The idea of receiving a baby as a Christmas present does not seem out of order to the recipients, and the donor's statement that he got it "from the bank" is merely "puzzling" to them. They calmly consume mulled wine without pursuing the question.

In the next, one-line paragraph it is curtly reported that "Eric was born" – we are not told, to whom, or in what temporal relationship to the arrival of Paul.

The third paragraph describes an affair between Hubert and Irene. There is a good deal of information about the couple's bed – indeed, rather more than we need – but little about their emotions, sexual pleasure, means of deceiving Charles, and all the other details that we expect of an adultery story. We don't know whether Hubert's gift of Paul preceded or followed his amorous interest in Irene. We infer that she took the infant along with her to their assignations, because "Paul regarded Hubert and Irene thoughtfully." Then we are told that "the affair lasted for twelve years and was considered very successful" – a judgment more usually applied to a marriage than an affair. The sequence of a sentence describing a particular moment in time, followed immediately by one summarizing the experience of twelve years, is highly disconcerting.

Another character, Hilda, is introduced in a one-word paragraph. From the next paragraph we infer that she is a child living nextdoor to Charles and Irene. Her growth from infancy to adolescence is summarized in a single sentence of stunning obviousness. If the adults act like children, the children seem disturbingly precocious: while Charles tritely registers that Hilda is a pretty girl, Paul has already "bitten the tips of Hilda's pretty breasts". In twenty-odd lines we have covered enough events to fill an entire novel in the hands of another writer. This kind of writing does indeed depend on the reader's familiarity with a more conventional and realistic fictional discourse to make its effect. Deviations can only be perceived against a norm.

42 Implication

"Don't you think you ought to come away from the window, darling?"

"Why?"

"You've got nothing on."

"All the better . . ." Out of respect for her delicacy I closed the window with a bang that drowned the end of my remark.

She was smiling at me. I went over and stood beside her. She looked appealing, resting on one elbow, with her dark hair sweeping over her smooth naked shoulder. I looked down on the top of her head.

Suddenly she blew.

"Wonderful Albert," she said.

I may say that my name is not Albert. It is Joe. Joe Lunn.

Myrtle looked up at me in sly inquiry.

I suppose I grinned.

After a while she paused.

"Men *are* lucky," she said, in a deep thoughtful tone. I said nothing: I thought it was no time for philosophical observations. I stared at the wall opposite.

Finally she stopped.

"Well?" I looked down just in time to catch her subsiding with a shocked expression on her face.

"Now," I said, "you'll have to wait again for your tea."

"Ah . . ." Myrtle gave a heavy, complacent sigh. Her eyes were closed.

In due course we had our tea.

WILLIAM COOPER *Scenes from Provincial Life* (1950)

A TRULY EXHAUSTIVE description of any event is impossible; from which it follows that all novels contain gaps and silences which the reader must fill, in order to "produce the text" (as poststructuralist critics say). But in some cases these gaps and silences are the result of unconscious evasions or suppressions on the writer's part (and no less interesting for that) while in others they are a conscious artistic strategy, to imply rather than state meaning.

Implication is a particularly useful technique in the treatment of sexuality. The novel has always been centrally concerned with erotic attraction and desire, but until recently the explicit description of sexual acts in literary fiction was prohibited. Innuendo was one solution.

> "Pray, my Dear," quoth my mother, "have you not forgot to wind up the clock?" . . . "Good God!" cried my father . . . "Did ever woman, since the creation of the world, interrupt a man with such a silly question." Pray, what was your father saying? . . . Nothing.

From this exchange between Tristram Shandy and his invented reader we may infer that his father was *doing* something, namely, begetting Tristram.

In the notoriously prudish Victorian period sex was treated with much greater reticence. Novels were for family reading, and could contain nothing that might, in the words of Dickens's Mr Podsnap, "bring a blush into the cheek of the young person." The scene in a recent BBC television adaptation of *Adam Bede*, depicting Arthur Donnithorne entwined on a couch with the half-naked Hetty Sorrel, has no equivalent in George Eliot's novel, the more innocent readers of which might well have assumed that Hetty was impregnated by a kiss. The non-consummation of Dorothea's marriage to Casaubon in *Middlemarch* is conveyed to the alert reader by the subtlest of hints, many of them metaphorical. As late as 1908, in *The Old Wives' Tale*, Arnold Bennett passes over Sophia's wedding night in silence, but suggests that it was an unpleasant and disillusioning experience by presenting it in a displaced form: the degrading spectacle of a public guillotining, all blood and phallic symbolism, which Gerald forces her to witness on their honeymoon.

By the time William Cooper published *Scenes from Provincial Life*, the boundaries of the permissible had been considerably extended, but it is unlikely that the particular activity in which his lovers are engaged here could have been plainly described in 1950 without attracting prosecution. Cooper goes to the very edge of explicitness, teasing his reader into the inferential construction of a scene that is both witty and erotic.

The narrator and his girlfriend have gone to bed in the country cottage that he shares with his friend Tom. He is just about to offer to make a cup of tea when he hears what he supposes to be the sound of Tom's car, and gets out of bed to check. Myrtle's remark tells us that he is naked. We can complete his reply, "All the better . . ." easily enough, since it seems to have the same structure as the Wolf's remarks to Red Riding Hood and we are told that the missing verbal phrase is indelicate. The next paragraph allows us to picture the naked narrator standing above his reclining, and also naked, mistress. "Suddenly she blew." With human subjects this verb usually takes an object, sometimes after a preposition like "on", but we must guess what it is. "'Wonderful Albert,' she said." Since the next paragraph eliminates the most obvious candidate for the identity of Albert, we are left in little doubt that it must be the familiar nickname of the object of "blew". (That this also provides an occasion for the narrator to introduce himself formally by name is an additional source of amusement.) We are not told what activity Myrtle "paused" from, but, as with Mr Shandy, it was not speaking, since she speaks after pausing. And so on. The abnormally short paragraphs emphasize the fact that much more is going on than is being said, or described.

Like Sterne's, Cooper's use of implication is not just an expedient: it carries a creative bonus of humour. A decade or so later, however, the *Lady Chatterley* trial swept away all the taboos that made such artful indirection mandatory, to the regret of many readers, and some writers. Kingsley Amis, for instance, though his stories are much concerned with sexual behaviour, has made something of a fetish of not attempting to describe the act itself.

There is a passage in his recent novel, *The Folks That Live on the Hill*, which makes the point and at the same time illustrates how implication is used in casual speech to refer to sex:

> "Let's have a nice early night tonight," said Desirée. This apparently straightforward proposal had several levels of meaning. An early night and no more meant something like what it said, was basically a temporal expression, advertised that there would be no later part to the evening, no social extension or excursion ... a *nice* early night meant not merely the exclusion of anything in the way of company but the inclusion of what it would be only fair, what it is indeed inescapable, to call sexual activity. This is ... better, much better, guessed at than described.

The explicit treatment of sexual acts is certainly another challenge to the novelist's artistry – how to avoid reiterating the language of pornography, how to defamiliarize the inherently limited repertoire of sexual acts – but not one that I propose to tackle in this book.

43 The Title

The last volume was written in fourteen days. In this achievement Reardon rose almost to heroic pitch, for he had much to contend with beyond the mere labour of composition. Scarcely had he begun when a sharp attack of lumbago fell upon him; for two or three days it was torture to support himself at the desk, and he moved about like a cripple. Upon this ensued headaches, sore throat, general enfeeblement. And before the end of the fortnight it was necessary to think of raising another small sum of money; he took his watch to the pawnbroker's (you can imagine that it would not stand as security for much), and sold a few more books. All this notwithstanding, here was the novel at length finished. When he had written "The End" he lay back, closed his eyes, and let time pass in blankness for a quarter of an hour.

It remained to determine the title. But his brain refused another effort; after a few minutes' feeble search he simply took the name of the chief female character, Margaret Home. That must do for the book. Already, with the penning of the last word, all its scenes, personages, dialogues had slipped away into oblivion; he knew and cared nothing more about them.

GEORGE GISSING *New Grub Street* (1891)

THE TITLE of a novel is part of the text – the first part of it, in fact, that we encounter – and therefore has considerable power to attract and condition the reader's attention. The titles of the earliest English novels were invariably the names of the central characters, *Moll Flanders*, *Tom Jones*, *Clarissa*. Fiction was modelling itself on, and sometimes disguising itself as, biography and autobiography. Later novelists realized that titles could indicate a theme (*Sense and Sensibility*), suggest an intriguing mystery (*The Woman in White*), or promise a certain kind of setting and atmosphere (*Wuthering Heights*). At some point in the nineteenth century they began to hitch their stories to resonant literary quotations (*Far From the Madding Crowd*), a practice that persists throughout the twentieth (*Where Angels Fear To Tread, A Handful of Dust, For Whom the Bell Tolls*), though it is now perhaps regarded as a little corny. The great modernists were drawn to symbolic or metaphorical titles – *Heart of Darkness, Ulysses, The Rainbow* – while more recent novelists often favour whimsical, riddling, off-beat titles, like *The Catcher in the Rye, A History of the World in 10½ Chapters, For Black Girls Who Consider Suicide When The Rainbow Is Not Enuf.*

For the novelist, choosing a title may be an important part of the creative process, bringing into sharper focus what the novel is supposed to be about. Charles Dickens, for instance, jotted down fourteen possible titles for the serial novel he planned to start early in 1854: *According to Cocker, Prove It, Stubborn Things, Mr Gradgrind's Facts, The Grindstone, Hard Times, Two and Two Are Four, Something Tangible, Our Hard-hearted Friend, Rust and Dust, Simple Arithmetic, A Matter of Calculation, A Mere Question of Figures, The Gradgrind Philosophy.* Most of these suggest that at this stage Dickens was preoccupied with the theme of Utilitarianism, as incarnated in Mr Gradgrind. His ultimate choice of *Hard Times* is consistent with the broader social concerns of the finished novel.

Edwin Reardon's indifference to the naming of his novel is a symptom of his loss of faith in his vocation. Having married imprudently after publishing a few novels of modest literary merit but limited circulation, he is compelled to churn out formulaic three-deckers, which he despises, at a crippling rate of production, to make ends meet. Gissing was expressing his own frustration as a struggling author in this book, and gave careful thought to its title. As he explained to a foreign correspondent, "Grub Street actually existed in London some hundred and fifty years ago. In Pope and his contemporaries it has become synonymous for wretched-authordom ... an abode not merely of poor, but of insignificant writers." By Gissing's time the literary market-place had become much bigger, more competitive, and publicity-conscious. Reardon is a memorable portrait of a writer who is not quite gifted enough, or cynical enough, to survive in this milieu. Neither is his idealistic young friend Biffen, who, still full of enthusiasm and idealism, plans to write a mould-breaking novel faithfully recording the banal life of an ordinary man. His announcement of its title provides one of *New Grub Street*'s few laughs: "I've decided to write a book called 'Mr Bailey, Grocer.'" When eventually published, it is admired by his friends but panned by the reviewers, and Biffen calmly commits suicide, Reardon having died from overwork in the meantime. *New Grub Street* is not a very cheerful book, but as a study in the pathology of the literary life it is unequalled, and still surprisingly relevant.

Novels have always been commodities as well as works of art, and commercial considerations can affect titles, or cause them to be changed. Thomas Hardy offered Macmillan a choice between *Fitzpiers at Hintock* and *The Woodlanders*; not surprisingly, they plumped for the latter. Ford Madox Ford's *The Good Soldier* was originally entitled *The Saddest Story* (of course); but it came out in the middle of the Great War, and his publishers persuaded him to go for a less depressing, more patriotic title. The title of Martin Amis's second novel, *Dead Babies* (1975) was apparently too shocking to his first paperback publishers, who issued it two years later as *Dark Secrets*. The American publishers of my *How Far Can You Go?* persuaded me to change its name to *Souls and Bodies* on the grounds that the British title would be shelved by American bookshops under How To Do It books, a silly argument to which I have always regretted yielding. (I don't know what they would have done with Carol Clewlow's *A Woman's Guide to Adultery*, or Georges Perec's *Life: a User's Manual*.) I wanted to call my third novel *The British Museum Had Lost Its Charm*, a line from the song, "A Foggy Day (in London Town)", but the Gershwin Publishing Corporation wouldn't let me; so I had to change it at the last minute to *The British Museum is Falling Down*, though the inspiration of the song left its trace in the fog-shrouded one-day action of the novel. Perhaps titles always mean more to authors than to readers, who, as every writer knows, frequently forget or garble the names of books they claim to admire. I have been credited with novels called *Changing Wives*, *Trading Places* and *Small Change*, and Professor Bernard Crick once mentioned in a letter that he had enjoyed my *Having It Off*, but perhaps he was having me on. (I couldn't tell which of my books he was referring to.)

44 Ideas

"Please, I must do something. Shall I clean your boots? Look, I'll get down and lick them." And, my brothers, believe it or kiss my sharries, I got down on my knees and pushed my red yahzick out a mile and half to lick his grahzny vonny boots. But all this veck did was to kick me not too hard on the rot. So then it seemed to me that it would not bring on the sickness and pain if I just gripped his ankles with my rookers tight round them and brought this grahzny bratchny down to the floor. So I did this and he got a real bolshy surprise, coming down crack amid loud laughter from the vonny audience. But viddying him on the floor I could feel the whole horrible feeling coming over me, so I gave him my rooker to lift him up skorry and up he came. Then just as he was going to give me a real nasty and earnest tolchock on the litso Dr Brodsky said:

"All right, that will do very well." Then this horrible veck sort of bowed and danced off like an actor while the lights came up on me blinking and with my rot square for howling. Dr Brodsky said to the audience: "Our subject is, you see, impelled towards the good by, paradoxically, being impelled towards evil. The intention to act violently is accompanied by strong feelings of physical distress. To counter these the subject has to switch to a diametrically opposed attitude. Any questions?"

"Choice," rumbled a rich deep goloss. I viddied it belonged to the prison charlie. "He has no real choice, has he? Self-interest, fear of physical pain, drove him to that grotesque act of self-abasement. Its insincerity was clearly to be seen. He ceases to be a wrongdoer. He ceases also to be a creature capable of moral choice."

ANTHONY BURGESS *A Clockwork Orange* (1962)

THE TERM "novel of ideas" usually suggests a book light on narrative interest, in which abnormally articulate characters bat philosophical questions back and forth between themselves, with brief intervals for eating, drinking and flirtation. It is a venerable tradition which goes back to Plato's Dialogues, but it has a high rate of obsolescence. In the nineteenth century, for example, hundreds of novels were published in which the rival claims and merits of High- and Low-Church Anglicanism, Roman Catholicism, Dissent and Honest Doubt were expounded in this fashion, with a dash of melodrama thrown in for the sake of the circulating libraries, and most of them are utterly and deservedly forgotten. The ideas no longer interest, and their exposition has deprived the characters and action of any life.

A name sometimes given to that kind of novel is *roman à thèse*, the novel with a thesis, and it is significant that we have borrowed it from the French language. The novel of ideas, whether it has a specific thesis, or is more broadly speculative and dialectical, has always seemed more at home in Continental European literature than in English. Perhaps this has something to do with the often-noted absence of a self-defined intelligentsia in English society, a fact sometimes attributed to the fact that Britain has not experienced a Revolution since the seventeenth century, and has remained comparatively untouched by the convulsions of modern European history. Whatever the reason, Dostoevsky, Thomas Mann, Robert Musil, Jean-Paul Sartre, are novelists for whom there is no real equivalent to be found in modern English literature. Perhaps D. H. Lawrence came closest, especially in *Women in Love*, but the ideas debated and expounded in his work were very personal, not to say eccentric, and sat at an odd angle to the main current of modern European thought.

Of course any novel worth more than a cursory glance contains ideas, provokes ideas, and can be discussed in terms of ideas. But by "novel of ideas" one means to denote a novel in which ideas seem to be the source of the work's energy, originating and shaping and maintaining its narrative momentum – rather than, say, emotions, moral choice, personal relationships, or the mutations of human fortune. In this sense English novelists have been more

198

comfortable dealing directly with ideas either in comic and satirical
fiction (including the campus novel) or in various forms of fable
and utopian or dystopian fantasy. I have glanced earlier at examples
of both types – Malcolm Bradbury's *The History Man* and Samuel
Butler's *Erewhon*, for instance. Anthony Burgess's *A Clockwork
Orange* belongs to the second type.

Anthony Burgess has recorded in his autobiography that this
novel was originally inspired by the delinquent behaviour of the
young hooligans who went under the tribal names of Mods and
Rockers in Britain *circa* 1960, and the perennial problem they
posed: how can a civilized society protect itself against anarchic
violence without compromising its own ethical standards? "I saw,"
the maverick Catholic Burgess recalls, "that the novel would have
to have a metaphysical or theological base ... the artificial
extirpation of free will through scientific conditioning; the question
whether this might not ... be a greater evil than the free choice of
evil."

The story is told in the confessional, colloquial mode, by Alex, a
vicious young hoodlum who is convicted of appalling crimes of sex
and violence. To obtain his release from prison, he agrees to
undergo Pavlovian aversion therapy, in which exposure to films
revelling in the kind of acts he committed is accompanied by
nausea-inducing drugs. The effectiveness of the treatment is
demonstrated in the scene from which this extract is taken. Before
an audience of criminologists, Alex is taunted and abused (by an
actor hired for the purpose), but as soon as he feels an urge to
retaliate he is overcome with nausea and reduced to grovelling
appeasement. The prison chaplain asks whether he has not been
dehumanized in the process.

Like many similar novels of ideas – Morris's *News from Nowhere*,
Huxley's *Brave New World*, Orwell's *Nineteen Eighty-four*, for
example – *A Clockwork Orange* is set in the future (though not very
far) so that the novelist can set up the terms of his ethical debate
with dramatic starkness, and without the constraints of social
realism. Burgess's masterstroke was to combine this well-tried
strategy with a highly inventive version of what I called, in
discussing Salinger's *The Catcher in the Rye*, "teenage *skaz*" (see

Section 4). Teenagers and criminals alike use slang as a tribal shibboleth, to distinguish themselves from adult, respectable society. Burgess imagines that in the England of the 1970s, youthful delinquents have adopted a style of speech heavily influenced by Russian (a conceit that would not have seemed so outlandish in the days of the Sputnik as it does now). Alex tells his story to an implied audience of "droogs" (Russian *drugi*: friends) in this argot, which is known as *nadsat* (the Russian suffix for "teen"), though he uses standard English in dialogue with officialdom. There is a bit of Cockney rhyming slang in the dialect ("charlie" = Charlie Chaplin = chaplain) but basically it's derived from Russian. You don't have to know Russian, however, to guess that, in the second sentence of this extract, "sharries" means buttocks, "yahzick" tongue, "grahzny" dirty and "vonny" stinking, especially if you've read the previous 99 pages of the novel. Burgess intended that his readers should gradually learn the language of *nadsat* as they went along, inferring the meaning of the loanwords from the context and other clues. The reader thus undergoes a kind of Pavlovian conditioning, though reinforced by reward (being able to follow the story) rather than punishment. A bonus is that the stylized language keeps the appalling acts that are described in it at a certain aesthetic distance, and protects us from being too revolted by them – or too excited. When the novel was made into a film by Stanley Kubrick, the power of conditioning was given a further ironic demonstration: Kubrick's brilliant translation of its violent action into the more illusionistic and accessible visual medium made the movie an incitement to the very hooliganism it was examining, and caused the director to withdraw it.

45 The Non-Fiction Novel

By and by, we note a thickset Individual, in round hat and
peruke, arm-and-arm with some servant, seemingly of the
Runner or Courier sort; he also issues through Villequier's
door; starts a shoebuckle as he passes one of the sentries,
stoops down to clasp it again; is however, by the Glass-
coachman, still more cheerfully admitted. And *now*, is his fare
complete? Not yet; the Glass-coachman still waits. – Alas! and
the false Chambermaid has warned Gouvion that she thinks
the Royal Family will fly this very night; and Gouvion, distrust-
ing his own glazed eyes, has sent express for Lafayette; and
Lafayette's Carriage, flaring with lights, rolls this moment
through the inner Arch of the Carrousel, – where a Lady
shaded in broad gypsy-hat, and leaning on the arm of a
servant, also of the Runner or Courier sort, stands aside to let
it pass, and has even the whim to touch a spoke of it with her
badine, – light little magic rod which she calls *badine*, such as
the Beautiful then wore. The flare of Lafayette's Carriage rolls
past: all is found quiet in the Court-of-Princes; sentries at
their post; Majesties' Apartments closed in smooth rest. Your
false Chambermaid must have been mistaken? Watch thou,
Gouvion, with Argus' vigilance; for, of a truth, treachery is
within these walls.

But where is the Lady that stood aside in gypsy-hat, and
touched the wheel-spoke with her *badine*? O Reader, that Lady
that touched the wheel-spoke was the Queen of France! She
has issued safe through that inner Arch, into the Carrousel
itself; but not into the Rue de l'Echelle. Flurried by the rattle
and rencounter, she took the right hand not the left; neither she
nor her Courier knows Paris; he indeed is no Courier, but a
loyal stupid *ci-devant* Bodyguard disguised as one. They are
off, quite wrong, over the Pont Royal and River; roaming
disconsolate in the Rue de Bac; far from the Glass-coachman,

who still waits. Waits, with flutter of heart; with thoughts –
which he must button close up, under his jarvie-surtout!

Midnight clangs from all the City-steeples; one precious
hour has been spent so; most mortals are asleep. The Glass-
coachman waits; and in what mood! A brother jarvie drives up,
enters into conversation; is answered cheerfully in jarvie-dia-
lect: the brothers of the whip exchange a pinch of snuff; decline
drinking together, and part with good night. Be the Heavens
blest! here at length is the Queen-lady, in gypsy-hat; safe after
perils; who has had to inquire her way. She too is admitted; her
Courier jumps aloft, as the other, who is also a disguised
Bodyguard, has done; and now, O Glass-coachman of a thousand, – Count Fersen, for the Reader sees it is thou, – drive!

THOMAS CARLYLE The French Revolution (1837)

THE "NON-FICTION NOVEL" is a term originally coined by Truman
Capote to describe his *In Cold Blood: A True Account of a Multiple
Murder and Its Consequences* (1966). In 1959 four members of a
model midwestern family were brutally and pointlessly murdered
by a pair of rootless psychopaths from America's underclass.
Capote investigated the family's history and its social milieu,
interviewed the criminals on Death Row and witnessed their
eventual execution. Then he wrote an account of the crime and its
aftermath in which these scrupulously researched facts were
integrated into a gripping narrative that in style and structure was
indistinguishable from a novel. It started something of a vogue for
documentary narrative in recent times, high points of which have
been books like Tom Wolfe's *Radical Chic* and *The Right Stuff*,
Norman Mailer's *Armies of the Night* and *The Executioner's Song*,
and Thomas Keneally's *Schindler's Ark*. "Non-fiction novel" is a
self-evidently paradoxical phrase, and it is not surprising that such
books are often the object of some suspicion and controversy as to
their generic identity. Are they works of history, reportage, or
imagination? *Schindler's Ark*, for instance (based on the true and

extraordinary story of a German businessman who used his position as an employer of forced labour in Nazi-occupied Poland to save the lives of many Jews) was published as non-fiction in America, but won the Booker prize for fiction in Britain.

Tom Wolfe began his literary career as a journalist covering the more bizarre manifestations of American popular culture, and then began to develop his themes in the form of extended narratives like *Radical Chic*, his wickedly funny account of trendy New York intellectuals hosting a fund-raising event for the Black Panthers. Other writers were working in a similar vein in America in the nineteen-sixties and -seventies, and Wolfe saw himself as leading a new literary movement which he called "The New Journalism", the title of an anthology he edited in 1973. In the Introduction to this volume he claimed that the New Journalism had taken over the novel's traditional task of describing contemporary social reality, which had been neglected by literary novelists too obsessed with myth, fabulation and metafictional tricks to notice what was going on around them. (Later Wolfe himself tried, with some success, to revive the panoramic social novel in *Bonfire of the Vanities*.)

In the non-fiction novel, new journalism, "faction", or whatever one calls it, the novelistic techniques generate an excitement, intensity and emotive power that orthodox reporting or historiography do not aspire to, while for the reader the guarantee that the story is "true" gives it a compulsion that no fiction can quite equal. Although it is a popular form of narrative today, it has in fact been around for quite a long time in various guises. The novel itself as a literary form evolved partly out of early journalism – broadsheets, pamphlets, criminals' "confessions", accounts of disasters, battles and extraordinary happenings, which were circulated to an eagerly credulous readership as true stories, though they almost certainly contained an element of invention. Daniel Defoe began his career as a novelist by imitating these allegedly documentary narratives, in works like *True Relation of the Apparition of one Mrs Veal*, and *Journal of the Plague Year*. Before the development of "scientific" historical method in the late nineteenth century there was a good deal of cross-fertilization between the novel and historiography:

Scott regarded himself as being as much a historian as a novelist, and in *The French Revolution* Carlyle wrote more like a novelist than a modern historian.

In the introduction to his anthology of New Journalism, Tom Wolfe distinguished four techniques it had borrowed from the novel: (1) telling the story through scenes rather than summary; (2) preferring dialogue to reported speech; (3) presenting events from the point of view of a participant rather than from some impersonal perspective; (4) incorporating the kind of detail about people's appearance, clothes, possessions, body language, etc. which act as indices of class, character, status and social milieu in the realistic novel. Carlyle used all these devices in *The French Revolution* (1837), and a few others that Wolfe omitted to mention, such as the "present historic" tense, and the involvement of the reader as narratee, to create the illusion that we are witnessing or eavesdropping on historical events.

The passage quoted describes the flight of Louis XVI, Marie-Antoinette and their children in June 1792 from the palace of The Tuileries where they had been confined by the National Assembly, partly as hostages against an invasion of France by neighbouring monarchist states. The Swedish Count Fersen masterminded the night escape, from which Carlyle extracts the maximum amount of narrative interest. First (just before the quoted passage) he describes a common "glass-coach" (privately-hired carriage) waiting in the Rue de l'Echelle near to the Tuileries. At intervals, unidentified and shrouded figures slip through an unguarded door of the palace and are admitted to this vehicle. One of them, who, we might guess, is the King in disguise, "starts a shoebuckle" as he passes a sentry – a suspense-enhancing device of a kind familiar in adventure-stories. Carlyle gives a narrative voice to suspense: "And *now*, is his fare complete? Not yet . . ." Meanwhile, inside the palace, suspicions have been aroused, jeopardizing the whole enterprise. In a series of rapid statements, telescoping time, Carlyle recapitulates these developments and brings his narrative back to the present, "this moment" when Lafayette, Commander of the National Guard, arrives to investigate. The last of the passengers awaited by the glass-coach, her face screened by a gypsy-hat, is

Marie-Antoinette, who has to stand aside as the coach of Lafayette wheels through the gate. As if to illustrate the narrowness of her escape, she touches the spoke of the wheel with a little ornamental rod called a *badine* "such as the Beautiful then wore". Throughout the passage Carlyle uses clothing in a way that Tom Wolfe would approve of, to indicate both the real status of the personages and the lengths they have to go to to disguise it.

The Queen and her bodyguard are so ignorant of the geography of their own capital that they immediately get lost, a nicely pointed irony which also increases the suspense, registered by the coachman's "flutter of heart . . . under his jarvie-surtout". The reader has probably already guessed that this person is Count Fersen himself, but by delaying the revelation of his identity Carlyle adds more mystery to the narrative brew. Fersen is the main point-of-view character in the second paragraph. "Be the Heavens blest!" is his exclamation or unvoiced thought when Marie-Antoinette finally appears. The effect of this narrative method is of course to make the reader identify with the plight of the fleeing royals, and perhaps the scene does betray Carlyle's fundamental emotional sympathies, although in the book as a whole he presents the Revolution as a Nemesis which the *ancien régime* brought down upon itself.

Carlyle steeped himself in the documents of the French Revolution like a historian, then synthesized and dramatized this mass of data like a moralizing novelist. No wonder Dickens was enraptured by the book, and carried it about with him everywhere on its first publication. Not only *A Tale of Two Cities*, but also Dickens's panoramic novels of English society were indebted to its example. Whether every detail in this extract had a documentary source, I do not know. Marie-Antoinette's gesture with her *badine* is so specific that I don't think Carlyle would have risked inventing it, though he cites no authority. The idea of Count Fersen having his impersonation of a cab-driver tested by conversation with the genuine article is more suspicious, because it heightens the suspense so conveniently. Perhaps anticipating this reaction, Carlyle gives two sources for the episode in a footnote. This kind of writing thrives on the old adage that truth is stranger than fiction.

46 Metafiction

Hunchbacks, fat ladies, fools – that no one chose what he was was unbearable. In the movies he'd meet a beautiful young girl in the funhouse; they'd have hairs-breadth escapes from real dangers; he'd do and say the right things; she also; in the end they'd be lovers: their dialogue lines would match up; he'd be perfectly at ease; she'd not only like him well enough, she'd think he was *marvellous*; she'd lie awake thinking about *him*, instead of vice versa – the way *his* face looked in different lights and how he stood and exactly what he'd said – and yet that would be only one small episode in his wonderful life, among many others. Not a *turning point* at all. What had happened in the toolshed was nothing. He hated, he loathed his parents! One reason for not writing a lost-in-the-funhouse story is that either everybody's felt what Ambrose feels, in which case it goes without saying, or else no normal person feels such things, in which case Ambrose is a freak. "Is anything more tiresome, in fiction, than the problems of sensitive adolescents?" And it's all too long and rambling, as if the author. For all a person knows the first time through, the end could be just around any corner; perhaps, *not impossibly* it's been within reach any number of times. On the other hand he may be scarcely past the start, with everything yet to get through, an intolerable idea.

JOHN BARTH *Lost in the Funhouse* (1968)

METAFICTION is fiction about fiction: novels and stories that call attention to their fictional status and their own compositional procedures. The grandaddy of all metafictional novels was *Tristram Shandy*, whose narrator's dialogues with his imaginary readers are only one of many ways in which Sterne foregrounds the gap between art and life that conventional realism seeks to conceal. Metafiction, then, is not a modern invention; but it is a mode that many contemporary writers find particularly appealing, weighed down, as they are, by their awareness of their literary antecedents, oppressed by the fear that whatever they might have to say has been said before, and condemned to self-consciousness by the climate of modern culture.

In the work of English novelists, metafictional discourse most commonly occurs in the form of "asides" in novels primarily focused on the traditional novelistic task of describing character and action. These passages acknowledge the artificiality of the conventions of realism even as they employ them; they disarm criticism by anticipating it; they flatter the reader by treating him or her as an intellectual equal, sophisticated enough not to be thrown by the admission that a work of fiction is a verbal construction rather than a slice of life. This, for instance, is how Margaret Drabble begins Part Three of her novel, *The Realms of Gold*, after a long, realistic and well-observed account of a suburban dinner party given by the more repressed of her two heroines:

And that is enough, for the moment, of Janet Bird. More than enough, you might reasonably think, for her life is slow, even slower than its description, and her dinner party seemed to go on too long to her, as it did to you. Frances Wingate's life moves much faster. (Though it began rather slowly, in these pages – a tactical error, perhaps, and the idea of starting her off in a more manic moment has frequently suggested itself, but the reasons against such an opening are stronger, finally, than the reasons for it.)

There are echoes here of *Tristram Shandy*, utterly different though Margaret Drabble's novel is in tone and subject matter, in the humorously apologetic address to the reader and the highlighting of the problems of narrative construction, especially in respect of "duration" (see Section 41). Such admissions however do not occur frequently enough to fundamentally disturb the novel's project, which is to examine the lot of educated women in modern society in a fictional story that is detailed, convincing and satisfying in a traditional way.

With other modern writers, mostly non-British – the Argentinian Borges, the Italian Calvino and the American John Barth come to mind, though John Fowles also belongs in this company – metafictional discourse is not so much a loophole or alibi by means of which the writer can occasionally escape the constraints of traditional realism; rather, it is a central preoccupation and source of inspiration. John Barth once wrote an influential essay entitled "The Literature of Exhaustion", in which, without actually using the word "metafiction", he invoked it as the means by which "an artist may paradoxically turn the felt ultimacies of our time into material and means for his work." There are, of course, dissenting voices, like Tom Wolfe's (see the preceding section), who see such writing as symptomatic of a decadent, narcissistic literary culture. "Another story about a writer writing a story! Another *regressus ad infinitum*! Who doesn't prefer art that at least overtly imitates something other than its own processes?" But that complaint was voiced by Barth himself, in "Life-Story", one of the pieces in his collection, *Lost in the Funhouse*. Metafictional writers have a sneaky habit of incorporating potential criticism into their texts and thus "fictionalizing" it. They also like to undermine the credibility of more orthodox fiction by means of parody.

The title story of *Lost in the Funhouse* traces Barth's attempt to write a story about a family outing to Atlantic City in the nineteen-forties. The central character is the adolescent Ambrose, who is accompanying his parents, his brother Peter, his uncle Karl, and Magda, a childhood playmate now a teenager like himself, and therefore an object of sexual interest. (Ambrose wistfully remembers a pre-pubescent game of Masters and Slaves in the course of which Magda led him to the toolshed and "purchased clemency at a surprising price set by herself.") Essentially it is a story of adolescent yearning for freedom and fulfilment, an "exhausted" footnote to the great tradition of the autobiographical-novel-about-boy-who-will-grow-up-to-be-a-writer, such as *A Portrait of the Artist as a Young Man* and *Sons and Lovers*. It is intended to reach

its climax in a boardwalk funhouse, where Ambrose is to get lost –
though in what circumstances, and with what outcome, the author
is never able to decide.

In the passage quoted here, the questioning of conventional
fictional representation is artfully doubled. First, Ambrose's
romantic longings are rendered through a parody of Hollywood's
wish-fulfilment fantasies: "In the movies he'd meet a beautiful
young girl in the funhouse; they'd have hairs-breadth escapes from
real dangers . . . their dialogue lines would match up . . ." This is
obviously bad art, in contrast to which the rendering of Ambrose's
actual frustrated, tongue-tied, alienated existence seems realistically authentic. But then *that* representation is undermined by a
typical metafictional move – what Erving Goffman has called
"breaking frame", an effect also illustrated by the passage from
Margaret Drabble's novel. The authorial voice abruptly intervenes
to comment that Ambrose's situation is either too familiar or too
deviant to be worth describing, which is as if a movie actor were to
turn to the camera suddenly and say, "This is a lousy script." In
the manner of *Tristram Shandy*, the voice of a carping critic is
heard, attacking the whole project: 'Is anything more tiresome, in
fiction, than the problems of sensitive adolescents?" The author
seems to be suddenly losing faith in his own story, and cannot even
summon up the energy to finish the sentence in which he confesses
that it is too long and rambling.

Writers of course often lose faith in what they are doing, but do
not normally admit this in their texts. To do so is to acknowledge
failure – but also tacitly to claim such failure as more interesting
and more truthful than conventional "success". Kurt Vonnegut
begins his *Slaughterhouse Five*, a novel as remarkable for its
stunning frame-breaking effects as for its imaginative use of time-
shift (see Section 16), by confessing: "I would hate to tell you what
this lousy little book cost me in money and anxiety and time." In
his first chapter he describes the difficulty of writing about an
event like the destruction of Dresden, and says, addressing the
man who commissioned it, "It is so short and jumbled and jangled,
Sam, because there is nothing intelligent to say about a massacre."
The personal experience on which it is based was so traumatic and

so painful to return to that Vonnegut compares his fate to that of Lot's wife in the Old Testament, who showed her human nature by looking back upon the destruction of Sodom and Gomorrah but was punished by being turned into a pillar of salt.

> I've finished my war book now. The next one I write is going to be fun.
> This one is a failure, and it had to be, since it was written by a pillar of salt.

In fact, so far from being a failure, *Slaughterhouse Five* is Vonnegut's masterpiece, and one of the most memorable novels of the postwar period in English.

47 The Uncanny

The contest was brief. I was frantic with every species of wild excitement, and felt within my single arm the energy and power of a multitude. In a few seconds I forced him by sheer strength against the wainscoting, and thus, getting him at mercy, plunged my sword, with brute ferocity, repeatedly through and through his bosom.

At that instant some person tried the latch of the door. I hastened to prevent an intrusion, and then immediately returned to my dying antagonist. But what human language can adequately portray *that* astonishment, *that* horror which possessed me at the spectacle then presented to view? The brief moment in which I averted my eyes had been sufficient to produce, apparently, a material change in the arrangements at the upper or farther end of the room. A large mirror, – so at first it seemed to me in my confusion – now stood where none had been perceptible before; and, as I stepped up to it in extremity of terror, mine own image, but with features all pale and dabbled in blood, advanced to meet me with a feeble and tottering gait.

Thus it appeared, I say, but was not. It was my antagonist – it was Wilson, who then stood before me in the agonies of his dissolution. His mask and cloak lay, where he had thrown them, upon the floor. Not a thread in all his raiment – not a line in all the marked and singular lineaments of his face which was not, even in the most absolute identity, *mine own!*

EDGAR ALLAN POE "William Wilson" (1839)

THE FRENCH (originally Bulgarian) structuralist critic Tzvetan Todorov has proposed that tales of the supernatural divide into three categories: the marvellous, in which no rational explanation of the supernatural phenomena is possible; the uncanny, in which it is; and the fantastic, in which the narrative hesitates undecidably between a natural and a supernatural explanation.

An example of the fantastic in this sense is Henry James's famous ghost story *The Turn of the Screw*. A young woman is appointed governess to two young orphaned children in an isolated country house, and sees figures who apparently resemble a former governess and the villainous manservant who seduced her, both now dead. She is convinced that these evil spirits have a hold over the young children in her care, from which she seeks to free them. In the climax she struggles with the male ghost for the possession of Miles's soul, and the boy dies: "his little heart, dispossessed, had stopped." The story (which is narrated by the governess) can be, and has been, read in two different ways, corresponding to Todorov's "marvellous" and "uncanny": either the ghosts are "real", and the governess is involved in a heroic struggle against supernatural evil, or they are projections of her own neuroses and sexual hang-ups, with which she frightens the little boy in her charge literally to death. Critics have vainly tried to prove the correctness of one or other of these readings. The point of the story is that everything in it is capable of a double interpretation, thus rendering it impervious to the reader's scepticism.

Todorov's typology is a useful provocation to thought on the subject, though his nomenclature (*le merveilleux, l'étrange, le fantastique*) is confusing when translated into English, in which "the fantastic" is usually in unambiguous opposition to "the real", and "the uncanny" seems a more appropriate term with which to characterize a story like *The Turn of the Screw*. One can also quibble about its application. Todorov himself is obliged to concede that there are borderline works which must be categorized as "fantastic-uncanny" or "fantastic-marvellous". Edgar Allan Poe's "William Wilson" is such a work. Though Todorov reads it as an allegory or parable of an uneasy conscience, therefore "uncanny" in his own terms, it contains that element of ambiguity which he sees as essential to the fantastic.

"William Wilson" is a *Doppelgänger* story. The eponymous narrator, who admits his own depravity at the outset, describes his first boarding-school as a quaint old building in which "it was difficult, at any given time, to say with certainty upon which of its two stories one happened to be" (the pun is surely intended). There he had a rival who bore the same name, was admitted to the school on the same day, had the same birthday, and bore a close physical resemblance to the narrator, which he exploited by satirically mimicking the latter's behaviour. The only respect in which this double differs from the narrator is in being unable to speak above a whisper.

Wilson graduates to Eton, and then Oxford, plunging deeper and deeper into dissipation. Whenever he commits some particularly heinous act, a man invariably turns up dressed in identical clothes, concealing his face, but hissing "William Wilson" in an unmistakable whisper. Exposed by his double for cheating at cards, Wilson flees abroad, but everywhere he is pursued by the *Doppelgänger*. "Again and again, in secret communion with my own spirit, I would demand the questions 'Who is he? – whence came he? – and what are his objects?'" In Venice, Wilson is just about to keep an adulterous assignation when he feels "a light hand placed upon my shoulder, and that ever-remembered, low, damnable *whisper* within my ear." Beside himself with rage, Wilson attacks his tormentor with his sword.

Obviously one can explain the double as Wilson's hallucinatory externalization of his own conscience or better self, and there are several clues to this effect in the text. For example, Wilson says that his schoolboy double had a "moral sense . . . far keener than my own," and nobody but himself seems to be struck by the physical resemblance between them. But the story would not have its haunting and suggestive power if it did not invest the uncanny phenomenon with a credible concreteness. The climax of the novel is particularly artful in its ambiguous reference to the mirror. From a rational standpoint, we might hypothesize that, in a delirium of guilt and self-hatred, Wilson has mistaken his own mirror-image for his double, attacked it and mutilated himself in the process; but from Wilson's point of view it seems that the reverse has happened – what he at first takes to be a reflection of himself turns out to be the bleeding, dying figure of his double.

Classic tales of the uncanny invariably use "I" narrators, and imitate documentary forms of discourse like confessions, letters and depositions to make the events more credible. (Compare Mary Shelley's *Frankenstein*, and Robert Louis Stevenson's *Dr Jekyll and Mr Hyde*.) And these narrators tend to write in a conventionally "literary" style which in another context one might find tiresomely cliché-ridden: for example, "wild excitement", "power of a multitude", "sheer strength", "brute ferocity" in the first paragraph of this extract. The whole Gothic-horror tradition to which Poe belongs, and to which he gave a powerful impetus, is replete with good–bad writing of this kind. The predictability of the rhetoric, its very lack of originality, guarantees the reliability of the narrator and makes his uncanny experience more believable.

48 Narrative Structure

THE HAND

I smacked my little boy. My anger was powerful. Like justice.
Then I discovered no feeling in the hand. I said, "Listen, I want
to explain the complexities to you." I spoke with seriousness
and care, particularly of fathers. He asked, when I finished, if I
wanted him to forgive me. I said yes. He said no. Like trumps.

ALL RIGHT

"I don't mind variations," she said, "but this feels wrong." I
said, "It feels all right to me." She said, "To you, wrong is right."
I said, "I didn't say right, I said all right." "Big difference," she
said. I said, "Yes, I'm critical. My mind never stops. To me
almost everything is always wrong. My standard is pleasure. To
me, this is all right." She said, "To me it stinks." I said, "What
do you like?" She said, "Like I don't like. I'm not interested in
being superior to my sensations. I won't live long enough for all
right."

MA

I said, "Ma, do you know what happened?" She said, "Oh, my
God."

LEONARD MICHAELS *I Would Have Saved Them
If I Could* (1975)

THE STRUCTURE of a narrative is like the framework of girders that holds up a modern high-rise building: you can't see it, but it determines the edifice's shape and character. The effects of a novel's structure, however, are experienced not in space but over time – often quite a long time. Henry Fielding's *Tom Jones*, for instance, which Coleridge thought had one of the three greatest plots in literature (the other two were both plays, *Oedipus Rex* and Ben Jonson's *The Alchemist*), runs to nearly 900 pages in the Penguin edition. As previously noted (Section 36) it has 198 Chapters, divided into eighteen Books, the first six of which are set in the country, the next six on the road, and the final six in London. Exactly in the middle of the novel most of the major characters pass through the same inn, but without meeting in combinations which would bring the story to a premature conclusion. The novel is packed with surprises, enigmas and suspense, and ends with a classic Reversal and Discovery.

It is impossible to illustrate the operation of such a complex plot with a short quotation, but the work of the American writer Leonard Michaels, who writes some of the shortest stories I know, allows us to examine the process in microcosm. I have cheated a little in as much as the pieces reproduced here were not designed to stand entirely alone, but belong to a cluster of short narratives, collectively entitled "Eating Out", some of which are interrelated by being concerned with the same character or characters. "Ma", for instance, is one of a series of dialogue-stories about the narrator and his mother. The whole sequence amounts to more than the sum of its parts. Nevertheless, each part is a self-contained narrative, with its own title. Even out of context the meaning of "Ma" is clear enough: the Jewish mother always expects the worst. Perhaps this text hovers on the boundary between the story and the joke. But there is no generic ambiguity about "The Hand", which conforms to the classic notion of narrative unity. It has a beginning, a middle and an end as defined by Aristotle: a beginning is what requires nothing to precede it, an end is what requires nothing to follow it, and a middle needs something both before and after it.

The beginning of "The Hand" consists of its first three sentences, describing the narrator's punishment of his son. We do not need to know what behaviour has provoked this act. The first sentence, "I smacked my little boy" establishes a familiar domestic context. The emphasis is all on the narrator's emotions. "My anger was powerful. Like justice." The verbless sentence is a kind of afterthought, justifying the relief of tension, the exercise of power.

The middle of the story describes the waning of the narrator's confidence in his own righteousness, and his attempt to justify his behaviour to his son. First there is a kind of psychosomatic symptom: "Then I discovered no feeling in the hand." The hand is both a synecdoche and a metaphor for the "unfeeling" parent. "I said, 'Listen, I want to explain the complexities to you.'" Structurally, the whole story turns on the axis of this line, the only direct speech in it. Formally it favours the narrator, because direct speech always conveys a stronger sense of the speaker's presence than reported speech. But the use of the adult word, "complexities", to a little boy gives the game away. In spite of his professed anxiety to communicate with his son ("I spoke with seriousness and care, particularly of fathers") the narrator is wrestling with his own conscience.

The ending contains a neat double reversal. First, the little boy proves to have a penetrating insight into his father's state of mind: "He asked me, when I finished, if I wanted him to forgive me." Secondly the normal power relations between father and son are reversed: "I said yes. He said no." The symmetry of these sentences echoes the symmetry of the plot. The narrator's "Like trumps" ruefully acknowledges defeat.

Plot has been defined by a modern disciple of Aristotle (R. S. Crane) as "a completed process of change". A good deal of modern fiction has, however, avoided the kind of closure implied in the word "completed" and has focused on states of being in which change is minimal. "All Right" is a case in point. It has a much more elusive narrative structure than "The Hand" – less obvious, less easy to follow, the divisions between beginning, middle, and end less certain. It uses techniques I discussed earlier under the headings of "Staying on the Surface" and "Implication", consisting almost entirely of dialogue, and withholding information about the characters' private thoughts and motives. We infer that the couple are engaged in some unconventional sexual act, but it is impossible and unnecessary to know what exactly it is. The beginning perhaps consists of the woman's statement of her uneasiness; the middle of the narrator's self-justification and the woman's reiteration of her displeasure ("To me it stinks"); and the ending of her refusal to play the game of sexual dilettantism. But the story lacks the reassuring movement of "The Hand" towards the narrator's moment of truth. It is not clear why he is telling us this story, for he reports the woman's harsh strictures on him without comment. Whereas "The Hand" is instantly comprehensible, we have to re-read "All Right" several times to make sense of it, sounding the dialogue in our heads. ("She said, '*Like* I don't like . . . I won't live long enough for *all right*.'") The text seems to be about deadlock rather than discovery, and its unity owes more to its internal verbal echoes, especially of the word "right" highlighted in the title, than to its narrative structure. In that respect it offers itself as a kind of prose poem – either that, or a tantalizing fragment of some longer story.

49 Aporia

Where now? Who now? When now? Unquestioning. I, say I.
Unbelieving. Questions, hypotheses, call them that. Keep going,
going on, call that going, call that on. Can it be that one day, off
it goes on, that one day I simply stayed in, in where, instead of
going out, in the old way, out to spend day and night as far away
as possible, it wasn't far. Perhaps that is how it began. You think
you are simply resting, the better to act when the time comes,
or for no reason, and you soon find yourself powerless ever to
do anything again. No matter how it happened. It, say it, not
knowing what. Perhaps I simply assented at last to an old thing.
But I did nothing. I seem to speak, it is not I, about me, it is not
about me. These few general remarks to begin with. What am I
to do, what shall I do, what should I do, in my situation, how
proceed? By aporia pure and simple? Or by affirmations and
negations invalidated as uttered, or sooner or later? Generally
speaking. There must be other shifts. Otherwise it would be
quite hopeless. But it is quite hopeless. I should mention before
going any further, any further on, that I say aporia without
knowing what it means.

SAMUEL BECKETT The Unnamable (1959)

APORIA is a Greek word meaning "difficulty, being at a loss",
literally, "a pathless path", a track that gives out. In classical
rhetoric it denotes real or pretended doubt about an issue,
uncertainty as to how to proceed in a discourse. Hamlet's "To be
or not to be" soliloquy is perhaps the best-known example in our
literature. In fiction, especially in texts that are framed by a
storytelling situation, aporia is a favourite device of narrators to

arouse curiosity in their audience, or to emphasize the extraordinary nature of the story they are telling. It is often combined with
another figure of rhetoric, "aposiopesis", the incomplete sentence
or unfinished utterance, usually indicated on the page by a trail of
dots ... In Conrad's *Heart of Darkness*, for instance, Marlow
frequently breaks off his narrative in this way:

> "It seems to me that I am trying to tell you a dream – making a
> vain attempt, because no relation of a dream can convey the
> dream-sensation, that commingling of absurdity, surprise, and
> bewilderment in a tremor of struggling revolt, that notion of
> being captured by the incredible which is of the very essence of
> dreams . . ."
> He was silent for a while.
> ". . . No it is impossible; it is impossible to convey the life-
> sensation of any given epoch of one's existence – that which
> makes its truth, its meaning – its subtle and penetrating essence.
> It is impossible. We live, as we dream – alone. . ."

In metafictional narratives like "Lost in the Funhouse" or *The
French Lieutenant's Woman* aporia becomes a structural principal,
as the authorial narrator wrestles with the insoluble problems of
adequately representing life in art, or confesses his own hesitation
about how to dispose of his fictional characters. In Chapter 55 of
The French Lieutenant's Woman, for instance, when Charles, having
discovered that Sarah has disappeared from the hotel in Exeter, is
travelling back to London to begin his search for her, the authorial
narrator intrudes into the narrative as a rudely staring stranger in
Charles's railway compartment:

> Now the question I am asking, as I stare at Charles, is . . . what
> the devil am I going to do with you? I have already thought of
> ending Charles's career here and now; of leaving him for eternity
> on his way to London. But the conventions of Victorian fiction
> allow, allowed no place for the open, the inconclusive ending;
> and I preached earlier of the freedom characters must be given.
> My problem is simple – what Charles wants is clear? It is indeed.
> But what the protagonist wants is not so clear; and I am not at all
> sure where she is at the moment.

In the fiction of Samuel Beckett, especially his later work, aporia is endemic. *The Unnamable* (originally published in French, as *L'Innommable*, in 1952) is a stream-of-consciousness novel, but not like Joyce's *Ulysses*, where the sights, sounds, smells and human bustle of Dublin are evoked for us, in vivid specificity, through the sense-impressions, thoughts and memories of the chief characters. All we have is a narrative voice talking to itself, or transcribing its own thoughts as they occur, longing for extinction and silence, but condemned to go on narrating, though it has no story worth telling, and is certain of nothing, not even of its own position in space and time.

The anonymous narrator is sitting in some vague, murky space, whose limits he can neither see nor touch, while dimly perceived figures, some of whom seem to be characters from Beckett's previous novels, move round him – or could it be that he is moving round them? He knows his eyes are open "because of the tears that fall from them unceasingly." Where is he? It could be hell. It could be senility. It could be the mind of a writer who has to go on writing though he has nothing to say, because there is nothing worth saying any longer about the human condition. Or are all these states essentially one and the same? *The Unnamable* seems to fit Roland Barthes' description of "zero degree writing", in which "literature is vanquished, the problematics of mankind is uncovered and presented without elaboration, the writer becomes irretrievably honest."

The discourse accretes rather than proceeds, by a kind of self-cancellation, one step forwards and one step back, contradictory statements separated only by commas, without the usual adversative *but* or *however*. "Keep going, going on," the narrator urges himself, and immediately adds the derisive rejoinder, "call that going, call that on?" How did he come to be where he is? "Can it be that one day . . . I simply stayed in." Immediately another question is raised: "in where"? He drops the original question: "No matter how it happened." But even this negative gesture presumes too much: "It, say it, not knowing what."

Beckett was a deconstructionist *avant la lettre*. "I seem to speak, it is not I, about me, it is not about me." That sentence attacks the foundations of the long humanist tradition of autobiographical fiction and fictional autobiography, from *Robinson Crusoe* through *Great Expectations* to *A La Recherche du temps perdu*, with its consoling promise of achieving self-knowledge. Beckett anticipated Derrida's notion of the inevitable *"différance"* (*sic*) of verbal discourse: the "I" that speaks always being different from the "I" that is spoken of, the precise fitting of language to reality always being deferred. "These few general remarks to begin with." That usually bland formula is blackly comic in this epistemological vacuum. How shall the narrator proceed, "by affirmations and negations invalidated as uttered" (i.e., self-contradiction) or "By aporia pure and simple?" Aporia is a favourite trope of deconstructionist critics, because it epitomizes the way in which all texts undermine their own claims to a determinate meaning; but the narrator's later admission, "that I say aporia without knowing what it means," is a trumping of aporia.

"There must be other shifts. Otherwise it would be quite hopeless. But it is quite hopeless." What is extraordinary is that this bleakly pessimistic and relentlessly sceptical text is not deeply depressing to read, but on the contrary funny, affecting, and in a surprising way affirmative of the survival of the human spirit *in extremis*. Its famous last words are: "you must go on, I can't go on, I'll go on."

50 Ending

The anxiety, which in this state of their attachment must be the portion of Henry and Catherine, and of all who loved either, as to its final event, can hardly extend, I fear, to the bosom of my readers, who will see in the tell-tale compression of the pages before them, that we are all hastening together to perfect felicity.

JANE AUSTEN Northanger Abbey (1818)

Ralph looked at him dumbly. For a moment he had a fleeting picture of the strange glamour that had once invested the beaches. But the island was scorched up like dead wood – Simon was dead – and Jack had ... The tears began to flow and sobs shook him. He gave himself up to them now for the first time on the island; great, shuddering spasms of grief that seemed to wrench his whole body. His voice rose under the black smoke before the burning wreckage of the island; and infected by that emotion, the other little boys began to shake and sob too. And in the middle of them, with filthy body, matted hair, and unwiped nose, Ralph wept for the end of innocence, the darkness of man's heart, and the fall through the air of the true, wise friend called Piggy.

The officer, surrounded by these noises, was moved and a little embarrassed. He turned away to give them time to pull themselves together; and waited, allowing his eyes to rest on the trim cruiser in the distance.

WILLIAM GOLDING Lord of the Flies (1954)

"CONCLUSIONS are the weak points of most authors," George Eliot remarked, "but some of the fault lies in the very nature of a conclusion, which is at best a negation." To Victorian novelists endings were apt to be particularly troublesome, because they were always under pressure from readers and publishers to provide a happy one. The last chapter was known in the trade as the "wind-up", which Henry James sarcastically described as "a distribution at the last of prizes, pensions, husbands, wives, babies, millions, appended paragraphs and cheerful remarks." James himself pioneered the "open" ending characteristic of modern fiction, often stopping the novel in the middle of a conversation, leaving a phrase hanging resonantly, but ambiguously, in the air: "'Then there we are,' said Strether." (*The Ambassadors*)

As Jane Austen pointed out in a metafictional aside in *Northanger Abbey*, a novelist cannot conceal the timing of the end of the story (as a dramatist or film-maker can, for instance) because of the tell-tale compression of the pages. When John Fowles provides a mock-Victorian wind-up to *The French Lieutenant's Woman* (in which Charles settles down happily with Ernestina) we are not deceived, for a quarter of the book remains to be read. Going on with the story of Charles's quest for Sarah, Fowles offers us two more alternative endings – one that ends happily for the hero, and the other unhappily. He invites us to choose between them, but tacitly encourages us to see the second as more authentic, not just because it is sadder, but because it is more open, with the sense of life going on into an uncertain future.

Perhaps we should distinguish between the end of a novel's story – the resolution or deliberate non-resolution of the narrative questions it has raised in the minds of its readers – and the last page or two of the text, which often act as a kind of epilogue or postscript, a gentle deceleration of the discourse as it draws to a halt. But this scarcely applies to the novels of Sir William Golding, whose last pages have a way of throwing everything that has gone before into a new and surprising light. *Pincher Martin* (1956), for instance, seems to be the story of a torpedoed sailor's desperate and finally unsuccessful struggle to survive on a bare rock in the middle of the Atlantic, but the final chapter reveals that he died with his boots on – so the whole narrative must be reinterpreted as some kind of drowning vision or purgatorial experience after death. The ending of *The Paper Men* (1984) reserves its final punch till the narrator's very last word, which is interrupted by a bullet: "How the devil did Rick L. Tucker manage to get hold of a gu "

That kind of last-minute twist is generally more typical of the short story than of the novel. Indeed one might say that the short story is essentially "end-oriented", inasmuch as one begins a short story in the expectation of soon reaching its conclusion, whereas one embarks upon a novel with no very precise idea of when one will finish it. We tend to read a short story in a single sitting, drawn along by the magnetic power of its anticipated conclusion; whereas we pick up and put down a novel at irregular intervals, and may be positively sorry to come to the end of it. Novelists of old used to exploit this sentimental bond formed between the reader and the novel during the reading experience. Fielding, for instance begins the last Book of *Tom Jones* with "A Farewell to the Reader":

> We are now, reader, arrived at the last stage of our long journey. As we have therefore, travelled together through so many pages, let us behave to one another like fellow-travellers, in a stage coach, who have passed several days in the company of each other; and who, notwithstanding any bickerings or little animosities which may have occurred on the road, generally make up at last, and mount, for the last time, into their vehicle with cheerfulness and good humour; since after this one stage, it may possibly happen to us, as it commonly happens to them, never to meet more.

The conclusion of *The Lord of the Flies* could easily have been a comfortable and reassuring one, because it introduces an adult perspective in the last few pages of what, up to that point, has been a "boys' story", a *Coral Island*-style adventure, that goes horribly wrong. A party of British schoolboys, who crash-land on a tropical island in unspecified circumstances (though there are hints of a war), rapidly revert to savagery and superstition. Freed from the restraints of civilized, adult society, and subject to hunger, loneliness and fear, the behaviour of the playground degenerates into

225

tribal violence. Two boys die, and the hero, Ralph, is fleeing for his life from a pack of bloodthirsty pursuers wielding wooden spears, and a deliberately started forest fire, when he runs full-tilt into a naval officer who has just landed on the beach, his ship alerted by the smoke. "Fun and games," the officer comments, regarding the boys with their makeshift weapons and warpaint.

For the reader, the apparition of the officer is almost as startling, and almost as great a relief, as it is for Ralph. We have been so absorbed in the story, and so involved in Ralph's plight, that we have forgotten that he and his cruel enemies are prepubescent boys. Suddenly, through the officer's eyes, we see them for what they really are, a bunch of dirty and unkempt children. But Golding does not allow this effect to undermine the essential truth of what has gone before, or make the restoration of "normality" into a comforting happy ending. The naval officer will never comprehend the experience that Ralph (and vicariously the reader) has undergone, eloquently recapitulated in the penultimate paragraph: "the end of innocence, the darkness of man's heart, and the fall through the air of the true, wise friend called Piggy." He will never understand why Ralph's sobbing spreads infectiously through the other boys. "He turned away, to give them time to pull themselves together; and waited, allowing his eyes to rest on the trim cruiser in the distance." The last sentence of any story acquires a certain resonance merely by virtue of being the last, but this one is particularly rich in irony. The adult's gaze at the "trim cruiser" implies complacency, evasion of the truth, and complicity in an institutionalized form of violence – modern warfare – that is equivalent to, as well as different from, the primitive violence of the castaway boys.

Readers acquainted with my *Changing Places* may recall that the passage from *Northanger Abbey* at the head of this section is cited by Philip Swallow and quoted by Morris Zapp on the last page of that novel. Philip invokes it to illustrate an important difference between an audience's experience of the end of a film, and a reader's experience of the end of a novel:

"That's something the novelist can't help giving away, isn't it, that his novel is shortly coming to an end? . . . he can't disguise the tell-tale compression of the pages . . . As you're reading, you're aware that there's only a page or two left in the book, and you get ready to close it. But with a film there's no way of telling, especially nowadays, when films are much more loosely structured, much more ambivalent, than they used to be. There's no way of telling which frame is going to be the last. The film is going along, just as life goes along, people are behaving, doing things, drinking, talking, and we're watching them, and at any point the director chooses, without warning, without anything being resolved, or explained, or wound up, it can just . . . end."

At this point in the book, Philip is represented as a character in a filmscript, and immediately after his speech the novel ends, thus:

PHILIP shrugs. The camera stops, freezing him in mid-gesture.

THE END

I ended the novel in this fashion for several, interrelated reasons. In one aspect, it is a sexual comedy of "long-range wifeswapping": the story concerns the fortunes of two academics, one British and one American, who, exchanging jobs in 1969, have affairs with each other's wives. But the two principal characters exchange much else in the course of the story – values, attitudes, language – and almost every incident in one location has its analogue or mirror-image in the other. Developing this highly symmetrical and perhaps predictable plot, I felt the need to provide some variety and surprise for the reader on another level of the text, and accordingly wrote each chapter in a different style or format. The first shift is comparatively inconspicuous – from present-tense narration in Chapter One to past-tense narration in Chapter Two. But the third chapter is in epistolary form, and the fourth consists of extracts from newspapers and other documents the characters are supposed to be reading. The fifth chapter is conventional in style, but deviates from the cross-cutting pattern of the previous chapters, presenting the interconnected experiences of the two main characters in consecutive chunks.

As the novel progressed I became increasingly conscious of the problem of how to end it in a way which would be satisfying on both the formal and the narrative levels. As regards the former, it was obvious that the final chapter must exhibit the most striking and surprising shift in narrative form, or risk being an aesthetic anticlimax. As regards the narrative level, I found myself unwilling to resolve the wife-swapping plot, partly because that would mean also resolving the cultural plot. A decision by Philip to stick with Desirée Zapp, for instance, would also entail a decision by him to stay in America or a willingness on her part to settle in England, and so on. I did not want to have to decide, as implied author, in favour of this partnership or that, this culture or that. But how could I "get away with" an ending of radical indeterminacy for a plot that had up till then been as regular and symmetrical in structure as a quadrille?

The idea of writing the last chapter (which is called "Ending") in the form of a filmscript seemed to solve all these problems at a stroke. First of all, such a format satisfied the need for a climactic deviation from "normal" fictional discourse. Secondly it freed me, as implied author, from the obligation to pass judgment on, or to arbitrate between, the claims of the four main characters, since there is no textual trace of the author's voice in a filmscript, consisting as it does of dialogue and impersonal, objective descriptions of the characters' outward behaviour. Philip, Desirée, Morris and Hilary meet in New York, halfway between the West Coast of America and the West Midlands of England, to discuss their marital problems, and in the course of a few days they discuss every possible resolution of the story – each couple to divorce and cross-marry, each couple to reunite, each couple to separate but not remarry, etc. etc. – but without reaching any conclusion. By having Philip draw attention to the fact that films are more amenable to unresolved endings than novels, while being represented as a character in a film inside a novel, I thought I had found a way to justify, by a kind of metafictional joke, my own refusal to resolve the story of *Changing Places*. In fact, so strong – atavistically strong – is the human desire for certainty, resolution and closure, that not all readers were satisfied by this ending, and some have complained to me that they felt cheated by it. But it satisfied *me* (and had the incidental bonus that when I decided to make further use of the principal characters in a subsequent novel, *Small World*, I had a free hand in developing their life-histories).

The point of this anecdote is, however, not to defend the ending of *Changing Places*, but to demonstrate that deciding how to handle it involved many other aspects of the novel, aspects that I have discussed elsewhere in this book under various headings. For example: (1) Point of View (the film-scenario form obviated the need to select a point of view, with the privileging of the p.o.v. character that is inevitably entailed) (2) Suspense (postponing till the very end an answer to the narrative question, how will the double adultery plot be resolved?) (3) Surprise (refusing to answer that question) (4) Intertextuality (the allusion to Jane Austen, which is natural and appropriate in that both Philip Swallow and Morris Zapp have specialized in the analysis of her work) (5) Staying on the Surface (another effect of the film-scenario format) (6) Titles and Chapters (the punning title of the novel – places that change, places where one changes, positions that are exchanged – suggested a series of cognate chapter headings – "Flying", "Settling", "Corresponding" etc. and finally "Ending", which is noun, participle and gerund: this is the end of the book, this is how it ends, this is how I am ending it) (7) Metafiction (the joke of the last lines is on the reader and his/her expectations, but also connects with a running metafictional joke about a how-to-do-it book called *Let's Write a Novel*, which Morris Zapp finds in Philip Swallow's office, and which provides a sardonic commentary on the novel's own shifting techniques. "Every novel must tell a story," it begins. "And there are three types of story, the story that ends happily, the story that ends unhappily, and the story that ends neither happily nor unhappily, or, in other words, doesn't really end at all.")

I could, without too much difficulty, discuss this ending under other headings, such as Defamiliarization, Repetition, The Experimental Novel, The Comic Novel, Epiphany, Coincidence, Irony, Motivation, Ideas, and Aporia, but I will not labour the point – which is, simply, that decisions about particular aspects or components of a novel are never taken in isolation, but affect, and are affected by, all its other aspects and components. A novel is a *Gestalt*, a German word for which there is no exact English equivalent, defined in my dictionary as "a perceptual pattern or structure possessing qualities as a whole that cannot be described merely as a sum of its parts."

THE END

Bibliography
of primary sources

This bibliography lists, alphabetically by author, the novels and short stories from which illustrative passages are quoted, either at the head of each section or in the body of the text. The following information is given: (1) Date of first publication. (2) In the case of modern texts, the place and publisher of first publication in the UK and USA. (3) Imprints of paperback editions (abbreviated as "pb") available in UK and USA at the time of compilation (May 1992).

Abish, Walter: *Alphabetical Africa*. New York, New Directions, 1974. US pb New Directions.

Amis, Kingsley: *Lucky Jim*. London, Gollancz, 1954. New York, Doubleday, 1954. UK pb Penguin; US pb Penguin.
The Folks that Live on the Hill. London, Hutchinson, 1990. New York, Summit, 1990. UK pb Penguin.

Amis, Martin: *Money*. London, Cape, 1984. New York, Viking, 1985. UK pb Penguin; US pb Penguin.

Austen, Jane: *Emma*. 1816. UK pb Penguin; US pb Penguin.
Northanger Abbey. 1818. UK pb Penguin; US pb Penguin.

Auster, Paul: *City of Glass*. London, Faber & Faber, 1987 (in *The New York Trilogy*). Los Angeles, Sun & Moon Press, 1985. UK pb Faber; US pb Penguin.

Barth, John: *Lost in the Funhouse*. London, Secker & Warburg, 1969. New York, Doubleday, 1968. US pb Anchor.

Barthelme, Donald: "Will You Tell Me?" in *Come Back, Dr Caligari*, London, Eyre & Spottiswoode, 1966. Boston, Little Brown, 1964. US pb Little Brown.

Beckett, Samuel: *Murphy*. London, Routledge, 1938. New York, Grove Press, 1938. UK pb Calder; US pb Grove Weidenfeld.
The Unnamable. [Paris, 1952, as *L'Innommable*] London, Calder, 1959. New York, Grove Press, 1958. UK pb Calder; US pb Grove Weidenfeld.

Bennett, Arnold: *The Old Wives' Tale*. 1908. UK pb Penguin; US pb Penguin.

Bradbury, Malcolm: *The History Man.* London, Secker & Warburg, 1975. Boston, Houghton Mifflin, 1976. UK pb Vintage; US pb Penguin.

Brontë, Charlotte: *Villette.* 1854. UK pb Penguin; US pb Penguin.

Bunyan, John: *The Pilgrim's Progress.* 1678. UK pb Penguin; US pb Penguin.

Burgess, Anthony: *A Clockwork Orange.* London, Heinemann, 1962. New York, Norton, 1963. UK pb Penguin; US pb Ballantine.

Butler, Samuel: *Erewhon.* 1872. UK pb Penguin; US pb Penguin.

Carlyle, Thomas: *The French Revolution.* 1837. UK pb Oxford World's Classics; US pb Oxford World's Classics.

Carrington, Leonora: *The Hearing Trumpet.* London, Routledge & Kegan Paul, 1977. New York, St Martin's, 1976. UK pb Virago; US pb City Lights Books.

Conrad, Joseph: *Heart of Darkness.* 1902. UK pb Penguin; US pb Penguin.
The Shadow-Line – A Confession. 1917. UK pb Penguin; US pb Penguin.

Cooper, William. *Scenes from Provincial Life.* London, Cape, 1950. New York NAL/Dutton, 1984. UK pb Methuen; US pb Avon.

Dickens, Charles: *Bleak House.* 1853. UK pb Penguin; US pb Penguin.
Hard Times. 1854. UK pb Penguin; US pb Penguin.
Oliver Twist. 1837–8. UK pb Penguin; US pb Penguin.

Drabble, Margaret: *The Realms of Gold.* London, Weidenfeld & Nicolson, 1975. New York, Knopf, 1975. UK pb Penguin; US pb Penguin.

Eliot, George: *Adam Bede.* 1859. UK pb Penguin; US pb Penguin.
Middlemarch. 1871–2. UK pb Penguin; US pb Penguin.

Fielding, Henry: *Joseph Andrews.* 1742. UK pb Penguin; US pb Penguin.
Tom Jones. 1749. UK pb Penguin; US pb Penguin.

Fitzgerald, F. Scott: *Tender is the Night.* London, Chatto & Windus, 1934. New York, Scribner's, 1934. UK pb Penguin; US pb Macmillan.

Ford, Ford Madox: *The Good Soldier.* 1915. UK pb Penguin; US pb Random House.

Forster, E. M.: *Howards End.* London, Arnold, 1910. New York, Putnam, 1911. UK pb Penguin; US pb Bantam.

Fowles, John: *The French Lieutenant's Woman.* London, Cape, 1969. Boston, Little Brown, 1969. UK pb Pan; US pb NAL/Dutton.

Frayn, Michael: *The Trick of It*. London, Viking, 1989. New York, Viking, 1990. UK pb Penguin; US pb Penguin.

Gissing, George: *New Grub Street*. 1891. UK pb Penguin; US pb Penguin.

Golding, William: *Lord of the Flies*. London, Faber & Faber, 1954. New York, Coward-McCann, 1955. UK pb Faber; US pb Putnam Perigee.

Green, Henry: *Living*. London, Hogarth Press, 1929. St Clair Shores, Mich., Scholarly, 1971. UK pb Picador; US pb Penguin.

Greene, Graham: *A Burnt-out Case*. London, Heinemann, 1961. New York, Viking, 1961. UK pb Penguin; US pb Penguin.
The Heart of the Matter. London, Heinemann, 1948. New York, Viking 1948. UK pb Penguin; US pb Penguin.

Hardy, Thomas: *A Pair of Blue Eyes*. 1873. UK pb Penguin; US pb Penguin.

Heller, Joseph: *Good As Gold*. London, Cape, 1979. New York, Simon & Schuster, 1979. US pb Dell.

Hemingway, Ernest. "In Another Country" in *Men Without Women*. London, Cape, 1928. New York, Scribner's, 1927. UK pb Panther; US pb Macmillan.

Isherwood, Christopher: *Goodbye to Berlin*. London, Hogarth Press, 1939. New York, Random House, 1939. UK pb Mandarin; US pb New Directions (in *The Berlin Stories*).

Ishiguro, Kazuo: *The Remains of the Day*. London, Faber & Faber, 1989. New York, Knopf, 1989. UK pb Faber; US pb Vintage.

James, Henry: *The Ambassadors*. 1903. UK pb Penguin; US pb Penguin.
What Maisie Knew. 1897. UK pb Penguin; US pb Penguin.

Joyce, James: *A Portrait of the Artist as a Young Man*. London, Egoist, 1916. New York, Huebsch, 1916. UK pb Penguin; US pb Penguin.
"Eveline", in *Dubliners*. London, Grant Richards 1914. New York, Modern Library 1926. UK pb Penguin; US pb Penguin.
Ulysses. [Paris, Shakespeare & Co, 1922] London, Bodley Head, 1937. New York, Random House, 1934. UK pb Penguin; US pb Random House.

Kipling, Rudyard: "Mrs Bathurst", in *Traffics and Discoveries*. 1904. UK pb Penguin (*Short Stories* Vol 1); US pb. Penguin.

Kundera, Milan: *The Book of Laughter and Forgetting*, trans. Michael Henry Heim. London, Faber & Faber, 1982. New York, Knopf, 1980. UK pb Faber; US pb Penguin.

Lawrence, D. H.: *Women in Love*. London, Secker, 1921. New York, Seltzer, 1921. UK pb Penguin; US pb Penguin.

Lodge, David: *Changing Places*. London, Secker & Warburg, 1975. New York, Penguin Books, 1980. UK pb Penguin; US pb Penguin.
How Far Can You Go? London, Secker & Warburg, 1980. New York, Morrow, 1982 (As *Souls and Bodies*). UK pb Penguin; US pb Penguin (*Souls and Bodies*).
Nice Work. London, Secker & Warburg, 1988. New York, Viking, 1989. UK pb Penguin ; US pb Penguin.
Small World. London, Secker & Warburg, 1984. New York, Macmillan, 1985. UK pb Penguin ; US pb Warner.
Lyly, John: *Euphues: the Anatomy of Wit*. 1578. US pb Saifer.
Michaels, Leonard: *I Would Have Saved Them If I Could*. New York, Farrar, Strauss & Giroux, 1975. US pb (forthcoming, 1993) Mercury.
Moore, Lorrie: "How To Be an Other Woman", in *Self-Help*. London, Faber, 1985. New York, Knopf, 1985. UK pb Faber; US pb Plume.
Nabokov, Vladimir: *Lolita*. [Paris, Olympia Press, 1955] London, Weidenfeld & Nicolson, 1959. New York, Putnam's, 1958. UK pb Penguin; US pb Random.
Orwell, George: *Nineteen Eighty-four*. London, Secker & Warburg, 1949. New York, Harcourt Brace, 1949. UK pb Penguin; US pb Penguin.
Poe, Edgar Allan: "William Wilson" 1839 (in *Burton's Gentlemen's Magazine*). UK pb Penguin (*Complete Tales and Poems*); US pb Penguin (*Fall of the House of Usher & Other Writings*).
Salinger, J. D: *The Catcher in the Rye*. London, Hamish Hamilton, 1951. Boston, Little Brown, 1951. UK pb Penguin; US pb Little Brown.
Scott, Sir Walter: *The Heart of Midlothian*. 1818. UK pb Oxford World's Classics; US pb Oxford World's Classics.
Smollett, Tobias: *The Adventures of Roderick Random*. 1748. UK pb Oxford World's Classics; US pb Oxford World's Classics.
Spark, Muriel: *The Prime of Miss Jean Brodie*. London, Macmillan, 1961. New York, *The New Yorker*, 1961. UK pb Penguin; US pb Penguin.
Sterne, Laurence: *The Life and Opinions of Tristram Shandy, Gent.* 1759–67. UK pb Penguin; US pb Penguin.
Thackeray, William Makepeace: *Vanity Fair*. 1848. UK pb Penguin; US pb Penguin.
Twain, Mark: *Huckleberry Finn*. 1884. UK pb Penguin; US pb Penguin.

Updike, John: *Rabbit Run*. London, Deutsch, 1961. New York, Knopf, 1960. UK pb Penguin; US pb Fawcett.

Vonnegut, Kurt: *Slaughterhouse Five*. London, Cape, 1970. New York, Delacorte, 1969. UK pb Vintage; US pb Dell.

Waugh, Evelyn: *A Handful of Dust*. London, Chapman & Hall, 1934. New York, Farrar & Rinehart, 1934. UK pb Penguin; US pb Little Brown.

Decline and Fall. London, Chapman & Hall, 1928. New York, Farrar & Rinehart, 1929. UK pb Penguin; US pb Little Brown.

Weldon, Fay: *Female Friends*. London, Heinemann, 1975. New York, St Martin's, 1974. UK pb Picador; US pb Academy.

Woolf, Virginia: *Mrs Dalloway*. London, Hogarth Press, 1925. New York, Harcourt, 1925. UK pb Oxford; US pb Harcourt Brace.

Index of Names

Note: numerals in **bold** indicate substantive quotation and/or discussion of a writer's work.